Jacques Rancière

Key Concepts

Key Concepts

Published

Theodor Adorno: Key Concepts
Edited by Deborah Cook

Alain Badiou: Key Concepts
Edited by A. J. Bartlett and
Justin Clemens

Pierre Bourdieu: Key Concepts
Edited by Michael Grenfell

Gilles Deleuze: Key Concepts
Edited by Charles J. Stivale

Martin Heidegger: Key Concepts
Edited by Bret W. Davis

Merleau-Ponty: Key Concepts
Edited by Rosalyn Diprose and
Jack Reynolds

Jacques Rancière: Key Concepts
Edited by Jean-Philippe Deranty

Wittgenstein: Key Concepts
Edited by Kelly Dean Jolley

Forthcoming

Michel Foucault: Key Concepts
Edited by Dianna Taylor

Jürgen Habermas: Key Concepts
Edited by Barbara Fultner

Immanuel Kant: Key Concepts
Edited by Will Dudley and
Kristina Engelhard

Jacques Rancière

Key Concepts

Edited by Jean-Philippe Deranty

LONDON AND NEW YORK

First published 2010 by Acumen

Published 2014 by Routledge
2 Park Square, Milton Park, Abingdon, Oxon OX14 4RN
711 Third Avenue, New York, NY 10017, USA

Routledge is an imprint of the Taylor & Francis Group, an informa business

© Editorial matter and selection, 2010 Jean-Philippe Deranty.
Individual contributions, the contributors.

This book is copyright under the Berne Convention.
No reproduction without permission.

All rights reserved. No part of this book may be reprinted or mechanical, reproduced or utilised in any form or by any electronic, or other means, now known or hereafter invented, including photocopying and recording, or in any information storage or retrieval system, without permission in writing from the publishers.

Notices
Practitioners and researchers must always rely on their own experience and knowledge in evaluating and using any information, methods, compounds, or experiments described herein. In using such information or methods they should be mindful of their own safety and the safety of others, including parties for whom they have a professional responsibility.

To the fullest extent of the law, neither the Publisher nor the authors, contributors, or editors, assume any liability for any injury and/or damage to persons or property as a matter of products liability, negligence or otherwise, or from any use or operation of any methods, products, instructions, or ideas contained in the material herein.

ISBN: 978-1-84465-232-7 (hardcover)
ISBN: 978-1-84465-233-4 (paperback)

British Library Cataloguing-in-Publication Data
A catalogue record for this book is available
from the British Library.

Designed and typeset in Classical Garamond and Myriad.

Contents

Contributors	vii
Abbreviations	xi
Introduction: a journey in equality *Jean-Philippe Deranty*	1

PART I: PHILOSOPHY

1	Logical revolts *Jean-Philippe Deranty*	17
2	"The ignorant schoolmaster": knowledge and authority *Yves Citton*	25
3	Philosophy and its poor: Rancière's critique of philosophy *Giuseppina Mecchia*	38

PART II: POLITICS

4	Police and oligarchy *Samuel A. Chambers*	57
5	Wrong, disagreement, subjectification *Todd May*	69
6	Archipolitics, parapolitics, metapolitics *Bruno Bosteels*	80

PART III: POETICS

7	*"Partage du sensible"*: the distribution of the sensible Davide Panagia	95
8	Heretical history and the poetics of knowledge Philip Watts	104
9	Regimes of the arts Jean-Philippe Deranty	116

PART IV: AESTHETICS

10	Expressivity, literarity, mute speech Alison Ross	133
11	Image, montage Toni Ross	151
12	Film fables Hassan Melehy	169
	Afterword Jean-Philippe Deranty	183
	Chronology	189
	Bibliography	193
	Index	203

Contributors

Bruno Bosteels is Associate Professor of Romance Studies at Cornell University, New York. He is the author most recently of *Alain Badiou, une trajectoire polémique* (2009). Two other books are forthcoming: *Badiou and Politics* and *Marx and Freud in Latin America*. He has published extensively on Latin American literature and politics, and on European philosophy and political theory. He is currently preparing *After Borges: Literature and Antiphilosophy* and a short book, *La Révolution de la honte*, on the twentieth-century uses of Marx's correspondence with Arnold Ruge. He also currently serves as general editor of the journal *diacritics*.

Samuel A. Chambers is Associate Professor of Political Science at Johns Hopkins University, Baltimore, USA, and co-editor of the journal *Contemporary Political Theory*. He has recently published *The Queer Politics of Television* (2009). His previous publications include the monographs *Untimely Politics* (2003) and *Judith Butler and Political Theory* (with Terrell Carver, 2008).

Yves Citton is Professor of French Literature at the University Grenoble-3 specializing in eighteenth-century literature, and a member of the CNRS research unit LIRE. His recent publications include: *Mythocratie: Storytelling et imaginaire de gauche* (2010), *Lire, interpréter, actualiser: Pourquoi les études littéraires?* (2007), *L'Envers de la liberté: L'invention d'un imaginaire spinoziste dans la France des Lumières* (2006) and, with Frédéric Lordon, *Spinoza et les sciences sociales: De la puissance de la multitude à l'économie des affects* (2008).

Jean-Philippe Deranty is Senior Lecturer in Philosophy at Macquarie University, Sydney, Australia, and co-editor of *Critical Horizons*. His recent publications include *Beyond Communication: A Critical Study of Axel Honneth's Social Philosophy* (2009).

Todd May is Class of 1941 Memorial Professor of the Humanities in the Department of Philosophy and Religion at Clemson University, South Carolina, USA. He is the author of ten books on continental philosophy, including most recently *Contemporary Movements* and *The Political Thought of Jacques Rancière: Creating Equality*. He has also been active for over two decades in egalitarian political movements.

Giuseppina Mecchia is Associate Professor of French and Italian and Director of the Graduate Program for Cultural Studies at the University of Pittsburgh, USA. Recently, she has published essays on Marcel Proust, the Italian writing collective Wu-Ming, the Austrian film director Michael Haneke and the concept of biopolitics in the works of Antonin Artaud, Felix Guattari and Michel Foucault.

Hassan Melehy is Associate Professor of French and Francophone Studies at the University of North Carolina at Chapel Hill, USA. A specialist in early modern literature and philosophy, he is the author of *Writing Cogito* (1997) and *The Poetics of Literary Transfer in Early Modern France and England* (2010). He is the translator of Jacques Rancière's *The Names of History* (1994).

Davide Panagia is a political and cultural theorist who holds the Canada Research Chair in Cultural Studies at Trent University (Canada) and is co-editor of the journal *Theory & Event*. His writings focus on the relationship between politics, aesthetics, popular culture and ethics, and include two books: *The Poetics of Political Thinking* (2006) and *The Political Life of Sensation* (2009).

Alison Ross is Senior Lecturer in Critical Theory and Director of the Centre for Comparative Literature and Cultural Studies, Monash University, Australia. She is the author of *The Aesthetic Paths of Philosophy: Presentation in Kant, Heidegger, Lacoue-Labarthe and Nancy* (2007).

Toni Ross is a Senior Lecturer in the School of Art History and Art Education, College of Fine Arts, University of New South Wales, Australia. Her most recent publications have appeared in the *Australian and New Zealand Journal of Arts*, the *Journal of Visual Arts Practice*, as well as in the anthology *Communities of Sense: Rethinking Aesthetics and Politics* (2009).

Philip Watts is Chair of the Department of French at Columbia University, New York, and specializes in the field of twentieth-century European literature and film. He is co-editor of the recent collection of essays *Jacques Rancière: History, Politics, Aesthetics* (2009).

Abbreviations

AaI	"Aesthetics against Incarnation: An Interview by Anne Marie Oliver" (2008).
AH	*Arrêt sur histoire* (with J.-L. Comolli) (1997)
AoP	"Art of the Possible: Fulvia Carnevale and John Kelsey in Conversation with Jacques Rancière" (2007).
AR	"The Aesthetic Revolution and Its Outcomes: Emplotments of Autonomy and Heteronomy" (2002).
CAPA	"Contemporary Art and the Politics of Aesthetics" (2009).
CR	"Comments and Responses" (2003)
D	*Disagreement: Politics and Philosophy* (1998).
DW	"Dissenting Words: A Conversation with Jacques Rancière" (2000).
ES	"The Emancipated Spectator" (2007)
FF	*Film Fables* (2006).
FI	*The Future of the Image* (2007).
FW	*The Flesh of Words: The Politics of Writing* (2004).
GE	"Going to the Expo: The Worker, his Wife and Machines" (1988).
GT	"Good Times, Or, Pleasure at the Barriers" (1988).
HD	*Hatred of Democracy* (2006).
HOW	"How to use *Lire le Capital*" (1989).
IE	*L'Inconscient esthétique* (2001).
IS	*The Ignorant Schoolmaster: Five Lessons in Intellectual Emancipation* (1991).
ITDA	"Is there a Deleuzian Aesthetics?" (2004).
LA	*La Leçon d'Althusser* (1974).

M *Mallarmé: Politique de la sirène* (1996).
MSDC "On Medium Specificity and Discipline Crossovers in Modern Art" (2007).
NH *The Names of History: On the Poetics of Knowledge* (1994).
NL *The Nights of Labour: The Workers' Dream in Nineteenth Century France* (1989).
OSP *On the Shores of Politics* (1995).
OTI "On the Theory of Ideology (the Politics of Althusser)" (1974).
PA *The Politics of Aesthetics* (2004).
PL *Politique de la littérature* (2007).
PM *La parole muette: Essai sur les contradictions de la littérature* (1998).
PO *La parole ouvrière, 1830/1851* (1975).
PoL "The Politics of Literature" (2004).
PP *The Philosopher and his Poor* (1991).
PtA "From Politics to Aesthetics" (2005).
SLS "The Sublime from Lyotard to Schiller: Two Readings of Kant and Their Political Significance" (2004).
SP *Les scènes du peuple* (2003).
SVLP *Short Voyages to the Land of the People* (1991).
TBD "Thinking Between Disciplines: An Aesthetics of Knowledge" (2006).
TI "Theatre of Images" (2007).
TT "Ten Theses on Politics" (2001).
WHO "Who is the Subject of the Rights of Man?" (2004).
WHY "Why Emma Bovary had to be Killed" (2008).

Introduction: a journey in equality
Jean-Philippe Deranty

It has taken several decades for the work of Jacques Rancière to find a wide audience. His first publications, in which he developed an alternative approach to the history of the labour movement, were known only to a few specialists in the mid-1970s. Interest in his writings started to grow with the publication of *Disagreement*, his major book of political philosophy (1995 in France, 1998 for the English translation). Since then, his unflinching defence of a radical version of democratic equality has made him one of the key references in contemporary political thought. Parallel to this work on democracy, his writings on literature and the visual arts, particularly film, have also gained increased attention in the last two decades. Of the more than twenty books he has published, only a handful are not yet translated into English. He now publishes regularly in international journals of politics and aesthetics and receives invitations all over the world from the most prestigious academic and artistic institutions.

Early Marxist years and the rupture of May '68

Rancière was born in 1940 in Algiers. He was therefore a decade younger than the generation of the most famous postwar French theorists, like Michel Foucault, Jacques Derrida, Jean-François Lyotard and Gilles Deleuze. Rancière's generation, of which Alain Badiou is the other very famous figure, was the one that would become engulfed by the revolutionary activism awakened by the events of May 1968.

The years leading to the 1968 conflagration were years of political radicalization. In 1965, at the age of 25, Rancière gave a long presentation in the most famous seminar of the time: the reading group on Marx's *Capital*, organized by the Marxist philosopher Louis Althusser at the École Normale Supérieure in Paris. The intellectual landscape was dominated by the reference to Marx, and Althusser was without a doubt one of the stellar figures in the field. In a rare retrospective note, Rancière has reminisced about the immense aura surrounding Althusser at the time. *Reading Capital*, the book that was published as a result of the Paris seminars, became for a couple years a central reference in Western academia, notably in the English-speaking world. As Rancière writes, he was living then "in the midst of Althusserian certitudes. Althusser had declared the necessity to return to Marx in order to retrieve all the incisiveness of his theoretical and political rupture" (PO 334, my trans.).

Rancière's Althusserian period came to a brutal halt in the agitation of May 1968. The year 1968 was one of revolutionary effervescence all around the world, but particularly so in France. The revolutionary tendencies that burst out in 1968 had been prepared by mounting political antagonisms and social, cultural dissatisfaction, particularly among the youth, in the two decades following the end of the war. Deep social–economic divisions, culminating in recurrent mass strikes (notably in 1945 and 1948; 1963 saw the first occupation of the Sorbonne by students) and brutal police repression, were relayed in the political arena by a sharp antagonism between parties of government and a powerful communist movement. The two decades between 1945 and 1968 also led to the end of the French empire, culminating in a bloody colonial war in Algeria (1954–62) and a near civil war in the homeland. Algeria gained its independence in 1962, but in 1968 the wounds opened up by this immensely traumatic period were still wide open. The international situation also played a direct role in fanning social and political antagonisms. For an increasingly radicalized youth, the war in Vietnam and the Cuban Revolution represented powerful models. The agitation that began at the end of March 1968 following police violence against anti-Vietnam demonstrations became the spark for a social and political explosion that had been brewing for many years.

While the student rebellion was quashed and state power re-established within a few months, the forces that had paved the way for the joint radicalization of the youth and the proletarian movement were still palpable. A significant part of the student and workers' bodies refused to abandon their hopes for a different future and took a radical leftist turn. The strong *gauchiste* movement that emerged on the left of the Communist Party was decisively influenced by the Cultural Revolution in China. It drew from its inspiration a series of fundamental demands: a radical rejection of the division of labour, especially between manual and intellectual labour; an emphasis on class struggle, in particular as it is relayed in intellectual production; and an emphasis on (revolutionary) practice as the factor in which antagonistic class lines, as well as the possibilities of collective action, are revealed. The year 1968 and those that immediately followed had a profound impact on Rancière on a theoretical, but also, judging from rare biographical indications, on an existential level. Throughout his writings, we hear the reverberation of the appeal made to intellectuals to "get off their horses" (SVLP 2), as a famous Mao aphorism put it: that is, to overcome class boundaries in real life as much as in thought, an injunction that led many *gauchiste* intellectuals to "establish" themselves in factories (SP 295; see a classic account in Linhart 1981).

Unlike the great majority of his colleagues, some of whom were to become important official figures in the Fifth Republic's establishment, Rancière has always remained true to the fundamental ideal of radical equality, which inspired the post-'68 movement. His whole work is characterized by the consistent attempt to scrupulously follow the implications of the idea that human beings are equal in all respects.

The immediate consequence of Rancière's embrace of radical egalitarianism was a definitive rupture with Althusser and orthodox Marxism, although not, for a while, with Marx himself. An article written in the summer of 1969 documents the sharp antagonism that from then on separated the young leftist intellectual from the official philosopher of the French Communist Party (OTI; see also the self-critical rejection of his 1965 article, in HOW). This early piece shows the immense disillusion, typical of a whole generation, felt by Rancière towards what he saw as the failure on the part of Althusser and the communist organizations to support and relay the hopes and ideals expressed in the 1968 movements. Five years later, *Althusser's Lesson* (1974) was an entire book dedicated to the account of this failed encounter. These first publications remained unequivocally dedicated to Marx as the central theoretical reference for the analysis of modern society and for the conceptualization of an alternative politics. A few years later, however, Rancière would become increasingly critical of Marx himself.

One of Althusser's most famous lessons was the radical distinction between science and ideology. According to this view, while bourgeois society justifies its domination through ideological constructs, communist thinkers, enlightened by Marx's revolutionary discovery of historical materialism, can see through ideological veils and develop a truly scientific analysis of history and society. Marx is credited with identifying the real structures of society and their interactions, explaining the specific character of given historical social orders. As a result, the revolution in practice is reliant upon Marx's revolution in theory. Rancière rejects this view because of its implications for the classes suffering from social domination. In the Althusserian construct, since the working classes are victims of ideological obfuscation, they are not in a position to see through to the reality of their situation. They need to be led by the Party and trust the Party's intellectuals to realize what their situation is and what kind of political action will liberate them from oppression. Their spontaneous expressions and their actions have no intrinsic value and must constantly be redirected by the Party and its theorists. In this Althusserian vision of the central role of the organization and its thinkers, Rancière finds the same logic at play as in traditional structures of domination and indeed, as he will argue later, in classical philosophy, including Marx: the social hierarchy, established through the division of labour (notably the division between manual and intellectual professions) is translated into a symbolic hierarchy, which amounts to making the working classes passive masses whose words and acts are meaningless. Only the individuals belonging to classes able to afford leisure are deemed able to express valuable thoughts and propose forms of collective action (economic, political, cultural) with real relevance. Already in the early publications, the critique of social domination and the goal of a truly egalitarian politics are intimately linked to questions relating to the transmission of knowledge and the positions of power of those who speak, and so to questions of education, knowledge, and the relationship between social value and meaning.

Logical revolts

From 1969 onwards, Rancière held a position in the newly created Université de Vincennes, just outside Paris (now Paris VIII at Saint-Denis). This university, which started as an experimental centre in the autumn of 1968 and was institutionally recognized in 1969, became the place where academics who had been involved in the post-'68 movements could find employment and experiment with teaching in non-hierarchical ways. Alain Badiou also found a post here. The University at Vincennes attracted some of the most prestigious intellectual leaders of the post-'68 period, like Deleuze, Foucault and Lyotard. Rancière was to spend his entire career at Vincennes, retiring in 2000 as a professor.

INTRODUCTION: A JOURNEY IN EQUALITY

The years following 1968 saw an immense disillusion gradually form for all those who had dreamt of an abolition of social hierarchies. This led many of the intellectuals involved in the events of 1968 to substantial reassessments and the development of new arguments and theoretical strategies to make sense of their past (although recent) engagement, explain the state of current disillusionment and map out a new course.

By contrast with many of his colleagues, who moved towards entirely new paradigms, or undertook stringent denunciations of their radicalism of yesterday (Lecourt 2001), Rancière's attitude towards the recess of revolutionary hopes was to remain true to the ideals expressed in 1968 and the transformations these demanded in the methods of the social sciences and philosophy (see Giuseppina Mecchia's study of Rancière's critical stance towards philosophy in Chapter 3).

The strike of the Lip factory workers in 1973 acted as a powerful reminder that the working class might not have taken state power, but was still, as always, able to denounce social domination and create new modes of collective life. This example convinced Rancière that it was a mistake to abandon the interest in workers' emancipation and class struggle (PO 337). But this had to be done differently.

Rancière dedicated himself to the concrete history of labour struggles, with particular attention to the specificities of each particular movement, below the theoretical preconceptions of Marxist and other socialist readings. As ever, it was necessary to let the voices and actions of the dominated speak for themselves. On the other hand, the disillusion that followed the immense hope of 1968 pointed precisely to the recurring limitations and contradictions of the labour movement, which one also had to study concretely, again in the specificity of each particular movement.

Several projects engaged in similar directions (Gossez 1968; Perrot 1987) confirmed for Rancière the validity of this approach, in particular E. P. Thompson's influential *The Making of the English Working Class*. For the next ten years, until 1981 and the publication of *The Nights of Labour*, Rancière's activity was wholly dedicated to archival work, aiming to produce a French version of "history from below". The first chapter of this book (by Jean-Philippe Deranty) focuses on this decade and Rancière's first publications following *Althusser's Lesson*.

Rancière's philosophy seminar at Vincennes was in fact "a research group into workers' history". It led to the formation of a research collective that named itself "Révoltes logiques" (Logical revolts), after one of Rimbaud's poems in *Illuminations* entitled "Democracy", in which Rimbaud renders the cruelty and corruption of soldiers planning a "massacre" of "logical revolts". The group published a journal under the collective's name until 1985 (see SP for Rancière's contributions).

Beside the yearly edition of *Révoltes logiques*, other publications arose from his substantial archival work. In 1975, Rancière edited *La parole ouvrière*, an anthology of workers' texts with Alain Faure, one of his students. In 1981, he published his doctoral thesis under the title "La nuit des prolétaires" (*The Nights of Labour*), a philosophical–historical account of some of the most original figures of the nineteenth-century labour movement. And in 1983, Rancière published an anthology of one the most unusual "plebeian philosophers", the carpenter Louis-Gabriel Gauny (PP).

The encounter with Joseph Jacotot

A significant expression used by the writers of the Révoltes logiques collective was that of "thought from below". While referring explicitly to the "history from below" perspective, the expression also contrasts with it in important ways. It points to the idea that human beings are equal not just in legal or moral terms, but also in terms of their intellectual and discursive capacities. This is the fundamental idea that Rancière retained from his involvement in the radical–egalitarian movement of the early 1970s: the dominated do not need masters or leaders to tell them what to think and what to say. Their plight is not due to false consciousness or ignorance, but to a social organization that systematically makes their voices and their achievements invisible and inaudible. This is the constant intuition inspiring Rancière's work. Accordingly, the political commitment to equality must not limit itself to political or historical studies, as in "history from below" writings, but must also include the study of the thoughts and modes of expression of the dominated. Further, these must be registered and studied not from a condescending sociological point of view, but as expressions of human thought as valid and as interesting as those of the socially recognized thinkers, writers and artists.

The fundamental idea that Rancière formed in those years was thus the "radical equality between human beings in terms of their intelligence". A decisive encounter he made during his archival research helped him to definitively establish this core intuition. In *The Ignorant Schoolmaster* (1987, English translation 1991), Rancière gives a thorough exposition and defence of the "method of intellectual emancipation" of the French revolutionary and educational philosopher Joseph Jacotot (1770–1840). The personal tone in which the book is written,

INTRODUCTION: A JOURNEY IN EQUALITY

with Rancière's own voice constantly meshing with that of Jacotot, often to the point of indistinction, makes it an extraordinarily revealing source for his deeply held convictions. In Chapter 2, Yves Citton describes the radical, yet thoroughly consistent, view of individual intelligence Jacotot developed. Rancière's work can be seen as a systematic exploration of Jacotot's axiom, according to which "the same intelligence is at work in all the acts of the human spirit" (IS 18). In *The Ignorant Schoolmaster*, the axiom is made to apply more specifically to issues in education. But the implications of Jacotot's axiom point in many other directions. In particular, the critical upshot of the radical equality thesis is the explanation of the fact of existing inequality as a result of hierarchically organized social structures. Rancière shares Jacotot's vision of social orders as being fundamentally structured on a divisive logic, which separates those who know from those who do not, those who work from those who think, adult from child, man from woman, and so on.

The Jacotot axiom also contained the roots of Rancière's shift towards poetics and aesthetics. The idea that "the same intelligence is at work in all the acts of the human spirit" is to be understood not just as a claim about capacities of individuals but also about the possibility of communication between human beings. Jacotot's method of teaching consisted in asking students to constantly describe and explain what they had read, seen, discovered, in other people's works or in the observation of nature. This was based on his idea that learning is first a matter of will and attention, which force intellectual capacities to find out for themselves how things work. But it was also premised on the idea that thinking is inherently an act of translation: of the words of another into one's own words; but also of external symbolic meanings (the meaning of a word, a mathematical formula, and so on) into internal ones (when one understands them) via their passage through the materiality of language (or other media, for instance a drawing). The materiality of communication media, in particular of language, provides a common resource through which different individuals can share thoughts they only had at first in the privacy of their individual minds. In Jacotot's insistence on the importance of material tools to mediate the learning of new knowledge (like the book he recommended to his students as the start of learning for the most different types of knowledge), Rancière already found the possibility of grounding his radical–democratic thinking in poetic and artistic practices, in particular, in the radical-egalitarian potentialities of word-use, that is, of literature. Jacotot enabled him to link his initial interest in the working class with the idea of equality as a work of radical communication: "in the act of speaking, man doesn't transmit his knowledge, he makes poetry; he translates and invites others to do the same. He communicates as an artisan: as a person who handles words like tools" (IS 65). The encounter with Jacotot encouraged subtle but significant shifts in the direction of Rancière's thought. Whereas his early archival work still aimed to retrieve something like a genuine "workers' voice", he became gradually aware of the pitfalls of an approach that would treat particular forms of expression as representative of a whole class. Increasingly, Rancière was attracted to the singular voices of isolated individuals who had attempted precisely to throw away the iron cast of class categorization. In these individual efforts at transcending class, Rancière gradually saw the most important social and political lesson. *The Nights of Labour* had already drawn attention to the specific ways in which singular voices could contest the logic of the category of "class". Jacotot's view that human intelligences are equal only inasmuch as they are compared individually, and his adjacent vision of social groupings as irreducibly governed by hierarchical logics, confirmed this new direction. This shift towards individual destinies also corroborated Rancière's increasing interest in the overlaps between politics, poetics and aesthetics. Many of those isolated voices of the workers' movement had attempted to transcend their condition by engaging in works normally reserved for the classes able to afford leisure. The structural inequality organizing social orders therefore turned out to be not only related to the organization of production, but also, and perhaps more fundamentally, to the implicit divisions in the realm of discourse, between those whose voices were deemed significant, and those whose voices remained inaudible. Class domination then would be rooted and expressed first and foremost in access to symbolic expression. Conversely, though, this focus on symbolic expression also started to show the emancipatory logic of modern poetics: underneath the social restrictions that seemed to regulate access to language, language itself, in the post-revolutionary ages, turned out to be open to all.

Interventions in political philosophy

The mid-1980s saw the demise of socialist experiments in real politics, culminating in the fall of the Berlin Wall in 1989. In France, Mitterrand's election to the presidency in 1981 had raised new hope on the Left. Based on a coalition between socialists and communists, it was the first major victory of the Left at the highest levels of power, reminiscent of the great electoral victory of the Popular Front in 1936. Soon,

INTRODUCTION: A JOURNEY IN EQUALITY

however, these hopes were dashed as the economic situation deteriorated and the socialist government began to return to the social–liberal orthodoxy of the time.

The rise of social–liberal and neoliberal policy thinking all around the world coincided with great shifts in the intellectual landscape. Marxism rapidly waned as the central conceptual matrix. It was replaced first by the style of normative political philosophy for which John Rawls's *Theory of Justice* represented the paradigm. For European thinkers, Habermas's communicative theory of democracy also presented a major model. Both Rawls's and Habermas's models contained sufficiently robust commitments to social equality to tempt many to embrace these new conceptual languages as appropriate political vocabularies for the times. The third major paradigm that emerged from the collapse of Marxist theory and practice was Foucault's genealogical method. In France, in particular, it became the method of choice for social and political theorists intent on continuing the task of radical critique through new categories.

In the face of these great shifts, Rancière remained steadfast in his fundamental commitment to equality. From his perspective, the major new paradigms all had something problematic about them. The problem was not their abandonment of Marx and of the rhetoric of the revolutionary years. The encounter with Jacotot showed precisely how one could hold on to the principle of radical equality without recourse to the Marxist rhetoric that was prevalent just a decade earlier. But, just as much as at the time of the struggle against Marxist orthodoxy, the concern to let "the people" speak in their own voices now too provided a critical vantage point on these newly emerging paradigms.

Rancière's interventions in political philosophy in the late 1980s and early 1990s therefore displayed a similar "out-of-left-field" aspect towards the dominant thinking of the day, as did the earlier research in the "logic of revolt". His writings in political theory, especially *Disagreement* (1995, English translation 1998), his major book in this area, started to make his name known beyond the small circles that were reading his work in the previous decade. Rancière developed a conceptual political vocabulary that was not directly antagonistic to, but rather shifted and displaced, the conceptual languages developed at the time, in order to focus specifically on the position of those excluded from political participation. His philosophy of radical equality thus became an explicit defence of radical democracy.

As Samuel A. Chambers shows in Chapter 4, against the general tendency of the new political philosophy to develop models without raising the problem of participation, Rancière generalized Jacotot's lesson and showed how what was discussed as politics was in fact mostly the smooth managing of the social order, premised on unquestioned social hierarchies. Thus his famous distinction between the "police" and "politics" emerged. The contrast between "*la police*", "*le politique*" and "*la politique*" made it look as though Rancière was situating himself within the paradigms and spoke the language developed by key figures in French philosophy at the time, most notably Foucault's genealogy of the liberal state, and Derridean deconstruction. But the "thought from below" perspective transformed these concepts and made them incommensurable with any of these references.

Similarly, his central concept of "disagreement", while an explicit critique of Habermas's politics of consensus, was also subtly critical of Jean-François Lyotard's "*différend*". Lyotard's "*différend*" postulates an incommensurability between types of discourse, whereas Rancière's stance is predicated on the opposite idea that it is always possible, in principle, and indeed, it is the very definition of democratic politics, to establish the commonality of experience and thinking between people, against the fact of social separation due to hierarchies. Equally, the logic of "heteronomy", the idea that political agency implies distancing oneself from one's social identity, sounded similar to the conceptualizations of ethics and politics that were being developed at the time following Jacques Derrida and Emmanuel Levinas (Rogozinski *et al.* 1983). But Rancière's "heteronomic" logic of politics is not premised, as these latter accounts are, on an ethics of alterity, itself underpinned by a radical critique of Western metaphysics. Instead, as Todd May demonstrates in Chapter 5, it revolves around the idea that political practice transcends the social destinies and identities imposed by social positions. The political disagreement, emerging on the basis of a hierarchical wrong, therefore creates political subjectivities, via processes of political "*subjectivation*" that are only contingently related to pre-existing social identities.

The first part of *Disagreement* allowed Rancière to make explicit and fully articulate the alternative social and political ontology that inspired his earlier interventions. In an important subsequent chapter, he used the perspective afforded by this alternative view to mount a vast, critical confrontation with the tradition of political philosophy. As Bruno Bosteels shows in Chapter 6, Rancière's aim in conducting such a confrontation was more systematic than historical. Rancière identified three fundamental strands, "archipolitics", "parapolitics" and "metapolitics", initially taking their roots in classical references: Plato, Aristotle and Marx. In each case, he showed how the classical author developed a mode of thinking about politics that still structured conceptually the contemporary field. The critical exegeses of the classics led to implicit, critical interventions in debates of the time, as well as indirect vindications of his claim that politics is synonymous with radical democracy. What unified these separate strands for Rancière was their attempt to circumvent, each in its own way, the "scandal" of politics, that is, the practical assertion of the axiom of equality. As Bosteels argues, the author to whom Rancière's thinking is most aptly contrasted here, as in other aspects of his work, is that of Alain Badiou.

From politics to poetics

Intimately linked with this sustained effort in political theory was Rancière's direct engagement with poetic and aesthetic issues. The conceptual link between the two areas was ensured by the notion of the "sharing", or "distributing", of the "sensible": *"partage du sensible"* (see Davide Panagia's account of it in Chapter 7). The concept basically names the critical intuition at play in the notion of "thought from below". As we saw, the central question for Rancière concerns the ways in which the thoughts, voices and actions of the dominated are made invisible and inaudible in the hierarchy of activities underpinning social orders. At the root of inequality therefore is a problem of perception, of *"aesthesis"*, in classical philosophical terms: the question of social domination can be rephrased in terms of which activities, and whose activities, can literally be seen and heard. The "sharing of the sensible" denotes the ambiguous logic whereby society relies on a bringing together of individuals and groups (sharing as having in common), while functioning on the basis of the separation between those whose voices and actions count, are meaningful, and those who remain invisible and inaudible (sharing as separating).

Throughout the 1990s, Rancière's work increasingly focused on this "aesthetic" aspect of social struggle and politics, to the point where he would soon invert the relationship between the two realms, and turn to the political dimensions implicit in aesthetic models and in artistic works.

The initial avenue for the study of this new dimension was his interest in the status of literature in the post-revolutionary context. Literature already had a privileged place in Rancière's early work, because of the centrality of speech and expression in his egalitarianism. Equality for him is primarily the equality people are afforded when they are taken seriously, as valid partners in a dialogue, as people who make sense. For instance, his archival research into workers' voices turned away from proletarian folklore and toward those proletarians who sought a place on the literary (poetic, philosophical, theatrical) stage of their time. Conversely, however, the romantic conception of literature also represents, in its own way, a striking illustration of the axiom of equality characteristic of the modern era. This conception is no longer premised on the strict division of genres and styles along the lines of social hierarchy (tragedy about kings for men of high rank versus comedy about everyday folk for people of low rank): it works on the assumption that everything speaks to everyone; that any form of discourse is in principle available to anyone. This converging of equality in the political and the literary explains a central claim already made in *Disagreement*, namely, that "the modern political animal is a literary animal" (D 37). With this turn of phrase Rancière meant to defend the claim that the primary mode through which equality is demanded is via actions whose main ends and means are discursive: by rejecting certain forms of social descriptions (for instance viewing workers, or women, or people of certain "races" as minors, as not being able to take part in certain activities); and by attempting to impose new descriptions (woman as mature citizen; worker as entitled to certain rights; migrant as equal, and so on). Already in his texts of political theory, Rancière connected directly the political and literary revolutions.

The evolution of Rancière's work in the 1990s corresponded to a more direct engagement with these discursive, "literary" aspects of politics. This shift in his work, from politics to poetics, or rather, the politics of poetics, was anticipated by *The Names of History: On the Poetics of Knowledge*, published in 1992 (English translation 1994). Philip Watts, in Chapter 8, studies this first substantial "poetic" enquiry in Rancière's work, and its significance for a good understanding of Rancière's critical intervention in the methodology of the social sciences. In this book, Rancière revisited his long-standing interest in the history of the labour movement and modern democratic struggles, from the new perspective of an interrogation into the stylistic and political decisions that underpin any attempt to write history. Just as he had unveiled, in *The Philosopher and his Poor*, the implicit assumptions about the divisions of the social upon which philosophical discourse relies, he uncovered in *The Names of History* the implicit views of "the people" at work in the writings of some of the major references in modern French historiography. At the end of the book, Rancière gave crucial indications about the literary dimensions of struggles for equality, that is, both how modern literature could provide a resource for these struggles, and how these struggles expressed themselves in literary ways. A study on Mallarmé, published in 1996, confirmed the new orientation in Rancière's work, that is, his attempt to find the pulse of radical equality in the very stylistic materiality of even the most sophisticated of modernist writings.

This research into the interrelations between poetics and politics culminated in the publication in 1998 of one of Rancière's most impressive and important books, *La parole muette: Essai sur les contradictions de la littérature*. Despite what the title might indicate, the book proposed not just a theory of modern literature; it effectively laid the foundations for a general theory of aesthetic modernity. The rich detail of this theory is well captured by the concept of "regimes of the arts". In Chapter 9, Jean-Philippe Deranty characterizes the basic features of this key Rancièrean concept, and presents the main differences between the three historical regimes identified by him: the ethical, the representative and the aesthetic.

From poetics to aesthetics

The last section of this book is dedicated to Rancière's writings on different art forms. This corresponds to the main focus of his work in the last decade. Apart from a small book published in 2007 in defence of the idea of democracy (*The Hatred of Democracy*) and the republication of his interviews (*Et tant pis pour les gens fatigués*) and newspaper articles (*Moments politiques*), the bulk of Rancière's activity since 2000 has been dedicated to poetics and aesthetics. He has been invited to deliver keynote addresses to many, increasingly prestigious, international exhibitions and conferences, and has contributed to a number of exhibition catalogues. He has also published lengthy film studies in French cinema journals, notably in *Trafic* and *Cahiers du cinéma*. While initially it was his writings in political theory that attracted interest, today his writings in aesthetics have become hugely influential.

In Chapter 10, Alison Ross focuses on Rancière's studies in literature. As she shows, the key concepts he has advanced in his study of literature also apply by extension to other arts, in particular the visual arts. These concepts, in particular "expressivity", "literarity" and "mute speech", are the aesthetic equivalents to the egalitarian revolutions in politics: they point to the idea that, in the post-Romantic paradigm, coinciding with the post-revolutionary paradigm in politics, it is not just social positions and social forms of expression that can in principle always demand to be treated as equal, but also aesthetic objects and expressions. The principle of radical equality extends to include the objects of representation themselves. For example a building, such as Notre-Dame Cathedral, can become a literary work's main character, as in Victor Hugo's novel.

Toni Ross (in Chapter 11 on painting) and Hassan Melehy (in Chapter 12 on film) detail the implications of this conceptual extension of key concepts and arguments from politics to the visual arts. In recent years, the concept of *"montage"*, borrowed from film technique, has become Rancière's central metaphor to think of particular art works or the aesthetic worlds of particular artists. The *montage* metaphor allows him to focus on the ways, each time different and specific, with which particular art works or artists deal with the new potentialities offered by the post-Romantic paradigm. Against the tendency of sweeping narratives to frame and contain the expressive potential of art works within predetermined directions, Rancière aims to retrieve in the field of the arts powers of creativity similar to the ones that he had earlier sought in historical social movements.

While so many thinkers of his generation are burning today what they adored yesterday, or the day before yesterday, Rancière's work proves remarkable for its consistency throughout the decades. His unflinching commitment to the ideas of equality and emancipatory action, first applied to social and political issues, then to literature and the arts, has produced a major body of work now celebrated all around the world. The ambition of this volume is to present some of the major concepts that punctuate that body of work in order to give a sense of its richness and sophistication.

PART I

Philosophy

ONE

Logical revolts

Jean-Philippe Deranty

This chapter deals with Rancière's first writings, following his rupture with Althusserian Marxism, whose *post mortem* is drawn in the 1974 book-length essay, *Althusser's Lesson*. Rancière's disillusionment with the orthodoxy of his time coincided with his involvement in the movements following the 1968 student and workers' revolts. The egalitarian spirit fuelling these movements led to a radical challenge of all social hierarchies. Rancière's research in that decade sought to apply this radical egalitarian acumen at the point where "*logos*", as the catchphrase for all the forms of reasoned discourse (from the arts and sciences to political deliberations), meets with the institutions of social life. This led him in particular to concentrate his research on "the workers' dream in nineteenth century France" (the sub-title of *The Nights of Labour*, the master work of that period). By recovering the theoretical and poetical writings, the organizational plans and political manifestos, the hopes and complaints of the nineteenth-century proletarians, Rancière aimed to achieve a double aim: on the positive side, to demonstrate the capacity of the dominated to use the resources of *logos*, their ability to articulate their own thoughts and feelings on the basis of their specific experiences; on the negative side, to unveil the boundaries and divisions that are projected from the social into the intellectual realms, and that prevent the dominated from having their discourses count as meaningful and significant.

The first key concepts in Rancière's work thus stem directly from his intensive research into the writings of the proletarian philosophers, poets and activists of the first half of the nineteenth century. Yet his general objective to bring class struggle into *logos*, to describe and accompany all the different "logical revolts" (*révoltes logiques*), also led to a radical gesture in terms of philosophical writing. Rancière refused to express the conclusions reached in studying the writings of the proletarian thinkers in the abstract languages, or using the canonical references, of academic philosophy and social theory. Rather, the key concepts encapsulating his initial approach were simple terms, down-to-earth words, but ones that contained deep and complex meanings. The general inversion of hierarchies was thus brought to bear on style itself. The concrete and the everyday, the simple material, that level, namely, at which working people are deemed by intellectuals and dominating classes to be stuck, was shown to hide magnificent thoughts and sublime feelings comparable to the established philosophy and poetry. Three such expressions in particular capture the constellations of ideas articulated in Rancière's initial research: the voice of workers (*la parole ouvrière*); the nights of proletarians (*la nuit des prolétaires*); the land of the people (*le pays du peuple*).

Logical revolts and the voice of workers

The expression that probably summarizes Rancière's overall theoretical practice most accurately is the early motto of the "*révoltes logiques*", *logical revolts*, a motto borrowed from the prose poem "Democracy" by Arthur Rimbaud (Rimbaud 1957: 128). When the young militants chose this title for their new journal, they were explicitly aiming to unite under the same banner the revolts of the early nineteenth-century workers and the creator of poetic modernity in France. This was an original research project, suggestive on many levels. It suggested that there is no qualitative gap between the poems of the glorified genius and the best writings of obscure proletarian poets, philosophers and reformers. It demanded therefore that the same intellectual application, care and sophistication be used in reading their writings as was demanded in reading the great poet, or indeed the established philosophers (see the later reading of Rimbaud in FW, but also the readings of Mallarmé in M and PL). It perhaps even suggested that Rimbaud, as a late child of the nineteenth century and a young witness of the Paris Commune, might have been an unconscious heir, together with the socialists of this generation, of these early proletarian writers. Altogether, it suggested that the early revolts of the proletarians were as much revolts in speaking, writing and thinking, "logical" revolts, revolts within *logos*, as political, social or economic ones. It set up already the constant to and fro between class positions, articulated around uses of language, that is the hallmark of Rancière's method.

Kristin Ross's indispensable book on May '68 in France documents the important editorial statement in the first issue of *Révoltes logiques*. One passage is worth quoting in full:

> *Révoltes logiques* wishes simply to listen again to what social history has shown, and resituate, in its debates and what it has at stake, the thought from below. The gap between the official genealogies of subversion – for example, the "history of the workers' movement" – and its real forms of elaboration, circulation, reappropriation, resurgence. The disparity in forms of revolt. Its contradictory characteristics. Its internal phenomena of micropowers. What is unexpected about it. With the simple idea that class struggle doesn't cease to exist, just because it doesn't conform to what one learns about it in school ... *Révoltes logiques* ... will try to follow the transversal paths of revolt, its contradictions, its lived experience and its dreams. (Ross 2002: 128)

Another document, the preface to the anthology of early proletarian writings published with Alain Faure (*La Parole ouvrière*), makes a comparable declaration of intent:

> to return to the concrete conditions of the elaboration of a revolutionary tradition that was specifically proletarian; to analyse the ways in which it encountered social theories in problematic fashion, from utopian socialisms to Marxism; but also to highlight the internal problems inherent in this tradition, its contradictions and its limits. (PO 338, my trans.)

The programme of research is clear: to undercut theoretical accounts of the social question that have been developed from outside and imposed from above, and instead, to let the workers speak for themselves, to read seriously and reconstruct painstakingly their own efforts of expression and organization. The theoretical opponents are numerous: Marxist dogmatism, which, starting with Marx himself, tends to pour contempt over much of these efforts of expression and organization because they do not conform to the ideal line that is supposed to lead from the formation of class consciousness to universal emancipation via party discipline; *gauchiste* spontaneism, nomadic desire or "*nouveaux philosophes*" line, which all overlook the intellectual sophistication of proletarian thinking in their search for the fantasmatic innocence of "the people"; the folkloric interest in "popular culture"; the Foucaldian method of genealogical reconstruction, always prompt to identify the logic of power hiding in discourses and practices seeking emancipation. Against these trends, Rancière wanted to retrieve the force and complexity of "*la parole ouvrière*", "the workers' voice", or "workers' speech". But doing justice to the sophistication and complexity of the "thought from below" is not to sacralize it. In some instances, the patient historical and exegetical work is able to demonstrate how refined this thought can be, how crude the intellectual reconstructions applied to it from outside. For instance, in an article of 1979, against the suspicions raised by genealogists of the time, Rancière retrieves the intellectual inventiveness and political courage of those women (notably Suzanne Voilquin) who, in the 1850s, strove to translate for themselves, from the specific perspective of their gender position, the Saint-Simonian religion of universal emancipatory love or the teachings of Fourier (SP 85–95). In other instances, however, the ambiguities and paradoxes of the thought from below must be highlighted, as when Rancière underlines the ambiguous relationship of an essentially male labour movement to female emancipation (SP 63–84; GE), or the compromising of twentieth-century unionism with the Vichy regime (SP 117–63). From the most sublime to the most ambiguous, however, in every case it is a matter of letting sense emerge from the speech and actions of the actors themselves.

The nights of labour

La parole ouvrière still had an implicit Marxist agenda. The anthology and the commentary organizing it aimed to study the reality of class consciousness, in the multiplicity of its forms, below the overbearing discourse of organized Marxism. This explains the book's focus on the 1830–51 period. This was a period when new forms of workers organization were devised in France; new forms of speech were created, and a true, collective "workers' voice" emerged. The workers' active participation in the regime change of 1830, followed by the first mass strikes of the 1830s (notably the Canut rebellion in Lyon in 1831), led directly to the creation of a proletarian political voice, which played a decisive role in the democratic revolution of 1848. Against the orthodoxy of science versus ideology, the concept of "*parole ouvrière*" aimed to uncover the great multiplicity of forms of speech, but it was still aiming to pursue the emergence of the unified consciousness of one class.

In the master work of this period, *The Nights of Labour*, the perspective has shifted. The period studied is the same. The book's three parts are organized chronologically, starting with the first attempts at self-expression following on from the workers' participation in the 1830 revolution; continuing with a study of the Saint-Simonian projects developed during in the 1830s and 1840s; and finishing with the great disillusionment following the failures of the Icarian colonies in Egypt and the USA, in the 1840s and 1850s. But this time, Rancière's intention is no longer simply to capture a collective proletarian discourse in the diversity of its voices. This time, the focus is on individual voices, like the philosopher–carpenter Gauny, the seamstress Désirée Véret, the laundry-maid Jeanne Deroin or the metal-worker Pierre Vinçard, to name but a few of the most unusual characters in the book, beside the names from the labour movement that history has remembered, like the leaders of the Saint-Simonian movement, Cabet and Enfantin. Later in the book, Rancière's analysis focuses more squarely on the paradoxes, contradictions, ambiguities, dialectical difficulties encountered by the proletarian thinkers in their attempts to articulate their experience, understand the mechanisms of oppression, organize new modes of work, and create new forms of community. The underlying intuition driving the project seems to have shifted. Now, there is no conclusion, not even, as in the other texts of the time, conclusions that could be drawn implicitly from the historical narratives and exegetical readings. The demonstration of the insoluble knots encountered by the proletarian writers seems to be the main point. This makes for a puzzling book. What is Rancière attempting to show with this series of allusive and aporetic readings of obscure, early proletarian writers?

It seems that the very impossibility to draw definitive, neat and consistent, black and white conclusions from the trials and tribulations of these isolated voices of the early labour movement is by itself the deep political, indeed the deep philosophical lesson Rancière wants to learn, and wants us to learn from his research into "the workers' dream". The book attempts to accomplish performatively through his reading of the obscure proletarian writers and our reading of his intricate renderings of them, the type of dis-identification that these workers were forced to experience in their flesh, in their militant action, and in their thinking. The ultimate logic of Rancière's paradoxical reading is therefore that there is no ultimate, essential grounding of a politics of emancipation. Every time emancipatory political action attempts to ground itself in some essential property, it falls into contradictions and paradoxes that make it miss its self-given target, transform it into its opposite: neither the ethical value of work, nor the demand for full employment or general education, nor individual needs, nor collective happiness, nor universal love, nor some specific proletarian identity, nor gender identities can by themselves stabilize the struggle against domination and make it a univocal, unambiguous project.

However, some positive lessons remain beyond the sceptical, aporetic, perhaps pessimistic, message drawn from the exemplary fates of these proletarian writers: the grandeur of the sentiments expressed in their writings; the unique beauty of their prose, despite their homage to the canons of their time; the sophistication of their political and organizational discussions, despite the paradoxes and contradictions they encountered. Precisely, Rancière implicitly shows that "real" thinkers avoid these contradictions only because they paper over them, mainly because they do not have to live them. All this combined leads to an important, positive political and theoretical message. It commands all the master thinkers, academics, experts and other well-wishers of the working classes to stop pontificating about them from above, and to simply let them speak, hear their voices, trust their capacity to spell out their needs and aspirations. The sceptical, pessimistic message is thus inverted into a message of political hope: the oppressed and the down-trodden already possess the intellectual means to articulate their plight and demand their rights. All they require are the opportunities (the allies, the material resources, the institutional openings) to make their speech public and implement their plans.

The concept of the "nights of labour", or rather, as Rancière's title says literally, the "nights of the proletarians", thus points to the other side of all that is supposed to exhaust proletarian reality: the reality of work, the clichés about working-life folklore, the economic or sociological truths about working classes, and so on. The "nights of labour" is only a vague signifier encapsulating all the different attempts by which those who were deemed unable to think, speak or write, mainly because they were tied to work, prove otherwise and thus escape the reifying categories through which they are viewed. But, as history shows, the content of those "nights" cannot be specified in advance. Different individuals, at different times, in different contexts, fill them differently. Indeed, this is one of the positive contents to be drawn from the empty concept: that beneath the clichés and reifying views, the "people" (the dominated, the exploited, the suffering classes, and so on) do not exist as such, always escape the definitions superimposed upon them. Despite the plasticity of the concept, however, some formal traits are common among all the different ways of filling these "nights" (i.e. of escaping the social destiny associated with working life): the desire to rebel; the courage needed to do so; the necessity to use intelligence, imagination and eloquence in order to implement the reversal of fortune.

The land of the people

In the years that followed the publication of his first master book, the shift in Rancière's position became more pronounced as he began to look at politics from the other side of the "barrier", to use another one of his key metaphors at the time (GT). That is, he no longer studied the possibilities and difficulties of political and intellectual emancipation by restricting himself to the discursive realm of those who had the most to gain from it. Rather, he combined this perspective (the "thought from below") with a more traditional critical dialogue with established writers and theorists.

Short Voyages to the Land of the People, which was published in 1990 (English translation 1991) but gathered studies written just a few years after *Nights of Labour*, signalled this shift from the immanent historical research into the labour movement and its obscure thinkers and poets, to more recognizable critical studies into politics and aesthetics.

The book describes a series of travels in which the geographical, the political and the literary are tightly interwoven. Most chapters are dedicated to artists (mostly poets, such as Wordsworth, Georg Büchner and Rainer Maria Rilke) whose geographical journeys lead them also to "the land of the people", in other words, to an encounter with the lower classes, in experiences of transgression of class boundaries. Other chapters recount the destinies of individuals "from the people" who transgressed class boundaries in the other direction, and did so not just spatially and sociologically, but also and crucially by reading and writing. This constellation of interests is representative of the development of Rancière's thought after his "proletarian" decade and captures the spirit of his later work. The singular voices of the proletarian poets and philosophers, beyond their limitations and contradictions, demonstrated the radical change brought about by the political revolutions characterizing modernity. Now, anyone can in principle speak about anything, even though the tendency to categorize forms of speech according to class distinctions remains ever-present and powerful. But this liberation of speech is not just of political relevance. Since speech is at play (expression and deliberation), the revolution ushering in modern society also has a direct aesthetic import. More specifically, Rancière was sensitive from the beginning to the fact that the disidentification operated by the proletarian voices was expressed in, and in fact required, reference to literary practices. Increasingly, Rancière links the drifting journeys of individuals disengaging from their social destinies with the radical freedom gained by literature in the wake of the Romantic revolution. He becomes fascinated with figures of individuals from the people who encounter "drifting" letters, that is texts that represent in their narrative, or incarnate in their themes or styles, the detachment of the written text from the traditional circuit that used to take it unequivocally from the well-identified authorial voice to a well-identified target audience, and the ways in which proletarian lives are transformed by this encounter with the drifting qualities of modern literature. Conversely, he is fascinated by modern writers who discover that the words they use can attach to places and people they had not foreseen when they wrote them.

The concept of "the land of the people" is the knot at which all these different threads are tied together. It designates first of all the place within society where traditional boundaries between classes, occupations, modes of thought and expression are radically challenged, as those "from below" demonstrate over and again how incorrect and unjust the assumptions were that relegated them to this position within the hierarchy. As a result, the concept also designates an aesthetic point of contestation: the point where the clear correspondences between words and reality are also challenged, and the letter is shown to be open for a multiplicity of uses and interpretations. This signals already one of the most striking aspects of Rancière's work, namely the seamless continuity, indeed the intimate link, it establishes between the equality of individuals in the political and the equality of materials and topics in the aesthetic.

TWO

"The ignorant schoolmaster": knowledge and authority
Yves Citton

Few endeavours could appear more self-contradictory (and self-defeating) than an attempt to *explain* the argument developed by Jacques Rancière in his 1987 book *The Ignorant Schoolmaster* (subtitled *Five Lessons in Intellectual Emancipation*, English translation 1991). The main assertion repeated in this remarkably subtle praise of equality is that the most perverse form of oppression and subjection is located in the very act of explaining. Most of us tend to take for granted that giving explanations – and what is teaching but "giving explanations"? – is a noble act of generosity and emancipation through which the explainer raises the explainee to a higher level of knowledge and understanding. I have spent a good amount of time reading, analyzing, discussing and teaching *The Ignorant Schoolmaster* over the last decades; I am eager to help more people discover and enjoy its power and its beauty. I hear people say that Rancière is not an easy philosopher to understand, and that his theory of emancipation is not an easy argument to grasp; therefore I am about to explain the main notions, assumptions and consequences of this book, as well as its charms and its stakes. But since the main lesson of the book is that explanation runs contrary to emancipation, I – along with my fellow contributors to a volume dedicated to "explaining" Rancière's key concepts – seem bound to betray the author and his ideas by the very nature of our explanatory gesture.

The paradox goes further. The anti-explanatory message advocated by *The Ignorant Schoolmaster* is carried out through the explanation of someone else's theories: Rancière has recovered the writings of a certain Joseph Jacotot (who first discovered that explanation runs contrary to emancipation), and he explains what Jacotot wrote in his theoretical works. A closer look, however, will reveal that, rather than "explaining" Jacotot's theory, Rancière *rewrites* it. This chapter may therefore not be so self-contradictory (nor self-defeating) in its attempt to rewrite Rancière's rewriting of Jacotot.

Joseph Jacotot's reversal of the explanatory model

While presenting Rancière as a philosopher is not inappropriate (for he is a great inventor of concepts), it tends nevertheless to downplay two essential features of his interventions in the philosophical field: their frailty and their literariness. In this regard, none of his books is more *tentative* than *The Ignorant Schoolmaster*: it is experimental (it resembles a thought-experiment), provisional (it sketches a theory still awaiting its full development), conceptually fragile, and argumentatively problematic (it thrives on a paradox). While Rancière has written a great deal about literature during his later career, rarely has he been as literary as in this early book, which takes the form of a narrative (the narrative of "an intellectual adventure") as much as that of a philosophical argument. Let us first survey its plot, centred on its protagonist, Joseph Jacotot.

Once upon a time, there was a teacher (who had previously been a soldier, an administrator and a deputy) who was exiled from France after the Restoration of Monarchy in 1815, and who became a lecturer in French literature at the University of Louvain in the Netherlands. Faced with students who did not speak French, and unable to speak Flemish himself, Jacotot came up with a practical fix: he handed his students a bilingual version of Fénelon's masterpiece *Télémaque* (one of the most widely read and admired didactic novels of the eighteenth century), and told them to learn French by figuring out this text in its original language with the help of the Flemish translation. This practical fix was the start of a philosophical experiment leading to an intellectual revolution: to Jacotot's surprise, the students soon managed – so we are told at least – to master enough of Fénelon's language to write essays (in French) about the book, achieving a very decent level of written expression. On the foundation provided by the fact that his students had managed to learn French without any form of explanation, Jacotot started building a radical reformation of all pedagogical methods under the title of "Universal Teaching" (*Enseignement universel*), later renamed "the panecastic system".

Such a reformation had a premise: every human being must necessarily be capable of learning by himself (through trial and error, guesses and self-correction), since this is how all of us learned our mother tongue. And since this is how we learned our first language, why could we not learn a second language in the same way? Beyond languages, why couldn't we learn piano or painting in the same fashion? Or mathematics, or chemistry, or economics?

It also had a far-reaching implication: the teacher's main function is not to transmit content (to give his knowledge to the ignorant pupils), but to drive the students' will. Indeed, the figure of the teacher was not to be dispensed with along this path of reformation: Jacotot *was* instrumental in the process that led this group of students to learn a language they did not originally know. However, the part he played in the process was not the one typically defined by the Old Testament of pedagogical theory, which Jacotot and Rancière simply refer to as "the Old Master" (or rather, in the French original, as "the Old Lady": *la Vieille*). In Jacotot's practice, the teacher's role was limited to *influencing the will*, and did not include any actual transfer of knowledge. His pedagogical act was not an explication (of the rules of French grammar), but a series of commands: "Read this book! Pay attention to these words!" If the Good News brought to mankind by the apostle Jacotot was that every child of man is intelligent enough to learn anything without the help of an explicator, the reformed Gospel of Universal Teaching was not meant to put all teachers out of a job: it tended only to recast them as Commanders instead of Explainers.

This implication, however, had a surprising but important corollary. Since a teacher did not need to (be able to) *explain* the content of the course, the teacher did not need to *know* nor *understand* what he was teaching. After having "taught" French (which he knew), Jacotot decided to teach piano or chemistry (in which he had no competence whatsoever). And it worked – or so we are told. A perfectly ignorant schoolmaster can teach a discipline that he has not mastered himself, since his role in the educational process is not to provide any specific content, but mainly to mobilize the learners' will. Hence the disturbing reversal of values suggested by Rancière's title. Far from naming and denouncing the disgrace of an impostor, *The Ignorant Schoolmaster* soon rings as a promise: there may be a blessed day of Intellectual Emancipation when "ignorant" people will be recognized as perfectly qualified schoolmasters; a day when children of human beings will have realized that they are intelligent enough to learn by themselves, without the need for any (superior) explicator, only with the commanding help (and encouragement) of their ignorant brothers.

A second, and even more disturbing, corollary followed: if the act of explication was in no way necessary to ensure proper learning, it did nevertheless fulfil a very important function in the process of socialization, by teaching the students that they were ignorant, incapable of escaping ignorance by their own means. For here is Jacotot's (and Rancière's) most subversive assertion: the true (if unconscious) function of all the generous, altruistic, philanthropic, enlightened and enlightening providers of explications is to instil a sense of inequality deep into the minds and souls of all the children of the Republic. These children all had the original experience of learning (their mother tongue, as well as most "life lessons") by themselves. They all spontaneously acted upon that premise of an equality of intelligence (according to which all of us are able to figure out, by trial and error, what we need to know in order to master the codes that surround and structure us). In light of this original experience, the School (the educational system, the Old Master, *la Vieille*, with its pedagogical practices and its armies of well-meaning Teachers, Instructors, Masters and Professors) appears as a tremendous machine devoted to neutralizing that spontaneous power to learn by oneself. The true (if untold) content of the teacher's explication has nothing to do with French grammar, fingering techniques on the piano or molecular interactions in chemistry: it is a monotonous chorus repeating, class after class: "You do not know how to learn", "You need me, i.e. my (superior) explications, in order properly to learn what you are learning". Against the practical evidence of the equality of all intelligences, as demonstrated by the mastery of our mother tongue, the very structure of the (modern) School, with its emphasis on the act of explaining, works as the most powerful machine of indoctrination geared towards convincing us of the incapacity (you cannot learn by yourself) and inequality (some are knowledgeable, others are ignorant) of our intelligence.

Jacotot's reversal of the explanatory model thus leads to a drastic and highly discomforting indictment of the progressive educator's best intents: far from promoting equality by raising the (formerly) ignorant pupil to the higher status of an enabled knower, the act of transmitting knowledge through explication tends to generate and perpetuate a structure of inequality between the explainer and the explainee. Far from being reduced by the act of explanation, this structure of inequality is (re-)enforced each time the educator reasserts his superiority by performing as a knowledge-provider. Far from contributing to the pupil's emancipation, the explanatory model is to be seen as a dramatic source of "stultification" (*abrutissement*). Jacotot's argument, closely followed by Rancière's rewriting, precisely defines stultification as inherent to any relation in which "one intelligence is subordinated to another", while, on the contrary, the possibility of emancipation rests on maintaining a clear difference between the equality of intelligence and the possible subordination of the will. In Jacotot's Universal Teaching, "the act of an intelligence obey[s] only itself, while the will obeys another will" (IS 13).

From a pedagogical experiment to its political implications

Beyond the special case of classroom interactions and of teachers' explications, *The Ignorant Schoolmaster* contains in a nutshell one of Rancière's most fundamental and obstinate political assertions – the definition of politics as the verification of the presupposition of the equality of intelligence. The political implications of Jacotot's gesture can be traced on at least three levels.

First, they lead us to question the political uses of expertise. Since Plato's *Republic* (a constant punch ball in Rancière's political reflection), "those who know" (theologians, philosophers, economists, and all of their fellow-experts) have claimed the right to be invested with political authority in the name of their superior knowledge. The division of labour delineated by Socrates as illustrating the essence of justice in the macroscopic case of the City demanded that each individual remain in the place and function attributed to him by an optimal distribution of specialized skills: those who are best suited for making bread should be (and remain) bakers, those best at fighting should be (and remain) soldiers, and those best at understanding how the world goes should advise the kings (or become kings themselves) (*Republic* 433a–444a). It seems common sense to admit that we would be best governed if "those who know" were put in the position of being those who decide – just as it seems commonsensical to recognize that the explicator performs a generous act of equalization when he raises his listener to a higher level of understanding by transmitting his knowledge. Yet it is against this misleadingly self-evident equation between authority and knowledge that Rancière constructed the core of his political reflection.

In showing that the explainer tends to stultify the explainee due to the structural inequality of the explanatory model, Jacotot helps us see that the expert tends to kill the democratic process because of the very position from which he pretends to enlighten it. No matter how well intended or knowledgeable he may be in his disciplinary field, the expert represents a potential threat to democratic politics in so far as his very enunciation divides the citizenry in two: those who have the knowledge (and who are entitled to command), and those who lack the knowledge (and must therefore obey). Throughout most of his books,

Rancière has constantly denounced not, of course, "those who have knowledge", but those who let their expert knowledge become a tool for silencing the claims and resistance expressed by "the ignorant ones". In symmetrical contradiction to Plato's philosophy, Rancière repeats, book after book, that the endlessly subversive nature of democracy consists in accepting that "the ignorant ones" should be entitled to rule the City. His close reading of Jacotot revealed that "the ignorant person" is never defined as such by a mere lack of knowledge, but by an oppressive structure that transforms a perfectly able intellectual agent into a powerless recipient (supposed passively to absorb forms of knowledge produced for him, but never by him) – an oppressive structure that is perverse enough to masquerade its very production of "the ignorant person" as a remedy against ignorance! "What stultifies the common people is not the lack of instruction, but the belief in the inferiority of their intelligence" (IS 39). The first political lesson to be drawn from Jacotot thus consists in spotting the stultifying side-effects that never fail to accompany any discourse of expertise, in so far as it is in the nature of explication and expertise to produce the very inequality of knowledge and power it pretends to correct.

The second political implication of Rancière's reading of Jacotot can be encapsulated in a term that has become trendy (in France) only several years after the publication of *The Ignorant Schoolmaster*, a term that Rancière has never really appropriated for himself but that nevertheless synthesizes a fundamental dimension of his thinking: *empowerment*. While the stultifying explicator pretends generously to give something that is lacking in "the ignorant person" (knowledge, understanding), the empowering emancipator mainly purports to reveal a power (to understand) that is already present in the agent – even though it may not be accessible to him without the mediation of the emancipator. The problem, in education, is not to transmit knowledge: "the problem is to reveal an intelligence to itself" (IS 28). Jacotot's pupils had it within themselves to learn (Fénelon's French) by themselves: the schoolteacher only provided an opportunity (a context, a situation, a framing structure) through which their power to learn found the chance to be actualized.

In this radical conception, empowerment consists not in a transmission of power (which would imply and would in fact produce an inequality of status between the giver and the receiver), but in the realization–actualization of a power whose source is located within the agent himself. All human children have the power to learn their mother tongue (and any other language) without the assistance of an explicator. The intervention of such an explicator, far from helping them to learn,

"THE IGNORANT SCHOOLMASTER": KNOWLEDGE AND AUTHORITY

"teaches" them that they are incapable of learning by themselves (it "stultifies" them; it constitutes them as "ignorant"). The emancipator's role, therefore, does not consist in providing the agents with anything they lack (knowledge, understanding, intelligence, power), but simply in helping them remove the obstacles that separate them from their own power. Emancipation, as we already saw, concerns the will (rather than knowledge or intelligence). Its main message fits perfectly with the motto of empowerment politics: "you already have the power; all you need is the will to use it for your own (common) good".

Slogans modelled on the "Yes, you can!" pattern can be both emancipatory and oppressive. Their empowering nature is often counterbalanced by an ideology of free will and unconditioned choice, which tends to blame the victims' fate on their lack of "will power", rather than on the situation that conditioned their choices. Few situations can be escaped by the mere will to *just do it!* "Universal teaching is not the key to success granted to the enterprising who explore the prodigious powers of the will. Nothing could be more opposed to the thought of emancipation than that advertising slogan" (IS 56). Politics, as Rancière defines it, consists in producing or in exploiting the practical conditions (context, situation, structural framework) that will solicit the agent's will to use the power at his disposal. When Rancière presents politics as a process of subjectification, he undermines in advance any appeal to a will that would be unconditioned, that is "free" to "just do" something if only the agent made "the right choice". His historical research in the nineteenth-century archives of the labour movement as well as in Jacotot's pedagogical enterprise describe and analyse socio-historical conditions that have allowed for a process of emancipatory subjectification to take place (i.e. for a certain type of will to be produced within a certain type of collective structure).

Hence the third main political lesson to be drawn from *The Ignorant Schoolmaster*: because it consists mainly in processes of subjectification, democratic politics revolves around the practical verification of the presupposition of the equality of intelligence. Since this principle is located at the very core of Jacques Rancière's philosophy, its complex articulation needs to be spelled out with some care and patience, in at least five different steps.

1. The basic assertion is a "principle of equality of all speaking beings" (IS 39): "everyone is of equal intelligence" (IS 101). If one can define "man as a will served by an intelligence" (IS 51), one should immediately add that, although there may be "inequality in the *manifestations* of intelligence ... there is no hierarchy of

intellectual capacity" (IS 27). All of Rancière's writings amount to a persistent and deepening reflection on equality in general, political equality in particular, with the principle of equality of intelligence as its foundation – a foundation drawn from his study of Jacotot's intellectual adventure.

2. The equality of intelligence, however, can never be observed as such. "We can never say: all intelligence is equal" (IS 46): phrenologists, neurobiologists, schoolmasters and other IQ-test designers will always find ways to measure something resembling intellectual capacity, and to rank the manifestations of intelligence according to the particular scale they happen to promote. This may be the reason why most progressive political agendas have tended to present equality as a goal (generally a never-fully achievable goal) for the future, rather than as a premise on which to build an egalitarian society.

3. This postponement of equality into a never-fully-achievable future constitutes the main trap of progressive politics Rancière has constantly denounced throughout his writings. Jacotot's (anti-)model of the explicator offers the blueprint for all such postponers of equality. Their common motto is: Accept to submit your (lower) intelligence to my (higher) understanding today, in order to be my equal tomorrow! Because it is based upon the principle of inequality of intelligence, this falsely emancipating (but actually stultifying) attitude, which has permeated most forms of modern progressive politics, defeats its stated purpose by relying on (and by perpetuating) the very inequality it pretends to abolish.

4. Since the equality of intelligence cannot be observed as such in its given manifestations, nor postponed as a goal only to be attained in the future, it has to be considered as a premise to egalitarian politics, a premise that needs to operate as a presupposition. Equality is "not an end to attain, but a point of departure, a *supposition* to maintain in every circumstance" (IS 138). The only truly emancipatory processes of subjectification that took place in modern history have received their dynamics from such a presupposition of equality of intelligence. Their slogans have been structured in the form of a "Yes, we already can", rather than as a "One day we will be able to". Their power has relied on the intuition that "We can" because we, as speaking beings, must declare and consider ourselves equal in intelligence to those deemed superior. This, in turn, has resulted from a self-declaration that has the form of a presupposition rooted in the will, rather than of an objective form of knowledge based on the collection of positive evidence.

5. Democratic politics will therefore consist in the practical verification of such a presupposition. "Equality is not a given, nor is it claimed; it is practiced, it is *verified*"; it will "never exist except in its verification and at the price of being verified always and everywhere" (IS 137–8). Since the equality of intelligence cannot be observed in its given manifestations, "we are reduced to multiplying the experiments inspired by that opinion" (IS 46). However, the self-emancipating agents might say, "our problem isn't proving that all intelligence is equal. It is seeing what can be done under that supposition" (*ibid.*). The presupposition has no worth in itself: its value is strictly limited to its effects, that is, to the practical experimentations produced by its attempted verifications. Contrary to the explicator's postponing device, the very structure of such verifications actually implements the equality they aim to foster: "for the only verified intelligence is the one that speaks to a fellow-man capable of verifying the equality of their intelligence" (IS 39).

Jacotot's practical experimentations (and theoretical reflections) in the field of pedagogy thus provided Rancière with a neat and original definition of democratic politics: to qualify as democratic, political agency must set in motion or fuel a practical verification of the equality of intelligence, that is, a process of subjectification through which all participating agents are empowered to find out for themselves how their conditions of living can be improved. By contrast, this definition raises suspicion towards the best-intentioned efforts through which progressively minded intellectuals (or parties) "explain" to the masses what is in their best interest from a superior position of expertise or scientificity.

As Kristin Ross skilfully showed in the introduction to her English translation of *The Ignorant Schoolmaster* (IS ix–xii), the book used Jacotot indirectly but sharply to criticize scientist attitudes that dominated a large spectrum of the French intelligentsia, from the remaining followers of Louis Althusser and Pierre Bourdieu to the neo-positivism of (ex)-socialists converted to the laws of free-market capitalism (on the contrasts and parallels between Rancière and Bourdieu, see Nordmann 2007; Pelletier 2009a,b). Rancière's intervention contributed to introducing a wedge within the left field of modern politics. From the early Enlighteners plotting the education of the masses, to the Marxist philosophers denouncing the illusions of "ideology" in the name of materialist "science", and all the way to the late twentieth-century sociologists theorizing the necessary "ignorance" of the social agent, all political projects explicitly geared towards the ideal of equality had to be reassessed in the new light shed by the long-forgotten Universal Teaching promoted in the 1820s by Jacotot. And, under this discriminating light, many emancipatory projects appear betrayed by large segments of an:

> intellectual hierarchy that has no other power except the rationalization of inequality. Progressivism is the modern form of that power, purified of any mixture with the material forms of traditional authority: progressives have *no power other* than that ignorance, that incapacity of the people on which their priesthood is based. How, without opening up an abyss under their own feet, can they say to working people that they don't need them in order to be free men, in order to be educated in everything suitable to their dignity as men? (IS 129)

From the contradictions of the explicator to the paradox of the spectator

If Rancière managed to operate such a theoretical tour de force in exhuming Jacotot's obscure writings, it is largely due to the literary devices he crafted to compose *The Ignorant Schoolmaster*. As Kristin Ross also notes, the reader of this highly sympathetic narrative of Jacotot's life and legend can hardly distinguish the moments when Rancière speaks for himself from the pages where he merely lends his voice to his protagonist (IS xxii). His most daring assertions are often prudently hidden behind the outrageous statements of the pedagogue; in return, tongue-in-cheek irony towards the provocative lunacy of the schoolmaster's claims pushes the reader to imagine Rancière himself smiling at the disturbingly radical and deliciously counter-intuitive positions he is led to defend in his effort to give an advantageous account of the doctrine of Universal Teaching. Far from trying to assess the "true value" (and limits) of Jacotot's theses, far from raising the numerous objections that jump to mind in the face of his declarations, Rancière adopts the posture of a humble advocate, espousing their logic as closely as possible, defending them as his own – even (or rather especially) in their most extreme and outrageous implications.

Such literary devices provide the narrow door that allows Rancière to escape what initially appeared to be a constitutive contradiction of his book: the account he provides of Jacotot's anti-explanatory system is in no way "an explication" of Jacotot's writings. Even though he often situates Jacotot within the intellectual debates of the early nineteenth century (bringing in quotes from Bonald, Maine de Biran, Destutt de Tracy, Lamennais), Rancière never attempts to second-guess Jacotot in "explaining" his behaviour and his assertions in causal terms, from a position of superiority towards the text. His presentation of Universal Teaching does not "explain" the doctrine, but merely rewrites it (by editing it, reassembling it, summarizing it, paraphrasing it) into a language that makes sense at the turn of the twenty-first century. Or rather, Rancière's gesture consists in translating Jacotot's writings into the vocabulary and framing of our own current problems and debates (with Althusser, Bourdieu, the economists and other advocates of political expertise). In doing so, *The Ignorant Schoolmaster* provides the most convincing example of an interpretation that endows an old book simultaneously with a renewal, a presentification and an actualization (Citton 2007).

Far from betraying the anti-explicator's message by an explication of his doctrine, Rancière remains deeply true to the founding experience on which Jacotot built his Universal Teaching. For the first success of the "panecastic system" consisted in a process of translation that took place between the Flemish pupils and Fénelon's French novel. As we recall:

> everything had perforce been played out between the intelligence of Fénelon who had wanted to make a particular use of the French language, the intelligence of the translator who had wanted to give a Flemish equivalent, and the intelligence of the apprentices who wanted to learn French. (IS 9)

In his gesture of situating himself on the same level (of advocacy) as Jacotot and of merging his translating voice into that of the nineteenth-century author, Rancière enacts one of the most important panecastic lessons, which therefore applies equally well to his relation to us as it applies to Jacotot's relation to his pupils:

> without thinking about it, he had made them discover this thing that he discovered with them: that all sentences, and consequently all the intelligences that produce them, are of the same nature. Understanding is never more than translating, that is: giving the equivalent of a text, but in no way its reason. There is nothing behind the written page, no false bottom that necessitates the work of an other intelligence, that of the explicator; no language of the master, no language of the language whose words and sentences are able to speak the reason of the words and sentences of

a text. The Flemish students had furnished the proof: to speak about *Télémaque*, they had at their disposition only the words of *Télémaque*. Fénelon's sentences alone are necessary to understand Fénelon's sentences and to express what one has understood about them. Learning and understanding are two ways of expressing the same act of translation. (IS 9)

Such an act of translation – in its etymological sense of "displacement" – has been pursued by Rancière long after the publication of *The Ignorant Schoolmaster*. Not only did he devote the two following decades to deepening and sharpening his reflection on the politics of equality, but he recently returned to the lessons of intellectual emancipation sketched by Jacotot in order to redefine the relation between politics and the arts in his 2008 book, *The Emancipated Spectator* (English translation 2009). In this case, the displacement consisted in applying to the spectator and the aesthetic experience provided in a theatre, a cinema, a museum, or at home in front of a television, the same presupposition of the equality of intelligence applied by Jacotot to his pupils in his Louvain classroom. The result of this further act of translation overturns two premises that are almost universally accepted in the current reflection on contemporary art. In reference to Denis Diderot's famous 1778 text entitled *The Paradox of the Comedian*, Rancière wrote *The Paradox of the Spectator* in order to debunk a double indictment frequently addressed to the traditional role of the audience.

First, as long as he sits in the darkness, watching the performance presented on the stage, the spectator is conceived as a passive being, whom countless scenographic devices, throughout the twentieth century, have desperately tried to "activate" (by blurring "the fourth wall" separating the stage from the audience, by exposing or unsettling him, by performing obscene acts supposed to raise his indignation, his outrage or any other form of (re)active participation). Secondly, all of the most significant currents in modern art, from Berthold Brecht and Antonin Artaud to the many reincarnations of agit-prop and "happenings", have attempted to pull the spectator out of his position of a watcher, who would return to his normal (and "real") life after the brief parenthesis of an entertaining or thought-provoking show, in order to push him to become a doer, most frequently a revolutionary agent geared up to take over the local Winter Palace.

On these two basic points, Rancière goes back to the lessons he drew from Jacotot in order to propose two drastic reversals. He first invites us to recognize in the spectator the same active power of intelligence that Jacotot revealed in his pupils: watching a show is in itself a form of

"THE IGNORANT SCHOOLMASTER": KNOWLEDGE AND AUTHORITY

(interpretive) activity, which triggers countless operations of attention, selection, retention, anticipation, retrospection, translation, adaptation and so on. He then suggests that a good number of modern artists (and art theorists) have indeed put themselves in the highly questionable position of the Explicator (i.e. of the Stultifier) by the very gesture through which they pretended to play the role of Emancipator. Many forms of "revolutionary" art – if not most of them – have treated their spectator with the type of condescendence Jacotot denounced in the explanatory system of *la Vieille*. Not only did the much-reviled apologists of Socialist Realism (in its multiple avatars) pretend to "explain" to the people what it ought to understand in Art and in Society, but the avant garde itself, because of the very wedge it introduced between the enlightened appreciators and the "ignorant" masses, ended up portraying the vast majority of the spectators as passive and powerless fools, endlessly numbed by the "Society of the Spectacle". Such attitudes reproduced the stultifying division between those who have Knowledge and Authority (in the arts) and those who lack the power to understand and make proper (aesthetic) judgements.

Presupposing the equality of intelligence, in this particular case, leads us to presuppose an intelligence at work in each spectator: the types, levels, intensities, qualities, and therefore the value of the operations generated by an aesthetic experience can obviously vary widely from the most conventional soap opera to the most transgressive theatre performance, but a truly emancipatory conception of the arts must recognize in each spectator of any genre of show an active translator who can – and more importantly still, who does – find for herself a meaningful and self-creative appropriation of the material presented to her.

"Understanding is never more than translating, that is: giving the equivalent of a text": understanding a work of art, understanding a book, understanding *The Ignorant Schoolmaster*, does not consist in explaining it from a position of superior knowledge and authority, but in translating it, in appropriating it within an activity of (self- as well as social) transformation that constantly *rewrites* the book according to the ever-changing demands of new situations. It could be said that Rancière has constantly rewritten Jacotot's tale and legend in his later publications on politics and aesthetics. It is up to our equally intelligent (though ever biased) readings to constantly rewrite his books according to our current needs and desires for emancipation.

THREE

Philosophy and its poor: Rancière's critique of philosophy
Giuseppina Mecchia

Few philosophers have entertained a more complex relation to the history of philosophy, both in terms of aesthetics and of political thought, than Jacques Rancière. His rigorous engagement with this tradition has allowed him to powerfully critique it, forcing us to reconsider what is at stake when intellectuals assume a position of authority in the name of their philosophical, and more generally theoretical, credentials. Rancière is ultimately able to show us that, in political philosophy, what always had to be defended, in the most different times and places, was the position of the philosopher himself, as bearer of a knowledge inaccessible to people outside specific pedagogical situations. For Rancière, this presupposed inaccessibility is not only a conceptual blind spot but also a historical fallacy.

In the following pages we shall follow three main lines of enquiry within Rancière's treatment of the philosophical tradition: the first will be his chronological point of entry into philosophical "disagreements", that is, the Marxist tradition; the second, the general philosophical heritage common to all Western "apprentices in philosophy", that is, the Greco-Roman Classics and the modern representatives of political philosophy from Hobbes to Sartre; the third and final line will try to situate Rancière with respect to the politics and philosophies of postmodernity.

Rancière shows us how, time and again, even extremely different philosophers tend to assume similar postures when faced with the independence of equal human beings claiming the same ability to reason as his or her own. It is the persistence and the freedom of a "people" newly defined as speaking subject that presents philosophy with its "poor", and calls it back to the equality of minds and bodies acting on the scene of history as the sole foundation for a renewed democratic ideal.

Marx's lessons: an ignorant schoolmaster?

As previous chapters have shown, Rancière came into contact with Marxism in the circle of Louis Althusser at the École Normale Supérieure. In *La Leçon d'Althusser*, however, he attempted to definitively "emancipate" himself not only from Althusser himself but more generally from the stranglehold that the French Communist Party was still trying to exert on master and disciples alike. Whether this emancipation implied an irrevocable distancing from Marxist theory is a much more difficult issue. Rancière's philosophical discourse evolved in a way that makes of Marxism only one of the many foundation stones on which to build a startlingly original conceptual framework. This new conceptual construction implies a decisive rethinking of some of Marx's own assumptions, particularly his extant belief in the scientific nature of social, economic and political analysis, as well as his use of a revised form of Hegelian dialectic that sees history largely as the manifestation of unconscious processes of actualization. It is precisely in *Althusser's Lesson* that Rancière's new conceptual landscape starts to take shape. If Rancière, however, does not appear, in this book, completely ungrateful towards his master, it is because the abjuration of Marxism was not his main political and philosophical focus.

One could even contend that one of the stakes of this first book was, in fact, to rescue several elements of *Marx's* lesson from Althusser's – and the Communist Party's – version of it: one of Rancière's tactics is to radically historicize supposedly "scientific" Marxist categories. One of the difficulties implicit in Althusser's political position between 1968 and the early 1970s was his inability to incorporate in his theoretical thought the fact that during the 1960s class composition had already undergone radical changes, and that theories of class struggle needed to be revised in view of present historical developments. Although perfectly aware of historical determinations, Althusser wrote *as if* the "working class" – also called the proletariat – and the "petty bourgeoisie" had not changed, in both economical and cultural terms. In turn, this explains Althusser's hesitancy to attribute full agency to the lower classes independently of the theoretical and organizational support provided by the Communist Party's *intelligentsia*. This is precisely the point at which Rancière intervenes, denouncing the implicit elitism of this brand of Marxist philosophy, which betrayed the very subjects that it claimed to liberate.

The tendency to treat Marx's descriptive categories as if they could ever be immutable concepts was another recurrent temptation for Althusser. His "voluntary servitude" as the Party's intellectual established once and for all Rancière's mistrust of an interpretation of the political as an ordering of minds and bodies, an ordering that could not but be nefarious both to historical agency and to philosophical thought: "philosophy entered into politics as one can enter into a religion: to expiate its sins" (LA 111, my trans.). This is also why Althusser, "in the last analysis", still thought of the students who mobilized in 1968 as ideological representatives of the "petty bourgeoisie" described by Marx in the mid-nineteenth century. For Althusser, only the workers were meaningful fighters in the class struggle between the owners of capital and its exploited underlings.

What Rancière can no longer accept is the vision of knowledge promoted by Althusser, who, unwittingly, reproduced a distinction between intellectual and productive forces – the infamous structure and superstructure – that other Marxist thinkers, and Antonio Gramsci in particular, had been undermining for a long time. For Rancière, it is not the original assignation of places within the social structure that determines the political and epistemic potential of a person or of a group of people, but rather the knowledge and the struggle that they consciously adopt as the foundation of their political demands.

This kind of position questions the very concept of ideology, even before emerging theories of postmodern societies and "cognitive" labour would render it particularly obsolete. For Rancière, it was already necessary to take into account the actual historical instances of autonomous political intervention on the part of the exploited classes who, since the very institution of the political arena, were able to make their voices heard even in extremely hostile ideological structures.

Gramsci's work, which was translated and published in French during the 1950s and whose reception by the French Communist Party was not uncontroversial, remains a largely understudied reference for both Althusser and Rancière. Arguably, though, Gramsci's study of cultural formations and of the political agency exerted by politically and economically subordinate classes is a vital precedent for the understanding of the "democratic" *agon* appearing in Rancière's later works. The Sardinian intellectual recommended and embraced the study both of folklore and of contemporary popular culture, making full use of historical, cultural and anthropological data. The proletariat as a social class is radically de-economicized by Gramsci, and its participation in the creation, conservation and transformation of cultural hegemonies occupies a pivotal role in his understanding of political struggle. In this respect, when Rancière said that it was necessary, at the end of the 1970s, to subtract the discourse on the working class produced by the French managerial and bureaucratic elites from "the economical necessity whose principle has been borrowed from the Marxist tradition" (SP 17, my trans.), Gramsci seemed to have expressed that necessity already in the 1920s.

Gramsci also defined the nature and modalities of intellectual labour in terms that are surprisingly close to Rancière's later positions:

> It must first be shown that all men are "philosophers", by defining the limits and the characteristics of the "spontaneous philosophy" which is proper to everybody. This philosophy is contained in: 1. Language itself, which is a totality of determined notions and concepts and not just words grammatically devoid of content; 2. "common sense" and "good sense"; 3. ...ways of seeing and acting, which are collectively bound together under the name of "folklore". (Gramsci 1996: 325)

The emphasis placed on the recognition that all men participate in the elaboration of thought and social life through their linguistic competence and social interactions cannot fail to evoke the self-teaching students and proletarian workers that occupy the centre stage of *The Nights of Labour* and *The Ignorant Schoolmaster*. By his recognition that the proletariat is a full cultural and epistemic actor, one can say that Gramsci had already presented the Philosopher with his Poor. Gramsci, operating in the context of the Bolshevik victory in the Russian Revolution and the subsequent foundation of the European Communist Parties, remained a Leninist, as he predicated the necessity of an institution such as the Party as the medium through which the intellectual potential of the proletariat could be realized in a revolutionary action. For Rancière, such mediation coming from the outside always risks becoming an obstacle to emancipative action. It is through the domain of aesthetics, social participation and abstract thought that emancipation is expressed as a fact and that its political potential comes to be realized. It is in these participative and dis-identificatory moments – in terms of economic and social assignation of status – that the passive victims of power become "a people" as historical subject. While this identification is neither stable nor predictable, it is nonetheless indisputably real when it occurs as public performance of one's ability to participate in any language-based human activity, be it politics, poetry or the fine arts. The Philosopher, therefore, should understand that his own role is not indispensable in the people's history, and that philosophy can never present itself as the knowledge of a truth that could not be shared by anyone else.

It is in search of these "spontaneous philosophers" and poets that Rancière abandoned, for a time, the theoretical disputes tied to the communist official thinkers in order to plunge in the archives of the French workers' publications dating from the mid-nineteenth century. What Rancière recognized in these "archives of the proletarian dream" reminds us of what Gramsci also said: "All men are intellectuals, one could therefore say: but not all men have in society the function of intellectuals" (1996: 304). For the accredited philosophers, for the mediatic intellectual, the most disconcerting part of class struggle, Rancière will argue, is not the one that sees the people fight for an improvement in wages or better parliamentary representation: the proletarian is only too readily recognized as an economically disadvantaged subject. What has proved inconceivable for many accredited thinkers and philosophers is the poor's mental and affective equality with their self-declared masters and superiors, even though this equality is the only rational foundation of any democratic constitution.

Going against the grain both of Marxist and anti-Marxist thought, Rancière is still willing to maintain some of his attachment to Marx himself, but only to the extent that he can purloin his texts not only from Althusser but also from the various parties and factions that used them as a guide for instituting "scientific" political programmes and to legitimize their own role as intellectual and political elites. The implication that only the bearer of the scientific awareness not only of capitalist exploitation but also of the laws of its historical unfolding can assess the opportunity and the success of the poor's struggles is the pitfall of Marxist theory.

In *The Philosopher and his Poor*, Rancière proposes a paradoxical reading of Marx, arguing that for him already, at least in certain parts of his work, it was actually aesthetic and intellectual engagement that mattered most, as tools to dis-identify oneself from a pre-assigned social role. Not unlike the "reactionary renter Flaubert" (PP 169), who entered the impersonal world of fiction to the point of tearing himself away from his gender- and class-based social determinations, Marx is said to have slowly abandoned his own identification with the First International as "communist intellectual". Precisely when the bourgeois were ready to see in Marx an agitator, Marx becomes a "scientist" and steps back from his more established role in order to devote himself to the writing of *Capital*: since intellectual endeavours are always profoundly disruptive of social assignations, Marx "was not a member of his own party" (PP 174).

Marx had famously presented Philosophy (in the face of Proudhon's egalitarian theory) with its Poor. For Rancière, Marx himself still had to be presented with his own Poor: the people who, forgetful of their assigned place in society, stubbornly continue to speak as human beings radically equal to anyone else.

In *Disagreement*, Rancière pursues his critique of Marxist economicism and the theory of ideology into a critique of contemporary sociology. In so far as they assert the supremacy of the social in all political conflict, critical sociologists also elevate themselves to the status of bearers of a "truth" inaccessible to those experiencing the social structures. When Rancière introduced in 2006 the second French edition of *The Philosopher and his Poor*, he openly recognized that the book that had prompted him to write it had been *La Distinction*, originally published by Pierre Bourdieu in 1981. Bourdieu occupies an important role in Rancière's argument, since after having dealt with Plato and Marx he shifts his interest toward two prominent figures in twentieth-century thought who still occupy what he calls "Marx's horizon": Jean-Paul Sartre and Pierre Bourdieu.

Taking the reader through a vertiginous excursus in the history of political philosophy, Rancière shows us how, far from deconstructing Plato's unwillingness to accept the free workers – the "artisans" of the *Republic* – as philosophical, political and even aesthetic subjects, Bourdieu actually ends up reproducing the Platonic interdiction, presenting it in even more extreme, quasi-absolute terms. While criticizing bourgeois forms of knowledge and even philosophy as a symbolic violence through which the ruling classes reproduce their own supremacy, sociology neutralizes all pedagogical, political and aesthetic recourse against the reproduction of the hierarchical structure of society: "[the sociologist] transforms in a necessity of the social body what Plato the philosopher had presented as the necessary 'lie' for the founding of a legal inferiority whose reproduction would anyway also be insured by its empirical reality" (PP viii).

In a way, even if sociology considers itself as a "human science", it fails to attribute full subjectivity to the objects of its enquiry, and therefore is literally incapable of conceiving the possibility of the political and aesthetic domains as an expression of the absolute equality of every speaking subject. This is why Rancière is extremely critical of the political use of sociological datas, as this science has become "the final form taken by the ... philosophical project of achieving politics by doing away with it" (D 92).

In that respect, the Marxist tradition is still presented, in later works, as closer to Rancière's concerns, since the theory of class struggle does stress the subjective role of all players on the socioeconomic stage. The intermittent nature of historical and political subjectivity had been asserted by Marx, at least in the way that Rancière wants to read him. As the German expatriate concerned himself on the one hand with the practice of revolutionary insurrections in contemporary France, Germany and England and on the other scientifically explaining why they failed in the 1830s and 1840s, he proceeded to

> deconstruct the social and economical figure of the worker, who needs to recognize herself as a "proletarian" in order to achieve historical subjectivity within the existing organization of Capital. No one is a "proletarian:, that is a historical subject, at all moments in their life: only when the "conjuncture" is right does this historical subject come to life. (D 90)

Even Sartre, this most sympathetically undisciplined of modern French philosophers, is seen by Rancière as a victim both of the sociological mirage and of a kind of dialectical thought that forbids him to renounce the belief in a supra-personal historical necessity that remains invisible to "practico-inert" subjectivities. Even this staunch believer in existential freedom cannot bring himself to concede that if such a human faculty existed, it would equally belong to all human subjects. The only entity capable to enact the "continuous creation" (WHO 139) of dialectical realization is once again the Party, which in the 1950s Sartre saw as a dialectical mediation between two negativities: the bad faith of the philosopher, always tainted by the contact with the petty bourgeoisie which legitimates his knowledge, and the exhaustion of the worker, who cannot independently become a historical agent because s/he lacks the time and the energy necessary to disentangle herself from her social determinations.

Moreover, Sartre's apparent "modesty" in his awareness of the philosopher's bad faith retains the egotistical posture historically associated with philosophy's practitioners. In his *Critique of Dialectical Reason*, workers' relations are apprehended by "the philosopher at his window" (PP 144). While the workers are prisoners of their worked matter, the philosopher who observes them knows that only by belonging to a "group" will they again conquer the power to perform a "pure Act". But the same philosopher – who after all had witnessed the rise of Stalinism and the repressive side of the Soviet socialist state – also thinks that he knows the reasons for the proletariat's supposed historical failures: the workers do not see the dialectical nature of historical processes. In the mind of the frustrated philosopher, the workers' repeated travails mirror his own loftier impotence: while the latter does not have the lived experience that would allow him to become a truly revolutionary subject, the former does not have the leisure to reflect. Clearly, the worker does not benefit at all by his assumption in such a degraded understanding of historical subjectivity, always tainted by blindness and impotence. Should not then the Philosopher speak for himself, and leave the Poor alone? Finally, according to Rancière, the only common ground between the philosopher and his poor is philosophically enunciated by Sartre as blindness and impotence. The philosopher becomes then a sort of deforming mirror-image for an imagined worker who truly does not benefit at all by his assumption into such a degraded form of political subjectivity.

The classics and modern political philosophy

In *The Philosopher and his Poor*, Rancière makes of Plato the inaugural classical reference that will serve as the basis for his ulterior critique of political philosophy. However, it is in the preface to *Disagreement* that we find another self-assessment on the part of Rancière with respect to his understanding of political philosophy. When, after the fall of the Berlin Wall, French leftist intellectuals seemed to have abandoned not only Marxism but also all reliance on "social" explanations of the political process, Rancière did not exult, because what emerged was an even more dangerous trend, consisting in a supposed return to "purely" philosophical investigations of the political field. Thence a return to the "classics", and more precisely to Plato and Aristotle as early thinkers of democracy:

> This return poses a few problems, however. When not limited to comment on certain texts, famous or forgotten, from out of its own history, this rejuvenated political philosophy seems most unwilling to go beyond the usual assortments of arguments trotted out by any state administration in thinking about democracy and the law ... In short, the main aim seems to be to ensure communication between the classical doctrines and the usual forms of state legitimization we know as liberal democracies. (D viii)

The alleged triumph of the "liberal" model of democratic organization over the so-called "socialist states" is the historical background against which Rancière wanted to raise a dissenting voice: when "political scientists" heralded the end of history and the triumph of liberal democracy, it was essential to reiterate that the claim to historical subjectivity is always not only a possibility, but a real though excessively rare actuality periodically emerging in the most different forms.

In order to tackle the new paradigm, Rancière retraced the modalities of the often nefarious encounter between politics and philosophy in classical models. He shows that the stakes of political philosophy have not fundamentally changed since the time of Plato and Aristotle, who first tried to come to terms with the historical reality of the *demos* as political actor. In fact, the clarity of their perception of what was at stake in the philosophical intervention on the scene of politics was often blurred by later thinkers, who all tried to theorize current forms of "state legitimization".

The differences between Plato and Aristotle help Rancière to identify two different but equally anti-democratic discursive modes within the field of political philosophy: the first he calls *archipolitics*, derives from Plato and is aimed at defining the principles of an ideal political arrangement devised by the "best" of society; the second he calls *parapolitics*, inspired by Aristotle and defines the rules of governing an inherently unruly and undesirable "body politics". Both these models found their followers in modernity, but they and their inheritors fail to understand their own insufficiencies when outlining the dynamics of political subjectivation.

Aristotle took Athens's democratic constitution as a *de facto* reality whose faulty nature derives essentially from the fact that it has ordered society into different but politically equivalent constituencies, who can claim a part in the *polis* without a just attribution of the proportional value that they create in it. Any *autochton* – that is, a person born in the *polis* – who is not a slave or a woman is a part of the citizenry, whose voice will carry equal weight in the public assembly independently of his inherent abilities.

The people who in Aristotle are excluded *a priori* from the *polis* are precisely those more directly engaged in the production of economic goods: whether slaves and women have or do not have a fully developed intellect, and therefore the ability to participate in public debates, is not so much a matter of fact, as of social necessity. Slavery and the exclusion of women continued to function in the same way well into the nineteenth century, and their consequences are still with us today. Even when manual labour was no longer performed by slaves or indentured servants, Rancière shows how the "worker" was still conceived as not being a fully competent linguistic subject even by its

Marxist defenders. From antiquity to postmodernity, the Philosopher never took his Poor seriously. In this sense, all limitations of citizenship functioned in ancient and modern societies as a convenient reduction of the actors involved in the political *agon*. The oligarchic nature of the original forms of democratic government is often forgotten. Rancière helps us remember how, from the very beginning, the equality of minds and bodies was never fully expressed in any historical form of representative democracy and never completely embraced by the philosophers of politics.

In Rancière's account, Aristotle sees the problem of democracy mostly as an issue of assigning value: "the pure and the impure are able to blend their effects. But how can they basically be compared with each other?" (D 7). Since nobody seems able to attribute such absolute value in a secular state, even the *"oligoi"* and the *"aristoi"* – that is, the wealthiest and the most accomplished individuals – will have to be part of inherently imperfect and contingent calculations trying to assign to each his rightful position within the representative bodies of the republic. In this way, politics becomes the art of giving to each one a "part" in the state, but the paradoxical nature of this arrangement is that in a democracy, a part is juridically attributed to those who have "no part" in it, that is, to people who do not have either the wealth or the superior qualities judged necessary to participate in fully rational political deliberations. The philosopher, then, is left with the task of lamenting this inevitable inadequacy, where knowledge and truth seem constantly betrayed in the political *agon* by actors who are neither the "best" nor the most "virtuous".

Plato is read by Rancière, both in the *Republic* and in the *Laws*, as describing Athens's current form of democratic government as a profoundly un-philosophical political arrangement. The Athenian democracy is incapable of mediating between the absolute value of the Law and the contingent and often undignified particularities of its subjects. The discourse of the Law, which the philosophers and the rulers cooperate to establish, is betrayed by its historical incarnation in the democratic constitution. Paradoxically, the democratic principle stating the representative equality of unequal constituents of the democratic state makes it vulnerable to injustice, corruption and even anarchy. According to Plato, only the best should govern, while the other inhabitants of the polis should be content with the virtue of *"sophrosyne"*, that is, the basic wisdom of literally "minding one's own business" while the really virtuous people – educated to become such from childhood – will take care of the state. The Philosopher becomes pedagogue and advisor to the rulers. From this point of view, it appears that the discipline of political philosophy itself is deeply compromised in its commitment to the truth because of its own reliance on the enlightened rulers who, for a time at least, consent to lend it their ear.

According to Rancière, the modern republican ideal, as it was embodied in the USA and then in other Western democracies, is constantly devising and enforcing "an education that would harmonize laws and behavior, the system of institutional forms and the dispositions of the social body" (HD 72). Even when the transcendent tendencies of Platonic theory have been replaced with the more "realist" spirit of Aristotle, the mistrust of governments with respect to their constituents remains the same. Rancière considers the belief in a knowable, generalized notion of human nature dividing humanity between different levels of political capacity as one of the basic tenets of modern political philosophy.

Foremost among the modern thinkers pursuing the tradition of political philosophy, Hobbes also anchored his political–philosophical meditations in the link between the state's constitution and general characteristics of human nature. Hobbes's positions are particularly interesting with respect to Rancière because he paradoxically starts from a principle dear to the latter – the natural equality of all men – in order to reach starkly different conclusions. Precisely because men are intellectually not that different from one another, competition and conflict are the main characters of the state of nature: if men enter a political covenant, it is precisely to protect themselves from the deadly potentialities of human equality, "that condition which is called Warre; … a warre, as is of every man, against every man" (1997: 70). In Hobbes, the philosopher appears once again, and even more radically than for the Ancients, as the denouncer of equality. With Hobbes is enshrined the philosopher's mission of helping the ruler keep his fellow human beings in check. A new, pressing concern makes its way into political philosophy: security, as the main motivation behind the renunciation to one's own decisional and deadly powers in the name of the Commonwealth.

For Hobbes and his many followers, the actual form of government that the common will adopt in order to ensure the conditions for social peace and prosperity seems to be of much lesser consequence. What needs to be achieved is transformation of the equal subjects of the Multitude into a single juridical Person able to express and enforce a common will. In the *De Cive*, Hobbes goes into describing different forms of "dominion" – democratic, aristocratic and monarchic – but for him what really matters is the establishment of sovereignty. From Rancière's perspective, however, sovereignty itself, as absolute power of life and death, is in fact a philosophical fallacy, since the insuppressible equality of all subjects, conveniently repressed and forgotten by modern and postmodern political philosophers, will always find a way to historical emergence. In history, however rarely, "a sphere of appearance of the demos is created, an element of kratos, the power of the people, exists" (D 88).

Rancière parts decisively from Hobbes and other moderns – Rousseau, of course, but also twentieth-century conservative thinkers of sovereignty like Carl Schmitt – in his rejection of the foundational nature of a theoretical "covenant" that would reduce conflicts to their minimum and ideally extinguish them in the name of security and commerce. What changes in Rancière is the valuation of equality, which is no longer considered a permanent threat to public order, but as the sole and welcome guarantee that this order cannot and will not ever become a fully realized totality. Efficiency and personal safety are indeed always compromised by political conflict, but far from decrying this phenomenon, Rancière embraces it while rejecting all hypostatized notions of sovereignty. For Rancière, the philosophers of sovereignty make a necessity of contingent, historically construed power structures. As a result, political philosophy always risks supporting totalitarian projects.

Rousseau's friendlier assessment of human equality and fundamental questioning concerning the ontological immateriality of social inequalities appears much closer to Rancière, and echoes of the *Discourse on the Origins of Inequality* can be heard throughout his works. On the other hand, Rousseau still falls into the traps of modern political philosophy when, in *The Social Contract*, he reduces the political space to a contractual agreement where equality will no longer need to be regularly demonstrated as it is already carried out by the collective sovereign. As Rancière says, "Rousseau is in agreement with the Hobbesian tautology of sovereignty: sovereignty rests solely on itself, for beyond it there are merely individuals" (D 78).

Rancière among the postmoderns

Generationally and historically, Rancière belongs fully to the postmodern era. However, postmodernism is constantly challenged in his texts. Armed with the solid "realism" deriving on the one hand from the classic Aristotelian notions of citizenship and democratic participation and on the other from the history of class struggle, Rancière does not conflate the philosophical deconstruction of historical narratives with the theoretical annihilation of the political space.

By contrast with postmodernist sociology (in particular Jean Beaudrillard), Rancière is not interested in theorizing the masses. Politically, they do not exist for him, since they are not a "subject" of political action but only the object of an *a*bjectifying philosophical reconstruction. Once again, sociology becomes an instrument for keeping the people outside of the philosophical arena, since according to postmodern philosophers the people in fact no longer exists. Equality is all but forgotten in an apocalyptic W*eltanschauung* that makes even the Althusserian notion of ideology look tame and open to historical contingencies. What Baudrillard calls the "inert matter of the social" (Baudrillard 1994: 3) had in fact already been theorized at the peak of the modern era in classical sociological theories (Le Bon, Durkheim, Tarde). Baudrillard himself, at an earlier stage of his reflection, had expressed the need to deconstruct the myth of the masses when he said that "the term mass is not a concept. It is a leitmotiv of political demagogy" (Baudrillard 1983: 4). The danger with this kind of focus on the disembodiment brought about by *mass* medias or – more recently – by the diffusion on a *mass*ive scale of digital information technologies, is that it slips easily into a conservative, pessimistic analysis of the possibilities for political subjectivation in contemporary societies. This is the reason for Rancière's recent demystification of theories of simulacra in his work on cinema and digital aesthetics. *The Future of the Image* argues precisely that our apprehension of visual data is deeply linked to linguistic functions and subject to critical reception by an "emancipated spectator".

Already at the end of the 1970s, Jean-François Lyotard had understood that the postmodern deconstruction of modern forms of knowledge and the dawn of the new digital era were inseparable from a political reflection on society and hierarchical structures of power. Lyotard was Rancière's senior by over a quarter-century. His political engagement during the Algerian War and later the events of May '68, as well as his philosophical activity in a group such as "Socialisme ou Barbarie" made him one of the leading figures in the French intellectual landscape to whom Rancière would appear to have been closest. This makes Lyotard's strong disinvestment in any project remotely resembling socialist or "proletarian"-centred movements even more significant, because this move away from politics to philosophy is precisely the anti-democratic step that Rancière judges dangerous and misguided.

When Lyotard started articulating his critique of knowledge, in the *The Postmodern Condition*, he identified two main ways of representing the social bond: one that considers society as a self-regulating system and resembles a cybernetic network, and another one that considers society as always "divided in two" (Lyotard 1984: 11). The first tendency is technocratic and unitary in nature, while the second retraces in class conflict a fundamental social constituent. Lyotard famously rejected the traditionally Marxist oppositional perspectives and theorized as postmodernity a cultural form where machines and technocratic oligarchies are making opposition itself an outdated model for thinking the social mechanism and thence the political scene. What appears in Lyotard's analysis is nothing less than the disappearance of political struggles.

Postmodernity does not allow social disputes, disagreements in Rancière's sense of the world, but only endless language-games that are still "agonistic" (Lyotard 1984: 16) in nature, but in a sterilized, abstract manner, since language is postulated as a purely self-referential activity. The social bond founded by these *agons* is not really threatened by them, as in fact they represent its very foundation. The risk of disembowelling the contents of the *agon* to the point of making political action completely unthinkable remains constant in this kind of approach to postmodernity. This explains why a few years later Rancière rejected any coincidence between Lyotard's "*différend*" and his own "disagreement". As Rancière himself states, politics is a matter of subjective recognition, of being able to recognize the opponent as such, as being an equal part of the same political universe:

> Disagreement clearly has not to do with words alone. It generally bears on the very situation in which speaking parties find themselves. In this, disagreement differs from what Jean-François Lyotard has conceptualized as *differend*. Disagreement is not concerned with issues such as the heterogeneity of regimes of sentences. (D xi)

For Rancière, Lyotard and his followers have made of postmodernity something decisively different from a historical category dependent on precise economical and cultural dynamics. Postmodernism can become a trans-historical approach to knowledge that in its renunciation to "grand narratives" and deconstruction of subjectivity runs the risk of dismissing the actual and continued persistence of political struggles. Notwithstanding his or her rejection of the philosopher's authority to speak for the other, the postmodern intellectual risks forgetting that the other is already speaking, and much too easily condemns him to the sublime silence of suffering. It is Rancière, and not Lyotard, who makes the very concept of philosophical authority obsolete in his absolute claim for equality and agency for all historical enactors of political conflict. In *The Future of the Image*, Lyotard's paradigmatically postmodern reconstruction of the Jews as the bearers of the ineffability of suffering and of artistic un-representability that as such needed to be silenced in the Holocaust, is violently attacked by Rancière, because it turns a historical event into "a law of the psychic apparatus" (FI 134). Nothing of the "concrete historical figures of a people or civilization" (*ibid.*) is deemed worthy of reflection. Philosophy, once again, presents itself as the theoretical enemy of language, and in its postmodern incarnation it even dismantles the very notion of historical event, as it connects it to unconscious psychic mechanisms that end up emptying out not only politics, but also art.

Equally distant from Rancière's positions are other strands of postmodern political philosophy, and in particular any account of the subaltern as sacrificial victim ontologically inscribed in the socius. What Giorgio Agamben compellingly described in the 1990s as *homo sacer* – a figure going back to ancient Greece, but epitomized in our times by the Jews caught in the Nazi regime – will never be, ontologically, a subject of politics: thence, once again, the "nihilistic" horizon that inscribes itself as the unsurpassable limit of this approach to postmodernity. For all of its conceptual value, this kind of "philosophical persona" makes of the political space a homogeneous surface that alterity can never dis-integrate but only harden even further.

For Rancière the universal value attributed to this model is not only historically inaccurate, but politically nefarious. The designation of a part of the population as expendable in the name of society is always inscribed in a "local" dispute, and politics is the universal name of the dispute, not of its victims.

> Politics is the art of warped deductions and mixed identities. It is the art of the local and singular construction of cases of universality. Such construction is only possible as long as the singularity of the wrong – the singularity of the local argument and expression of law – is ... separate from the naked relationship between humanity and inhumanity. (D 139)

In Rancière's analysis, the designation of someone as *homo sacer* is always localized and it is a name and a function attributed to a subject who, far from accepting it, tries to reject it in refusing the identity attributed to him. This is why politics is different from religion, for only in the latter are sacrificial roles legitimated by a transcendent reference. In politics, the stripping of one's citizen's rights in order to be reduced to naked life, simple *zoas*, is not an ontological necessity, but a political strategy that can be challenged in multiple fashions, depending on how much political and juridical room is left for such a resistance. The apocalyptic, quasi-mystical "dérives" implicit in Agamben's discourse are then another risk undergone by political philosophy "in its nihilistic age" (D 123–39). In his essay "Who is the Subject of the Rights of Man", Rancière deepens his critique of Agamben, showing how the latter still relies on absolutist theorists of sovereignty derived from Hobbes and his modern followers such as Schmitt, and then conflates the totalitarian state with Michel Foucault's theories of the modern democratic state as biopolitical apparatus. In Agamben, nobody fully escapes the space of the camps, because the camps are modernity itself.

For Rancière, this latter-day philosophical position "would prove quite effective for depoliticizing matters on power and repression and setting them in a sphere of exceptionality that is no longer political … situated beyond the reach of political dissensus" (WHO 299). The infinite injustice of the state in Agamben, the inhuman alterity that threatens all public space in Lyotard: finally, our postmodern philosophers sanction the vanity of politics and of democracy with the same conviction of their ancient and modern predecessors. Some other way of thinking is necessary if we want to "understand who is the subject of the Rights of Man" (WHO 309).

Democratic politics today

There is no eschatological, apocalyptic horizon in Rancière's understanding of the political. Always too ready to enumerate the necessary conditions for meaningful political action – and more often, of its impossibility – philosophers pontificate while history goes on. History, in this sense, is not a grand narrative that needs to be undermined, but the material struggle for democracy that the people have undertaken since the very beginning of politics. In *The Hatred of Democracy*, Rancière takes one last jab at what he calls the "*imprécateurs*" – the "cursers" – of democracy, who are always too ready to denounce the inadequacies of democratic forms of government because they do not see that democracy is not a form of government but the contested stake of every political arrangement.

Democracy cannot but be the object of philosophical hatred, says Rancière, because it provokes the ire both of the disappointed leftists who cannot accept that the people still do not "understand" how they are duped every day by the oligarchic, media-supported, capitalist "democracies", and of the pessimist reactionaries who would rather have it done with the sovereignty of a people in such dire need of ethical and political guidance. Luckily, if the intellectuals do not listen to the people, the opposite is also true: while political events are indeed rare and far between, they keep occurring notwithstanding the intellectuals' disbelief. "We don't live in real democracies. We don't live in concentration camps either, as certain authors, who see us all subjected to the law of exception of biopolitical governance, try to make us believe" (HD 81). The reality of the oligarchies that keep reproducing themselves in contemporary representative democracies is not contested by Rancière, but the personal freedoms dearly conquered by the people in the course of their historical struggles are still there, and from time to time they allow us to talk back to oligarchic powers in a meaningful and successful way. That political philosophy has often been unable to think this cannot but be attributed to its own lack, deriving either from elitist conceit or from political complicity with historically determined structures of power.

Paradoxically, though, it is precisely because of the fallacies of political philosophy that Rancière can end his long confrontation with the history of political philosophy and of the people's continued interventions in their own historical existence, on a happily contrarian optimistic note. If political philosophers are still entrenched in the habit of exerting an intellectual authority that condemns them to repeating the oppressive structures of the *polis*, history periodically reminds them that a better pedagogical path is possible, one that builds subjects able to recognize and cultivate their equal apprehension of the world. The final passage of *Hatred of Democracy* constitutes the most appropriate end to our excursus:

> Democracy is as bare in its relation to the power of wealth as it is to the power of kinship that today comes to assist and to rival it. It is not based on any nature of things nor guaranteed by any institutional form. It is not borne along by any historical necessity and does not bear any. It is only entrusted to the constancy of its specific acts. This can provoke fear, and so hatred, among those who are used to exercising the *magisterium* of thought. But among those who know how to share with anybody and everybody the equal power of intelligence, it can conversely inspire courage, and hence joy. (HD 97)

PART II
Politics

FOUR

Police and oligarchy
Samuel A. Chambers

The three chapters of this part of the book are devoted to elucidating the key concepts that constitute Rancière's work on politics. And doubtless, Rancière has made a crucial contribution to debates over how to understand or theorize politics. Indeed, his work gained much wider circulation outside France when his writings specifically on politics from the 1990s were quickly translated into English and powerfully affected a series of debates within contemporary critical and political theory. For these reasons, Rancière's readers may be tempted to take up his writings as works in the tradition of political philosophy. Matters prove less than simple, however, since Rancière states directly, and with critical force: "I am not a political philosopher" (CR 10).

Rancière refuses this label not merely for the sake of avoiding disciplinary confines, but for two interrelated reasons. First, political philosophy has a very particular meaning within Rancière's arguments: he entirely rejects the idea of taking "*political* philosophy" as a branch or "natural division" of the broader field of philosophy (D ix). More than this, Rancière argues that the ultimate aim of the project of political philosophy has been precisely the *elimination of politics*. This claim holds, according to Rancière, across the canon. From Plato to Aristotle, from Marx to Arendt, political philosophers have sought to supplant the anarchic disorder of politics with a hierarchical order of the philosopher. Secondly, the so-called "return of political philosophy" has a particular resonance in the context of French politics. Political philosophy was reputedly "reborn" in North America thanks to the work of John Rawls, his followers, and the debates his work spawned. While the conversations surrounding Rawls's work in North America remained mostly academic, the importation of American political philosophers into France was carried out by thinkers such as Alain Renaut and Luc Ferry (minister under Chirac), who not only taught "political philosophy" but also brought it to bear directly on political debates. For Rancière, then, political philosophy played a key part in an ideological struggle against any contestation of "pure republicanism". Thus we might say that Rancière disavows political philosophy on both philosophical and political grounds. But for precisely these reasons, Rancière remains committed to a thorough analysis of the relation between politics and philosophy, and herein lies his most significant theorization of politics.

This chapter explicates two key concepts that prove essential to Rancière's overall project and that play a pivotal role in his understanding of politics: police and oligarchy. These are not standard terms within a contemporary theory of politics. Indeed, the list of "key concepts" for most contemporary political theorists would not include them, and therefore it may seem somewhat strange to begin the discussion of politics here. More than this, one might even worry that Rancière defends some sort of authoritarian vision of politics – centred on policing and committed to oligarchic rule. Of course, in Rancière's own case, nothing could be further from the truth. In order to work towards Rancière's radically democratic thinking of politics (see Chapter 5), we must begin with his own preparatory work. Rancière proceeds by way of a process that might best be called "re-definition". That is, he starts with phenomena and ideas that his readers already have a clear sense of, those they can easily name. He then swiftly *renames* these phenomena – a conceptual move that has significant consequences for his theory of politics. This chapter focuses on two of the new names that Rancière gives to the familiar. To state the case succinctly at the outset: where we would see politics, Rancière sees "police"; where we would identify democracy, Rancière recognizes only oligarchy. This chapter will provide concise articulations of the key concepts "police" and "oligarchy". But it will also clarify these concepts against the background of Rancière's broader understanding of philosophy, and it will link these concepts to his radical defence of democracy as the essence of politics.

Philosophy versus politics

Chapter 3 has already shown how Rancière's arguments emerge from his engagement with the philosophical tradition. In the context of developing Rancière's concepts of police and oligarchy, it proves particularly important to grasp his critique of Plato. Articulating the relationship between politics and philosophy (through his reading of Plato) leads Rancière directly to an analysis of society as a hierarchical order. The Platonic philosophic order is, as we shall see, the police order *par excellence*. Plato's Republic turns out to be an oligarchy.

On Rancière's reading, Plato remains paramount not for the usual reasons: not because Plato's teacher Socrates was the first philosopher and Plato himself was the first philosopher who wrote; not because Plato was the first *political* philosopher; not even because, as the first to answer the question "what is the best regime?", he was the pre-eminent "classical" political philosopher (see Strauss 1959). Instead, Rancière argues for the importance of Platonic philosophy along a different register; Plato's thought proves so significant because it is Plato who establishes a powerful and historically dominant relation between politics and philosophy. As will be developed below, Plato paradigmatically reduces politics to police.

This relationship depends on the connection that Plato draws between, on the one hand, the social order that he seeks to establish and maintain and, on the other, the threatening power of language to subvert that order. First, Plato builds his ideal regime upon a rigid, *hierarchical* social order: one very small group will be rulers of the regime (philosopher-kings); one slightly larger group will be soldiers and protectors (guardians); and one much larger group will be constituted by farmers and craftsmen. For Plato the justice of the city depends upon this order. Put more precisely, *justice is this order*, this structure, this hierarchy. In other words, justice for Plato proves to be a certain respect – a certain allegiance – to a social order of hierarchical inequality. Domination thus lies not just at the centre of Plato's ideal regime, but at the heart of his conception of justice.

Plato injects hierarchy into the very structure of his account of justice by having the founders of the ideal city tell a "noble lie" through the construction of a myth. According to this myth, each member of the regime is born with a particular metal in his or her soul and the type of metal determines their station in the social order: gold for guardians, silver for auxiliaries, and iron and bronze for workers. More important for Rancière than the mere fact that Plato must lie in order to create a "just" regime is what he must do in order to preserve the order he has constructed. Rancière focuses on a much less famous passage of the *Republic*, one in which Plato argues rather viciously against the idea that mere workers would take up the noble discourse of philosophy. For Plato, says Rancière, the order of the city can be protected only if the "order of discourse" is kept out of the hands of the workers (PP 31–2). Plato understands well a point that proves central to Rancière:

writing cannot be controlled. Writing gets in the hands of just about anyone and they can then choose to do just about anything with it. It is precisely this contaminating capacity of both philosophic discourse and poetic writing that runs the risk of disrupting and eventually tearing apart Plato's carefully constructed city. The city is precarious because its foundation must make commensurate the hierarchical social order and justice itself. Because they threaten this foundation, Plato banishes both the sophists and the poets from his perfect regime: the former would circulate philosophical discourse among everyone, while the latter would circulate poetic writing freely and widely. In either case the purity of Plato's philosophical order would come under threat.

Rancière wishes to associate this very disorder that threatens Platonic political philosophy, the impurity caused by the circulation of writing, the anarchy waiting at the gates of the Platonic *kallipolis* – Rancière associates all of this with democratic politics. For just this reason, he will argue that the project of constructing a philosophical order (and the commitment to order remains the *raison d'être* of philosophy) must always lead to one central (if often unintended) consequence: *politics' eradication*. In other words, and as the next two sections will expound, Plato's philosophy constructs a police order that eliminates politics, but that, at the same time, always remains exposed to the risk of politics. Thus, for Rancière politics is always *impure*, and for that reason always scandalous. But philosophy tries above all else to "suppress" any such scandal as this; it aims to eliminate all impurity. Hence, "philosophy tries to rid itself of politics" (D xii). Thus the conclusion of the story as told through Platonic philosophy looks like this: the relation between philosophy and politics turns out not merely to be one of trade-offs and tensions, but one of conflict and antagonism. If philosophy would banish politics from the city in order to strengthen and support the hierarchical social order that the philosopher has constructed, then this is only because of a more fundamental conflict between politics and "police".

The order of the police

The above allusions to politics make it sound as if perhaps Rancière does not quite understand what everyday politics is really all about. But Rancière has no illusions whatsoever about what "politics", as we comprehend it, actually looks like. He states the point quite clearly in *Disagreement* when he takes the time to identify just those "regular" sort of phenomena: "Politics is generally seen as the set of procedures whereby the aggregation and consent of collectivities is achieved, [it denotes] the organization of powers, the distribution of places and roles, and the systems for legitimizing this distribution" (D 28). It is not that Rancière does not understand that this is how we typically see politics – as if someone needed to explain it to him. Instead, he wishes to resist this reduction of politics to bureaucratic administration and economic management. Therefore Rancière takes everything he describes above and renames it: he calls the system of distribution "the police".

Rancière repeatedly invokes the phrase "police order" to refer to *any* hierarchical social order – the orders in which we all circulate, each and every day. He uses "policing" to designate not only policy-making – as the term in English, though not in French, already connotes – but also parliamentary legislation, executive orders, judicial decisions, and the vast array of economic arrangements. Most of what we would take to be politics turns out to be police: from the principles of interest-group liberalism to the actions of bureaucrats and executives; from elections to welfare. Today's technocracy proves to be a prime contemporary example of policing, for Rancière, and he repeatedly refers to the opinion poll as "the normal form" that policing takes today (D 31).

After introducing the term "police", Rancière quickly adds that it "no doubt poses a few problems", and this because we typically take "police" to refer to uniformed officers, to patrol cars, to "the truncheon blows of the forces of law and order" (D 28). But Rancière reminds us, as Michel Foucault had done before him, that a much broader idea of "police" arises earlier, in seventeenth-century German and Italian discourses on the state, coming to some prominence with the emergence of political economy in Germany (*ibid*.; cf. Foucault 1979). "Police orders"' therefore cut across culture, politics and economics; as Foucault says, "the police includes everything", to the extent that any police order determines relationships between human beings (thus it creates a hierarchy) and determines the relations between "men and things" (thus it determines a material order as well) (Foucault 1979: 248). At the core of his argument, Rancière uses police to refer to the organization of society, the dividing up and distribution of the various parts that make up the social whole. Hence we see that police is Rancière's term for what we usually understand by everyday interest-group politics. The distribution of goods and services, the allotment of roles and occupations, the management of the economy – all are part and parcel of the police order. Police, says Rancière succinctly, names "a symbolic constitution of the social" (TT 20).

Therefore, on the one hand, Rancière's concept of police must be understood as quite distinct from the common notion of cops on the street. On the other hand, we can trace an important relation between police in the specific sense of those who enforce law and, above all, maintain order, and "police" as a core principle that names the primary arrangement of parts that make up this order in the first place. Rancière's concept of police points to the general order that, in our everyday understanding, "the police" are meant to maintain. In terms of this relation between Rancière's general and specialized understanding and our own particular and ordinary sense, we might say that a powerful *police order* will have less use for *police officers*. In other words, the "truncheon blows" of police officers become necessary only when a general police order has somehow been threatened or called into question.

Rancière maintains the distinction between his "broader sense" of police and particular understandings of or critiques of the police. For this reason he frequently emphasizes that, as it functions in his writings, police has little if anything to do with repression or overt physical violence. He also insists that the identification of a police order does not constitute a critique of police orders in general. For Rancière, such a critique would make no sense. A police order, *some* police order, is inevitable. Thus to think, understand or analyse any particular police order, we must refuse the temptation to project a realm of pure freedom as existing outside that order; there is no pure "outside" to the police order. Drawing all these points together helps to make sense of Rancière's description of his own concept of police as "non-pejorative" (D 29). Rancière seeks neither an elimination of the police order nor a mobilization against police in general, and for this reason we must resist the notion of challenging the police order writ large. Hence Rancière's project does not oppose itself to police in the way that, for example, an orthodox Marxist project would oppose capitalism.

But to say that some police order proves unavoidable, to maintain neutrality against the idea of a police order, is neither to abandon a critical position on the police nor to reduce all police orders to the same level. While there may well be no pure "outside" of the police order, this does not mean that the "inside" of all police orders is equivalent. Rancière keenly describes the order of police that he sees around him in European democracies; he insists that much of what we take for "politics" is best described as police. He thereby shows that we live in police orders, but he nevertheless reminds us that "we do not live in camps" (HD 73). And such a reminder serves to emphasize the fact that not all police orders are the same. Rancière formulates this argument succinctly: "there is a worse and a better police" (D 30–31). While Rancière himself does not explore the differences, his framework makes possible and gives value to an analysis of the variations and differences between and among given police orders. As we shall see below, such a project might not concern itself directly with politics, but it would be no less valuable for that.

Rancière focuses on explicating the concept of "police" in such a way as to throw into relief a distinct conception of politics. This sort of project depends upon "police" consistently referring to a particular arrangement of bodies – the arrangement of the social order, the allocation of places, roles, occupations. The police thereby "defines the allocation of ways of doing, ways of being, and ways of saying" and for this reason any police order determines who has a part in society and who does not (D 29). This understanding of police as determining a distribution of roles within society, links the concept centrally to two other key concepts: politics (Chapter 5) and *Partage du sensible* (Chapter 7). Because of these links, an unexpected term like "police" proves to be the lynchpin of Rancière's theoretical and conceptual work on politics. And the concept of "police" also reveals the powerful, necessary, but not always obvious connections between Rancière's work "on politics" and his writings "on aesthetics".

The arguments of Chapter 7 will make clear the tie between police and Rancière's "politics of aesthetics": as a distribution of bodies, the police order must be understood as one particular "distribution/partition of the sensible" – a way of determining the order of appearance, of what can be apprehended by the senses. Rancière insists that a police order is also "an order of the visible and the sayable" (D 29). This logic can be completed as follows: police determines not just the part that any party has in society; it also determines the *intelligibility* of any party at all. To have no place within the police order means to be *unintelligible* – not just marginalized within the system, but made invisible by the system. Police orders thereby distribute both roles and the lack of roles; they determine who counts and they decide that some do not count at all.

This notion of those who "do not count", those who have "no part" in the given police order, connects Rancière's concept of "police" to his novel understanding of politics. For Rancière, his radical redefinition of the term politics makes sense only in relation to police. But to explain this relation is to get ahead of the story to be told here. Chapter 5 will take up the task of explicating Rancière's concept of politics. Before that, this chapter needs to complete the logic of the police in Rancière by extending the discussion to his other central concept in this project of redefining ordinary phenomena. If so much of what we take to be politics turns out be nothing more than "police", then the analysis begs at least two decisive and essential questions. First, the question for the next chapter: what is politics? Secondly, the question for the next section: how do we understand the system of political rule under which we all live? In other words, if what we thought was politics turns out to be police, then can we still so easily and simply describe our political regime as "democratic", or must we, in redefining much of politics, also redefine the systems of police under which we live?

The rule of oligarchy

In his more recent *Hatred of Democracy*, Rancière offers a vigorous defence of democracy against all the critiques of democracy – as individualist consumer society run amok – that have circulated in recent years, especially in France. In making this defence, however, Rancière also forwards a clear and powerfully polemical answer to the questions posed above. He states plainly, yet repeatedly, that "we do not live in democracies". He offers his alternative formulation just as plainly: "we live in States of oligarchic rule" (HD 73). Rancière's logic here parallels the move he makes from politics to police: all social orders are marked by hierarchy and domination, and all political orders (all political regimes) seek to naturalize the very inequality that the police order presupposes and enacts. The concept of "oligarchy" therefore proves central to Rancière's understanding of the political and social worlds we inhabit, but it should be stressed that "oligarchy" emerges sharply only in some of Rancière's most recent writings. Thus, while some of the "centrality" of this term comes about retrospectively for Rancière – as he reinterprets early arguments in light of this newer concept – Rancière's conceptualization of oligarchy has become crucial to his overall project.

To understand what it means to say that we live under oligarchic rule, Rancière first exposes what he names the "*scandal* of democracy" (HD 51). This phrase must be interpreted carefully. "Scandal of democracy" refers not to a scandal that happens *to* democracy, not to some non-necessary incident that would mar an otherwise good or pure democracy (thus not to the type of scandal that marks a particular political administration). Rather, "scandal of democracy" names the scandal that *is* democracy. This scandal has to do with the right or the title to rule. Any political regime, says Rancière, is made up of those who rule and those who are ruled. In Greek, *arkhe* names the principle that identifies the rulers and the ruled; *arkhe* is the principle that designates who will take up which of the two categories. Rancière offers an important reading of Plato's *Laws*, designed to sort out the various titles to *arkhe* – that is, legitimate claims to rule, to be a governor rather than merely to be governed. Plato lists seven titles to rule. The first four are titles of birth: parents over children, old over young, masters over slaves, nobles over commoners. The next two titles, says Rancière, "express nature if not birth": strong over weak, intelligent over ignorant (HD 39–40). These first six titles express (and indeed, exhaust) the different forms that oligarchy can take. These six titles express six different principles of *arkhe*: all of them are, obviously, non-democratic, but they are also the principles that still rule in politics today. Nonetheless, for Rancière, the last title, the seventh title – a seemingly "extra" title – matters most. In his reading of Plato, Rancière describes the seventh title as "a title that is not a title, and that, … is nevertheless considered to be the most just". It is the drawing of lots, the principle of randomness as the principle of rule (HD 40). *It is a claim to rule that is not actually based on any principle at all.* Thus, to clarify terms, this seventh title to rule is no *arkhe* at all. It is not an *arkhe* (a *principle* of rule), but a *kratos* (a mere *prevailing*) (OSP 94).

This seventh title that is not a title provides, of course, the only "title" to rule that can justify democracy. This should not be surprising since, as any student of politics or political theory knows, democracy means "rule by the people", but the word comes from the Greek *demokratia*, a compound of *demos* (people) and *kratos*. Etymologically, *arkhe* plays no part in democracy. Rancière wishes to show that it also plays no part conceptually. Thus democracy is a *kratos*, a manner of prevailing, based on no natural principle. Democracy is rule by the people in the sense of "rule by those who rule", that is, rule by those who have no other claim to rule than random luck – the throw of the dice. Here we see precisely why democracy is scandalous: because it is rule without principle (*kratos* without *arkhe*). Because a democrat's title to rule is only this seventh "title that is not a title", democracy separates political rule from *any* social order whatsoever. The first four titles to rule link a political regime directly to an order of birth: one is born a master, born a noble, and hence one rules. The second two titles disconnect rule from birth, but only so as to reconnect it to nature: one rules because one is best. But in democracy, rule itself is scandalous because it can be shored up in no social order. Rancière writes: "the scandal lies in the disjoining of entitlements to govern from any analogy to those that order social relations. … It is the scandal of a superiority based on no other title than the very absence of superiority" (HD 41). Unlike bureaucracy, which Hannah Arendt famously defined as "rule by no one" (1958: 40), democracy is indeed rule by someone, by the people. But since the people have no title to rule, democracy, we might say, is therefore "rule by anyone at all".

To clarify the stakes of this argument, we can stress that while Rancière draws out his argument about oligarchy from ancient sources, one should not conclude that he confines his analysis to the ancient world: the very same principles of oligarchy remain prevalent throughout history. Indeed, the technocratic nature of modern policy-making only gives oligarchic principles more force and resonance. And while oligarchic principles of rule seem rather banal – oligarchy is surely not scandalous – oligarchy proves crucial to Rancière's work precisely because he insists upon the scandalous nature of democracy. Democracy is not a regime, nor is it a form of society. It is not an arrangement of a state, nor is it a system of political institutions. "There is, strictly speaking, no such thing as democratic government. *Government is always exercised by the minority over a majority*" (HD 52, emphasis added). In one sense, then, all government is oligarchic.

Rancière knows the typical response to this claim quite well. In the face of the argument that nowhere in the world today can we genuinely say that the people rule, most commentators tell the same story. It is a standard narrative, frequently taught in the classroom, and easily locatable on any number of Wikipedia pages, including that of "democracy". I have covered the narrative many times myself, and it always goes something like this. Ancient societies were ruled by direct democracies, wherein all citizens legislated directly; but modern mass societies prove ill suited to this form of rule. Put simply, they are too big, making it both financially and logistically impossible to implement direct democracy. In the face of this challenge, it proves imperative to distinguish carefully between direct democracy (practised in the ancient world but impossible today) from representative democracy. The latter, it is said, seeks to implement many of the same goals and principles of ancient democracy while paying full attention to modern realities. Thus one cannot criticize or dismiss democracy today by saying that "a minority rules" (one cannot call it oligarchy), since that minority is democratically elected and serves to represent the people as a whole.

Rancière has a powerful response to this standard narrative: it is very bad history. Representation was a system that emerged in Europe not in order to democratize regimes, but rather so that state power could be extended and more efficiently implemented. Representation "is, by all rights, an oligarchic form". The same goes for voting: "originally the expression of a consent" and certainly not a device of democracy (HD 53). In the end, Rancière concludes that far from being redundant, as it often sounds to our ears today, the phrase "representative democracy" started off as an oxymoron.

Therefore, one cannot merely dismiss the crucial, even if obvious, empirical observation that today it is always a minority that rules. Rather than somehow cover over this fact with faulty historical narratives about democratic progress or mask it by way of technical distinctions between direct democracy and republican principles, Rancière proposes instead to tell it as he sees it. Democracy is not a regime, because all political regimes are oligarchic. "What we call democracy is a statist and government functioning that is exactly the contrary" (HD 72, emphasis added). Hence Rancière's claim that "we live in States of oligarchic law". We live in oligarchies, and only in oligarchies, precisely because that is all we can live in. Some rule while others are ruled, with the ruling group always smaller than the group being ruled. Yet, again, Rancière does not intend his claim to have some sort of levelling effect, as if to say that all regimes are oligarchies and are therefore all the "same". As he puts it, the states of oligarchic law that North Americans and Europeans live in are always more or less constrained by a discourse of civil liberty and popular sovereignty. These limits surely have "advantages", and, significantly, various manifestations of oligarchy "can give democracy more or less room" (HD 72-3). Thus oligarchies can be evaluated, challenged and transformed in various ways, but they cannot merely be praised for being democracies – that is exactly what they are not.

Rancière's insistence that we live in oligarchies, like his insistence that we always live under particular police orders, serves not to narrow political possibilities, but rather to specify the form that democratic politics would take were it to occur. More to the point, by showing precisely that democracy is not a regime, and that all regimes are oligarchies, Rancière opens up a different space for thinking democracy. He separates out "the democratic" from interest-group competition, civil rights, liberal constitutionalism, and all the other institutional and legal forms with which democracy is so frequently conflated. By revealing the rule of oligarchy, Rancière broaches the possibility of democracy. Such a possibility depends on seeing that democracy is not a question of regimes; it is a question of politics.

On the way to politics

Politics can come about only by opposing a given police order. Politics occurs when the logic of the police order (domination) finds itself challenged by a wholly different logic – that of equality (see Part I of this volume). Democracy can only emerge as something that thwarts the oligarchic rule that is the norm. Democratic struggle bases its claim to rule not on a principle different from that operative within the oligarchy, but on no principle at all. Democracy thereby undermines the principle of oligarchy, rather than replacing it with a new one. Thus democracy is the essence of politics (OSP 94).

While these statements all seem to take the form of simple and direct definitions of politics and democracy, they work instead, and more forcefully, to illustrate that politics and democracy are both relational concepts within Rancière's writings. As such, they depend upon a full understanding of the terms that they oppose – police and oligarchy. Rancière's theory requires a prior sense of how he redefines our ordinary understanding of democratic politics under the conceptual framework announced by "police" and "oligarchy". A reader who can make sense of Rancière's claims that so-called democratic regimes are actually oligarchies, and that much of what passes for politics is actually policing – that reader now sees the need to offer distinct and counterintuitive conceptualizations of both politics and democracy. In reading Rancière it is always important not to lose sight of the fact that, according to his account, the world is made up of, if not dominated by, police and oligarchy. And that explains why these concepts – surely less exciting or radical-sounding than many others in Rancière's corpus – must come first in any account of his politics. They play a more fundamental role because these two concepts illuminate the world we live in.

Moreover, the democratic struggle that Rancière both joins and defends can be advanced only with a keen awareness of the dilemmas of police and oligarchy. In other words, to grasp the concept of police reveals the impossibility of eliminating police in favour of politics. Any effort to disrupt the police order will always be subject to co-optation by that very police order. Challenges to the police order will always be heard merely as calls to adjust its terms. And understanding what Rancière means by oligarchy exposes the obvious fact that we could never simply replace oligarchy with democracy. Rancière calls this latter paradox the "quandary of oligarchy". It is a quandary proper to oligarchy yet unavoidable even by democracy. Just as every democracy for Plato risks being reduced to a tyranny (because mob rule was the perfect context for takeover by a tyrant), so for Rancière any effort to bring about democratic action, to mobilize democratic struggle, may fall prey to the dangers of oligarchy (HD 84). Rather that rejecting *arkhe* for *kratos* as democratic struggle intends, it may only replace one *arkhe* with another.

This is not to suggest that such paradoxes could ever be eradicated, solved or eliminated. The paradoxes of democratic politics can only ever be *navigated*, *managed* or *engaged*. To do so, however, will require intimate knowledge of police and oligarchy – terms that set the foundation for the chapters to follow.

FIVE

Wrong, disagreement, subjectification
Todd May

The central divide in traditional political theory runs between those theories that advocate for liberty and those that advocate for equality. On the one side, theories that advocate for liberty argue that the most important human ability is autonomy: the ability to fashion life as one sees fit. In order to do that, people must be free to create themselves. Therefore liberty is the key political value. On the other side are theorists who argue that an unequal society is an unjust one. Societies that countenance inequality are unfair to their members. In addition, they deny real liberty to those who are less than equal, since without resources one cannot fashion life as one sees fit.

There is another way to cast this debate, one that will be helpful in understanding Jacques Rancière's thought. We can think of the dividing line as one that runs, not between liberty and equality, but within equality itself. Theories of liberty can be seen as a type of theory of equality. What theorists of liberty seek is, in fact, equal liberty for everyone. Theorists of liberty do not endorse unequal liberty; they allow inequalities in other things, for example income or resources, in order to preserve equal liberty. For them, since liberty is the key value, we must maximize it for everyone. Moreover, to permit one person to have more liberty at the expense of another is to violate the autonomy of that other person. Everyone should have maximal equal liberty.

If we put matters this way, then the question for most traditional political theories is not: liberty or equality? Rather, it is: equality in what? What is it that everyone is to be equal in? What should be the central value? Should we be equal in liberty, in opportunity, in income, in access to goods (and what goods?), in some combination of these, or in something else altogether? Most traditional theories can be seen as casting their lot with some particular answer to that question. Libertarian theories endorse liberty. Liberal theories endorse a combination of liberty and opportunity. Socialist theories tend to opt for access to goods or income. But all these theories agree that there is something we should all be equal in.

There is another common element to these theories as well. They all endorse the idea that the state bears the ultimate responsibility for ensuring access to the value we should be equal in. Equality, for these theories, is something to be granted, protected or created by the state. (Some socialist theories do not ratify the central role of the state; they turn out to be closer to Rancière's view.) For libertarians, the state protects liberty and does nothing more. For liberals, it both protects liberty and ensures (and sometimes creates) opportunity. For most socialists, the state ensures and creates access to goods and/or income equality.

We might put this idea another way. Equality, according to most traditional political theories, is something people receive from the state or some state-like institution. It is not something they create; it is not something they guide; it is not something they do. Equality happens to them. To be sure, they may utilize that equality in any number of ways. But the equality itself comes to them (or is protected for them) from a source outside themselves.

That presupposition – that equality is received rather than created – is inherent to most political theories, from right to left. And it is that presupposition that Rancière's political view places in question. For Rancière, as for other political theories, equality is the central value. However, equality, for him, is created *by* people rather than *for* them. A democratic politics is a politics of the *demos*, of the people. It belongs to them, and not to anyone who claims to represent them. "[P]olitical activity", Rancière writes, in a difficult passage we shall examine presently:

> is always a mode of expression that undoes the perceptible divisions of the police order by implementing a basically heterogeneous assumption, that of a part of those who have no part, an assumption that, at the end of the day, itself demonstrates the sheer contingency of the order, the equality of any speaking being with any other speaking being. (D 30)

Politics, in short, a truly democratic politics, is collective action emerging from the presupposition of equality.

In order to understand how Rancière thinks of this democratic politics, we should recall briefly his idea of the police discussed in the previous chapter. Before that, we should comment in passing on his use of the term *politics*. When Rancière contrasts politics with police, he does not mean to say that the police is nothing political. Instead, he is marking the difference between a democratic politics – a politics of the *demos* – and a hierarchical politics of the police order. Sometimes he indicates this distinction in French by reserving the term *la politique* for a democratic politics and *le politique* for the politics of the police order. We shall keep this distinction by using the term "democratic politics" for Rancière's politics of the *demos*, except, of course, when citing his writings.

In any case, a police order, as explained in the previous chapter, is hierarchical. It is based upon the presupposition that some are fit to govern and some are not. Otherwise put, a police order distinguishes between those who have a part and those who do not. In Rancière's writing, that distinction is a fluid one. It is not that there are simply two groups of people lying on either side of the divide. In a particular society, there can be many types of hierarchy: gender, race, class, sexual orientation and so on. A complex police order will be characterized not by a single hierarchy but by a number of (often intersecting) hierarchies. However, in each hierarchy there is always the distinction between those who have a part and those who do not, between those who are fit to make decisions and to create lives and those whose lives are to be created for them.

This is true not only of societies. It is also true of traditional political theories. The equality they seek is not an equality presupposed by those who act, but instead one granted or guaranteed by those who govern. Traditional political theories rely on the state or some other governing institution to distribute whatever type of equality is valued. That is why these theories are called distributive theories of justice. They embrace a value or small set of values, justify it, and argue that that value should be equally distributed to each member of the society. This, in itself, implies a hierarchy between those who govern and distribute, and those who are governed and receive.

This hierarchy is no different in kind from the hierarchies of the police order. Like social hierarchies, the hierarchy of traditional liberal political theory divides those who have a part – those who distribute and make decisions about that distribution – from those who do not. Even if, as in most liberal theories, those who distribute and make decisions must be voted into that position by those who do not, the hierarchy persists. Moreover, from the experience we have of elections in nominally democratic countries, we know that those who are voted into the position of distributors generally come from the class of people who already have a part.

A politics of the Rancièrean kind, a politics that presupposes rather than distributes equality, is in an important way the inverse of traditional liberal political theory. Where the latter sees equality coming from the distributor to the people, Rancière sees equality coming from the people. It is a presupposition out of which they act, the presupposition of their equality. In democratic political action, people take the hierarchies of a given political and social order to be, as Rancière says, contingent rather than natural or inevitable. The *demos* works against those hierarchies in the name of its equality. It is not that people necessarily demand equality, or even think of themselves consciously as presupposing equality (although often they do). Rather, it is there, in their political practices. If one looks, one can see it as an inherent presupposition lying within what they do. "Equality", Rancière argues, "is not a given that politics then presses into service, an essence embodied in the law or a goal politics sets itself the task of attaining. It is a mere assumption that needs to be discerned within the practices implementing it" (D 33).

An example would help clarify this idea. One tactic of the US civil rights movement of the 1960s was the lunch-counter sit-in. At the time, there were many lunch counters in the South that did not serve African Americans. As a protest, integrated groups of three or four people would go to a discriminatory lunch counter, sit together, and wait to order lunch. They did not carry placards or shout slogans. They acted like customers, asking for menus and seeking to order a meal. They were usually followed into the restaurant by segregationists who taunted and sometimes beat them, and then by police who arrested them. But they did not fight back. They made it clear that they were there to order lunch like other people, and that they expected to be served.

In this example, the civil rights workers acted out of the presupposition of equality. They took themselves to be equal to those who were allowed to order lunch, and acted collectively out of that presupposition.

One might argue that equality was not a presupposition of their action but rather a goal. In that sense, one might say, the lunch-counter sit-ins were more characteristic of traditional political theories of equality. What the protestors sought, on this view, was to be treated equally by others. They wanted to *receive* equality, to have it distributed to them.

This would be too superficial a view of their actions. To be sure, those who sat in at lunch counters did seek to be treated equally. But they did not do so simply by asking for such treatment. They did so by acting as though they were *already* equal. They presupposed their equality and, through their actions, brought the social order into conflict with that presupposition. To be sure, many actions and movements that Rancière might be willing to call democratic seek to change a police order by means of recognizing equality. However, there is a difference between asking to be treated equally in order to think of oneself as equal and demanding to be treated equally by acting as though one is equal. In the first case, the power of equality lay with the distributor. In the second case, it lay with the actors, with the people or the *demos*.

In every democratic political movement, there is a conflict between those who act in the name of their equality (and those in solidarity with them) and the social order that presupposes their inequality. That conflict Rancière calls a *disagreement* (*une mésentente*), a term that he uses to name his most comprehensive political book. He defines a disagreement this way: "We should take disagreement to mean a determined kind of speech situation: one in which one of the interlocutors at once understands and does not understand what the other is saying" (D x). A bit further on he writes:

> An extreme form of disagreement is where X cannot see the common object Y is presenting because X cannot comprehend that the sounds uttered by Y form words and chains of words similar to X's own. This extreme situation – first and foremost – concerns politics. (D xii)

This is an unusual way to define a disagreement in general and a political disagreement in particular, and we should unpack what Rancière means by it.

Rancière's definition of a disagreement is indebted to a passage in Aristotle's *Politics*, where Aristotle argues that what makes man alone a political animal is the capacity for speech.

> Speech is something different from voice, which is possessed by other animals also and used by them to express pain or pleasure; for their nature does indeed enable them not only to feel pleasure and pain but to communicated these feelings to each other. Speech, on the other hand, serves to indicate what is useful and what is harmful, and so also what is just and what is unjust.
> (Aristotle, *Politics*, 1253a)

Slaves, for Aristotle, do not engage in speech, properly understood; they are more like animals that can emit sounds but do not engage in language, although they can recognize language in men enough to follow orders. Or better, what sounds like language among slaves is only really a series of brute noises and cries. In Aristotle's words, "the 'slave by nature' is he that can and therefore does belong to another, and he that participates in reason so far as to recognize it but not so as to possess it (whereas the other animals obey not reason but emotions)" (Aristotle, *Politics*, 1254b16).

Of course, when slaves make these noises, they certainly sound as if they are speaking. But the elites or the oligarchs cannot recognize these sounds as speech, because they cannot recognize their authors as speaking beings. If those same noises were uttered by someone they recognized as an equal, they would understand them as human speech. To put the point another way, those at the top of the police order do recognize the uttered noises as sounds that would be words, but cannot be because of who is uttering them: they at once understand and do not understand what the other is saying. And the reason for this is that they do not recognize the other as capable of forming words and chains of words similar to their own.

This is a disagreement. A disagreement does not concern, or does not primarily concern, competing views over an issue, for example whether a group of workers is underpaid. It concerns who gets to speak, whose voice counts. And, more deeply, it concerns who actually has a voice, who is capable of speech. Workers' demands, women's demands, the demands of those who are marginalized by race, class, immigration status and so on are not recognized as demands because they are not recognized as issuing from people capable of making real demands.

Now one might argue that, in contrast to Aristotle's time, those at the top of a police order, particularly in contemporary societies that are usually thought of as democratic, do not really think that the *demos* is incapable of speech. Strictly speaking, this is true. However, we are not so far from Aristotle's view as we might think. For most of the elites, whether in politics, business or elsewhere, even if the *demos* is capable of speech, it is not capable of saying anything worth hearing. The *demos* remains populated by people who do not understand and therefore have to have their interests watched over by those who do understand. This view is rarely articulated so boldly in public, but it does make an appearance every once in a while. A recent example is President George W. Bush's advice to the American people after the plane crashes of 9/11 that the best thing they could do for the country would be to go about their business and, especially, to shop.

A disagreement, then, does not centre primarily on any set of demands that are made, but rather on who gets to speak and make demands. Therefore it centres on the equality of those who are making demands. We can see, then, why it is that a democratic politics is collective action issuing from or expressing the presupposition of equality. What is at issue in politics is the equality of those who seek to participate. If the *demos*, the people, are less than equal, then their participation is unnecessary. They can justifiably remain, as Rancière says, a part that has no part. However, if they are equal, then being treated as less than equal is unjustified. A democratic politics is a matter of confronting a disagreement. The term Rancière uses for this confrontation is a *wrong*.

"Wrong", Rancière says:

> is simply the mode of subjectification in which the assertion of equality takes its political shape ... Wrong institutes a singular universal, a polemical universal, by tying the presentation of equality, as the part of those who have no part, to the conflict between parts of society. (D 39)

This passage, although abstract in character, captures the core of democratic politics movements. In considering it, we shall leave the term *subjectification* to the side for a moment. It is an important term that we shall return to below.

When a wrong ties the presentation of equality to a conflict between parts of society, it asserts the equality of the part of society that is not recognized in the police order as being equal. The wrongness lies precisely in the failure of the police order to recognize this equality. In this sense, a wrong is not so much claimed as it is displayed. We hear a great deal these days about politics being a matter of victimization. Everyone complains that he or she is a victim and therefore deserves recognition from the governing powers of a society. Rancière denies that the concept of a wrong is one of victimization. In some ways, the concept of wrong as he understands it is the opposite of victimization. With victimization, one claims to be wronged and demands compensation. The onus of recognizing equality lies on those who are supposed to provide that compensation. With a wrong as Rancière defines it, the project of recognizing equality lies first with the *demos*, with those who act on their own behalf. By expressing their equality, they display for all to see that the police order has all along denied it.

In order to understand this, we can return to the example of the lunch-counter sit-ins. The sit-ins were a staging of a wrong. The participants in the sit-in movement did not primarily ask for recognition of their equality. They acted as though they were already equal. In doing so, they confronted a social order that did not recognize them as equal. In effect, rather than saying, "You have wronged us and you need to do something about it," their message was, "We are equal to you, and now we're going to see whether or not you recognize that." The failure of the social order to recognize that equality displays the wrong. It stages it, in a theatrical sense. And when it is displayed or staged as a wrong, what Rancière calls a single or polemical universal emerges. That universal is one of equality. It is a singular universal because it is the equality of a particular group in a particular set of social circumstances. The people sitting at lunch counters did not display the general idea that all people are equal, although they probably thought that. Their actions were more local in character. Their message was, more specifically: we are equal to others who sit here. The wrong, then, lies in the failure of the police order to incorporate that equality into itself.

What is this equality that is presupposed in democratic political action? What is its character? In one way, it has no particular character. It operates instead by undercutting the particular characters assigned by a police order. If a police order distinguishes men and women, blacks and whites, gays and straights, immigrants and citizens, it does so for the purpose of constructing hierarchies. We might see these terms as purely descriptive, but that is not how they operate in constructing a police order. These distinctions serve to divide those who have a part from those who do not. If this is so, then equality is, in a particular sense, an empty term. It signifies the rejection of classifications characteristic of a given police order. As Rancière puts it, "The essence of equality is in fact not so much to unify as to declassify, to undo the supposed naturalness of orders and replace it with the controversial figures of division" (OSP 32–3). (The division Rancière refers to here does not refer to the divisions posited by the police order, but to the dissent of one group from the consensus sought by the police order for those divisions.)

In this sense, the term *equality* has no content. It serves instead to mark the refusal of a particular content posited by the police order. In another, more pedestrian, sense, however, we can say that the term does have content. If the distinctions posited by the police order are unjustified, this is because we are all equal. But what is it we are equal in that undermines the justification of a police order? It is that each of us is capable of constructing a meaningful life alongside others. We can think for ourselves, converse with others, and together and separately create lives that have significance. We do not need an authority to tell us who we ought to be or where our good lies.

If we were incapable of this, then a police order would indeed be justified. It would be necessary for those who are competent to have a part, and for others, less competent, not to have a part. Rancière does not argue this particular point, but does hint at it in a couple of places. In *Disagreement*, he says:

There is order in society because some people command and others obey, but in order to obey at least two things are required: you must understand the order and you must understand that you must obey it. And to do that, you must already be the equal of the person who is ordering you. It is this equality that gnaws away at any natural order. (D 16)

If we take this argument as concluding that equality means identity of intellectual ability, it is not a very good one. However, if we take it more as a rejoinder to Aristotle – that speech is characteristic of both those who give and those who receive orders – and as claiming the ability of everyone to give and receive orders, then it can stand for the rejection of any justification for others to order our lives.

The other place where this equality is given content is in *The Ignorant Schoolmaster*, discussed in Chapter 2. If we think of the equal intelligence posited by Joseph Jacotot as indicating that everyone is equally capable of solving Fermat's last theorem or writing brilliant poetry, then it is plainly wrong that we are all equally intelligent. It is certainly true that we are more nearly equally intelligent than our police orders recognize, and the educational experiments performed by Jacotot are evidence of that. However, we are not equally capable of performing high-level abstract tasks, any more than we are equally capable of performing high-level athletic feats. On the other hand, if we take equal intelligence in a more pedestrian sense to indicate that we are capable of building meaningful lives alongside and in interaction with others, then the concept of equal intelligence becomes both more compelling and more politically relevant. This is the underlying theme of *The Ignorant Schoolmaster*: not just the equality (or near equality) of intelligence required to perform well in school, but the equality of intelligence required to undercut any justification for the hierarchical divisions of a police order.

So far, we have discussed the underlying character of a democratic politics. We have said nothing about its results. This is for good reason. If a democratic politics were defined by its results, then its democratic character would be founded on the success (or failure) of its goals. This would shift things away from Rancière's own framework of thought in two ways. First, it would found the democratic character of a movement not in its motivation but in its end-point. This would, in effect, deny that democratic movements emerge out of the presupposition of equality. If, for Rancière, equality lies at the source of political action, and if we define the democratic character of a movement by reference to its goal or its results, then equality would no longer be that by which a democratic movement is defined.

Secondly, and related, to focus on results would hold the democratic character of the movement hostage to the context in which it is undertaken. If that context is not conducive to success, then that would damage the character of the movement as democratic. This is a position very much counter to the spirit of Rancière's thought. Imagine a movement that emerges out of the presupposition of equality, but struggling against a police order that is so entrenched that it fails to make changes in that order. If that lack of success were relevant to the question of whether the movement is democratic, then the democratic character of political engagement would no longer be defined by the *demos* but by outside forces. It is better, then, to leave results to the side when asking about what constitutes a democratic politics. A movement that arises from the presupposition of equality but that does not have an impact is a failed, but nevertheless democratic, movement. And even then, the fact of the movement itself probably introduces changes into the lives of those who participate in it (and those who may come later and refer to it as a touchstone in their own struggle), even where they fall short of their goals. To count a movement as failed because it does not achieve its goals is often to view the effects of that movement in overly simplistic terms.

There is a phenomenon, however, that emerges, not *from* but *within* a democratic movement. Rancière calls it *subjectification*. It is not the type of subjectification discussed, for example, by Michel Foucault, where the power relations around us turn us into subjects. In some sense, it is the opposite. Subjectification is the process of becoming a collective subject through acting out of the presupposition of equality.

> By *subjectification* I mean the production through a series of actions of a body and a capacity for enunciation not previously identifiable within a given field of experience, whose identification is thus part of the reconfiguration of the field of experience.
>
> (D 35)

The process of subjectification will be a familiar one to those who have studied the history of democratic political movements. Previous to these movements, the lives of people in the *demos* are disparate and isolated. Those who have no part are each trying to survive, often taking on the denigrating character the police order assigns them. As Rancière says, "There is only the order of domination or the disorder of revolt" (D 12). As a democratic political movement begins to take hold, a *we* emerges that was not there before. A group begins to emerge where there was none before. In that sense, the social field of experience is reconfigured. It is reconfigured for those who have a part, since they are forced to see others they have not seen before, or at least not in that particular way. And it is is reconfigured for the *demos*, who see a social order in which they may have a part. As a result, within the *demos* people begin to feel empowered. This empowerment is not individual but collective. Rather than seeing others among the *demos* as competitors for the same scarce goods (whether those goods be material or abstract – beauty, for example, in the case of women), one begins to see them as just like oneself, engaged in the same struggle, confronting the same adversary. For instance, I was on a human rights delegation in Palestine in 1988, during the first *intifada*, where this process was on display first hand. People described how they were coming together for a common purpose – ending the Israeli occupation – whereas before they were often at odds, each trying to make the best for himself or herself from within the stranglehold Israel placed upon their lives. As an example of this, during curfews imposed by the Israeli army, people would pass food from door to door to make sure everyone was fed. This would have been largely unthinkable in many places before the *intifada* began.

We should not see subjectification as a result of a democratic movement, but rather as part of one. We noted above that Rancière defines a wrong as "the mode of subjecification in which the assertion of equality takes its political shape". Subjectification, then, is not the result of a democratic politics but one of its elements. It is the element that is constituted by a collective *we* that is co-extensive with collective action. The *we* is neither the source of the action nor its outcome. It emerges alongside the ongoing activity, feeding and being fed by it.

For Rancière, then, politics – a democratic politics – has nothing to do with what people are given or what they can expect. It has nothing, at least nothing directly, to do with fair treatment. Democratic politics is not something that happens to people. It is something they do. They do it when they act together, alongside those in solidarity with them, under the presupposition of their equality within a police order that does not recognize that equality. Such a thought of politics is timely. In a period in which we are encouraged to become passive, to expect rather than to act, to shop rather than to organize, there are fewer theoretical tasks more urgent than that of reminding us that for politics to become *our* politics, we cannot be its audience; we must instead be its actors.

SIX
Archipolitics, parapolitics, metapolitics

Bruno Bosteels

Archipolitics, parapolitics and metapolitics are three neologisms with which Jacques Rancière, in a central chapter of his 1995 book *Disagreement: Politics and Philosophy* (English translation 1998), proposes to reflect upon the dominant figures of what he calls "the politics of the philosophers", from Plato to Hobbes and from Marx to Bourdieu. Precisely what is at stake in this reflection – whence the chapter's centrality in the book – is the very question of the relation between politics and philosophy, which is but one instance among others of the relation between the real and the thought of the real. The ultimate goal is to come to an understanding of politics without prefixes, of the real of politics set free from the typical efforts of philosophers to appropriate, displace, cover up and/or unmask its essential scandal, which is none other than the scandal of democracy when properly understood, that is, the staging of equality in the form of an empty liberty, over and against the purported naturalness of the existing order of domination. "This equality is simply the equality of anyone at all with anyone else: in other words, in the final instance, the absence of *arkhê*, the sheer contingency of any social order," writes Rancière. "Every politics is democratic in this precise sense: not in the sense of a set of institutions, but in the sense of forms of expression that confront the logic of equality with the logic of the police order" (D 15, 101). The discussion of these three key concepts from *Disagreement* thus offers a major opportunity to raise the thorny question of the exact status of Rancière's own discourse, in so far as he claims to avoid the trappings of "political philosophy", including the recently much-acclaimed "return of the political", all the while refusing at the same time to join in on the celebratory consensus about the "end of politics" that would signal the beginning of the era of so-called postpolitics. In a characteristic move, he proposes to follow neither the traditionalists nor the apocalyptical extremists. In order to do so, however, he nevertheless seems to continue relying surreptitiously on some of the radical energy afforded philosophy by the different perspectives of archipolitics, parapolitics and metapolitics. Rancière's use of these neologisms, finally, can be contrasted in interesting directions with the way in which some of these very same terms are deployed, for instance, in the work of his contemporary Alain Badiou.

Political philosophy and politics

Before we take a closer look at the specific characterizations of archipolitics, parapolitics and metapolitics in *Disagreement*, two methodological principles are worth keeping in mind as they affect the treatment of each of these key concepts. Rancière posits first of all that political philosophy is always the belated response to an already-existing form of what we might call militant politics. "It is first in relation to politics that philosophy, from the very beginning, 'comes too late.' Only for philosophy this 'lateness' is the wrong of democracy," as in the case of Plato's *Republic*, which is the philosopher's reply to the scandalous appearance of the people or *demos* on the scene of the Athenian city-state. "In the form of democracy, politics is already in place, without waiting for its theoretical underpinnings or its *arkhê*, without waiting for the proper beginning that will give birth to it as performance of its own principle" (D 62). This antecedence of factual or empirical politics, then, is what political philosophy will set out to correct. Archipolitics, from Plato to modern-day republicanism, for instance, will consist entirely in the endeavour to steer political thought back in the direction of a proper realization of the *arkhê* of politics, both as beginning or initial cause and as guiding principle of order.

None of these philosophical attempts at displacement and obfuscation, however, will ever prove to be completely successful. This is due to a second methodological insight that runs through this part of Rancière's work, namely, the notion that actual forms of politics may always take back certain categories and paradoxes from political philosophy so as to put them to radical emancipatory uses: "The concepts that political philosophy subtracts from politics in order to belabor the rules of a community without conflict are endlessly reclaimed by politics to work up a new dispute" (D 76, trans. mod.). A good example of this kind of reappropriation is the split between "man" and "citizen" in the tradition of modern-day human rights doctrines, a split that far from constituting an obstacle or shortcoming, turns out to provide crucial leverage for what can become a truly revolutionary denunciation of the insufficiency of merely political emancipation, on one hand, and a powerful argument in favour of total human emancipation, on the other.

Thus, according to Rancière, all political philosophies – whether archipolitical, parapolitical or metapolitical – undoubtedly lead to some kind of negation, denial or disavowal of politics properly speaking. And yet, in spite of their negative rapport with the real of political action, each of these three figures can nonetheless be tied back to, and thereby indirectly still reveal, the true nature of emancipatory politics, which consists in making a part out of those who have no part and verifying the latter's paradoxical effects on the existing order of domination. "Political philosophies, at least those worthy of the name, the name of this particular paradox, are philosophies that offer a solution to the paradox of the part of those who have no part, either by substituting an equivalent role for it, or by creating a simulacrum of it, by performing an imitation of politics in negating it," Rancière writes. He continues: "The solution, in a word, is to achieve the essence of politics by eliminating this difference from itself that politics consists of, to achieve politics by eliminating politics, by achieving philosophy 'in place' of politics" (D 65, 63). But, on the other hand, those same categories with which philosophy seeks to outstrip politics can be reinterpreted, in the theatrical sense of the term, as part of a constant process of repoliticization.

The result is that, between politics and philosophy, between the real and the thought of this real in its different figures, there develops what Rancière calls a network of inter-interpretations, a field of mutual rivalry and mimicry, in which every disagreement or misunderstanding can open the way to a renewed agreement or understanding. In fact, the notion of "disagreement" (with *mésentente* in French also meaning "misunderstanding" or "dissension") operates both *between* philosophy and politics and *within* the domain of politics as such, in so far as politics involves the staging of a productive disagreement that interrupts the seemingly natural distribution of the dominators and the dominated, by following a set of logical and rhetorical moves or tropes that political philosophers then in turn prefer to misunderstand. Consequently, all political philosophy can even be defined in terms of what Rancière writes about Marx's metapolitical figure, when he speaks of "an ambiguity in which all the philosophical *disagreement* about political *disagreement* is concentrated" (D 84; this is one instance where perhaps *mésentente* might be better translated as "misunderstanding").

Another way of capturing this ambiguity would require that we come to grips with political philosophy as a *réplique* in the double sense of the French term, that is, both as a "reply" to the always-already existing scandal of democratic politics and as a "replica" thereof, the philosopher's mimicry or simulacrum of politics: a "true" politics, which by definition would also be a "politics of truth", in lieu of the always troubled, always precarious, rare but really existing acts of political subjectivization.

Archipolitics

Plato, in this sense, can be said to inaugurate political philosophy in so far as he proposes a "true" politics over and above all "merely" democratic factionalism. In the *Republic*, Socrates thus seeks not only to define the philosophical idea of justice as the true essence of politics, but he also presents philosophy itself as the genuine accomplishment of this essence, an ideal realization that ought to take the place of democracy, whose nature by contrast would be essentially unfounded. This is why Rancière coins the neologism "archipolitics" to describe Plato's figure of political philosophy: it seeks to return politics to its proper beginning or foundation, all the while suppressing those forms of really existing politics that fall short of this beginning or foundation. More specifically, the aim is to substitute a well-ordered community, a community whose order is somehow inscribed in nature in a cosmic sense, for the random appearance and literally anarchic multitudinousness of the people as *demos*.

> Archipolitics, whose model is supplied by Plato, reveals in all its radicality the project of a community based on the complete realization of the *arkhê* of community, on its integral sensibilization, replacing without any leftover the democratic configuration of politics. (D 65, trans. mod.)

The myth of the metals invoked by Socrates, which assigns each member of the republic to a hierarchically prescribed task as worker, guardian or philosopher, is the fictitious legitimization of this process whereby archipolitics seeks to make nature into law: "Archipolitics is the complete realization of *phusis* into *nomos*, the total becoming-sensible of the law of the community. There can be no time off, no empty space in the fabric of the community" (D 68, trans. mod.). In this ideal community, with which the republic opposes the unrest of democracy, people are (only) who they are and they do (only) what they are supposed to do. Such is the tautological truth of politics when it is reduced to archipolitics. Instead of the empty category of the people (*demos*), the philosopher proposes the fully particularized body of the community accomplishing its inner essence or character; instead of the power of paradoxical speech acts, in which the part of those who have no part claims to be equal to the whole, the philosopher propounds the truth of a discourse that claims to be seamlessly derived from an ideal nature; and instead of a polemical universality, the philosopher seeks to breathe life into particular ways of doing, speaking and living as moulded into the fragile bodies of each of the community's members.

Modern-day republicanism, no less than sociological readings in the style of Pierre Bourdieu, in this sense continues the legacy of Plato's archipolitics as defined by Rancière. In fact, in his view the success of the social sciences is in no small measure due to an ongoing desire to be done with the disorderliness of subjects who stubbornly refuse to stay in their assigned place and time or fail to stick to their prescribed task. Likewise, those political philosophers who today seek to define a pure concept of politics and complain about the encroachment of the social and human sciences on the terrain of the political are merely forgetting the extent to which the integral becoming-sensible of the individual and collective soul was already key to ancient archipolitics with its stark alternative of either unruly democracy or the common good of the republic. The typically French debate over the republican value of education and the need for reforms of the school system, thus, would be a modern, unwitting, repetition of Plato's pedagogical apparatus for the formation of the soul both individually and collectively. Despite what the defenders of universalist republicanism argue:

> The school system and the republic have not just recently been perverted by psychology and sociology. They have merely changed brands of psychology and sociology, and the way these sciences of individual and collective soul work within the system of knowledge distribution. They have merely combined in a different way the relationship of pedagogical mastery, the an-archy of the democratic circulation of knowledge and the republican development of harmony between personalities and moralities.
> (D 68, trans. mod.)

But for Rancière this whole argumentation, which is constantly invoked by France's ministers of education, already defines the agenda of Plato's *Republic*:

The "republican" project, as it is elaborated in Plato's archipolitics, is the complete psychologizing and sociologizing of the elements of the political apparatus. In place of the disturbing elements of political subjectivization, the *politeia* puts the roles, aptitudes, and feelings of the community conceived as a body animated by the one soul of the whole. (D 69, trans. mod.)

Even in the Anglo-American world, all appearances and claims to the contrary notwithstanding, the dominant use of standardized testing is not foreign to Plato's anti-democratic ideal. After all, what do these tests seek to bring out if not the different aptitudes that nature seems to have inscribed into each individual's mental and bodily frame?

Finally, Rancière's diagnosis of the operations involved in ancient and modern archipolitics, from Plato to Jules Ferry (twice France's prime minister in the 1880s, responsible, among others, for the policies defining the secular educational system of the French Republic) to Bourdieu (the sociologist whose study of cultural and symbolical "distinction" according to Rancière ultimately has the effect of keeping individuals in their place), at the same time allows him to rehearse his own understanding of politics already laid out in previous chapters of *Disagreement*. This is an understanding of politics as radically contingent and anarchic, not one allegedly rooted in the necessary order of nature – whether this nature is seen as cosmic, as is the case in ancient times, or else as strictly human, as for us moderns. And it is an understanding of politics as the disruptive effect of equality when verified as the freedom of anyone whatsoever to speak in the name of the people. "The specificity of politics is disruption, the effect of equality as the litigious 'freedom' of the people. It is the original division of *phusis* that is called on to be achieved as community *nomos*," Rancière writes, before offering a formula typical of the peculiar assertive style of *Disagreement*: "There is politics because equality comes along and carries out this originary split in the 'nature' of politics, which is the condition for even being able to imagine any such 'nature' to begin with" (D 70, trans. mod.). Such a definition of politics can be read, as in a photographic negative, in the radical alternative that seeks to take its place in the guise of Plato's archipolitics.

Badiou, interestingly enough, uses the exact same term of "archipolitics" to discuss the case of Nietzsche. This may seem surprising in so far as the philosopher of the overman (*der Übermensch*) sees himself as the quintessential anti-Platonist. And yet there can be no doubt that this overturning of the "malady" of Platonism also leads to a kind of "true" politics that is the inverted mirror-image of that presented by

Socrates in the *Republic*. Thus, what Nietzsche imagined as the "grand style" of "grand politics" in Badiou's diagnosis comes extremely close to Rancière's account of the tension between politics and philosophy in archipolitics. For Badiou, too, this tension is one marked by rivalry and mimicry. Nietzsche, to be more precise, is seen as wanting to absorb the energy of revolutionary upheavals such as the French Revolution or the Paris Commune into the conceptual apparatus of a purely philosophical act, as when the author of *Ecce Homo*, calling himself dynamite, pretends to break in two the history of humanity. This act, then, is archipolitical in the extent to which it lays claims to being truer than any really existing political event, even as it repeats the power of such an absolutely radical event in an imitation, within philosophy, of the revolutionary act. In this way, philosophy – which in the process begins to look rather like an anti-philosophy – promises to be able to transcend the mere administration of the existing order of things. "The philosophical act is *archipolitical* in the sense that it seeks to revolutionize humanity at a more radical level than the calculations of politics," Badiou says about Nietzsche. He continues: "He proposes to make formally equivalent the philosophical act as an act of thinking with the explosive potentiality that is apparent in the politico-historical revolution" (Badiou 1994, 11, my trans.). Nietzsche's grand politics, in this sense, would still fall in line with the reading of archipolitics presented in *Disagreement*.

Parapolitics

If archipolitics, modelled on Plato's example, involves a simultaneous displacement and replacement of politics, then parapolitics, for which Aristotle serves as the model according to Rancière, takes rather the form of a *recouvrement*, a recovery of and from politics that is at the same time a stealthy cover-up.

> Just as Plato instantly achieves the perfection of archipolitics, so Aristotle instantly accomplishes the telos of a parapolitics that will function as the normal, honest regime of "political philosophy": transforming the actors and forms of the political conflict into the parts and forms of distribution of the policing apparatus.
> (D 72, trans. mod.)

Logically, if not also historically, moreover, parapolitics can be seen as a partial answer to the limits and shortcomings of archipolitics.

Thus, whereas Plato's *Republic* bans all internal strife from the community in the name of an ideal fusion of the individual into the collective soul, Aristotle's *Politics* at least starts out by acknowledging not just the intrinsically political nature of the human animal but also the presence of conflict, even war, between rich and poor at the heart of the city-state. And yet this recognition of the antagonistic kernel of politics is once again obfuscated as soon as the problem shifts toward a question of distributing groups, orders or offices of power into a stable constitutional regime. Parapolitics consists in thus translating all politics into a question of power and command. Put differently, as the exemplary figure of what today is considered the task of "political philosophy", parapolitics proposes to centre "politics" (*la politique*) on "the political" (*le politique*) (on the importance of the distinction between "*la politique*" and "*le politique*"; see Bosteels 2009b: 235–51).

"Such centering seems obvious to a modernity for whom the issue of politics is quite naturally one of power, of the principles that legitimize power, the forms in which power is distributed, and the types of personality specific to it," adds Rancière.

> But it is important for us to see that it is a peculiar response to the specific paradox of politics, to the confrontation between the police logic of the distribution of parts and the political logic of the part of those who have no part. Aristotle displaces the singular knot that ties the effect of equality to the inegalitarian logic of social bodies, the knot that is proper to politics, toward *the political* as the specific place of institutions. (D 73, trans. mod.)

Thus we find both a confirmation of the methodological principle according to which all political philosophy comes in response to an already-existing paradox of political subjectivization and, concurrently, another indication of what is proper to politics, as opposed to the political, according to Rancière himself.

For a modern reader, however, the figure of parapolitics may well be the most deceptive and difficult to unravel, in so far as we tend to identify political philosophy precisely with such a definition of the essence of the political, whether in terms of the delimitation of a specific social sphere different from the economical or the moral, for example, or in terms of a specific human faculty, right or aptitude. It is for this very reason that Aristotle, instead of covering up the specificity of political action in the guise of parapolitics, which is what he really does according to Rancière, may appear to represent the essential determination of politics as such. Rancière writes:

Whatever we may say about the Ancients and their city of the common good, Aristotle introduces a decisive break into this common good, thereby initiating a new modality of "political philosophy." That this new modality comes to be identified with the quintessence of political philosophy and that Aristotle is always the last resort of all its "restorers" is not too hard to understand … It is Aristotle who managed to square the circle, to propose the realization of a natural order of politics as a constitutional order by the very inclusion of what blocked any such realization: the *demos*, either as the form of exposure of the war between the "rich" and the "poor," or finally as the effectiveness of an egalitarian an-archy. (D 71–2, trans. mod.)

Hobbes, who in this reading emerges as the principal proponent of modern parapolitics, at the same time would seem to want to counteract the subversive potential hidden in the ancient version handed down to us from Aristotle. If people are all equally political animals by nature, which is a hypothesis that even the exclusion of slaves cannot refute completely, and if all political constitutions are delivered over to popular judgement as to their capacity to match their norm, then ancient "political philosophy" paradoxically begins to look at once utopian and seditious.

For Hobbes, the Ancients' position is utopian in its affirmation of an inherent "politicity" of human nature and it is seditious in making this natural bent for politics the norm by which the first person who comes along can presume to judge whether a regime conforms to such an underlying politicity and to the good government that is its ideal accomplishment. (D 76, trans. mod.)

For Hobbes, consequently, the human being must not be said to be political by nature; instead, politics comes in second place, as the outcome of a decision in the face of a prior state of nature. Modern parapolitics thus serves as a reply to the potential threat inherent in ancient parapolitics, in so far as the latter, reclaimed by politics, always risks opening the door to a popular rebellious appropriation.

In terms of the actual content of its propositions, though, modern parapolitics still follows the path of its ancient forerunner. Politics continues to be defined in terms of power, except that now the fundamental question tends to revolve around the enigma of the origins of power, legitimate or otherwise. Whatever the specific answer involves as far as the theories of sovereignty or the alienation of rights are concerned, the different treatments of this question ultimately coincide in reformulating the terms of the debate along the lines of a stark opposition between the individual and the sovereign. However, like all versions of political philosophy, this presentation of the problem of political power still serves to liquidate the paradoxical appearing of a part of those who have no part, which is the only practice that names the effectiveness of actual politics for Rancière. What vanishes from this presentation, in other words, is anything resembling a truly collective act that would cut across the purely theoretical if not imaginary divide between individuals and the sovereign state. "The problematization of the 'origins' of power and the terms in which it is framed – the social contract, alienation, and sovereignty – declare first that there is no part of those who have no part. There are only individuals and the power of the state," writes Rancière. He continues:

> Modern parapolitics begins by inventing a specific nature, an "individuality," strictly correlating to the absolute of a sovereign power that must exclude quarreling between fractions, quarreling between parts and parties. It begins by initially breaking down the people into individuals, which, in one go, exorcises the class war of which politics consists, in the war of all against all.
>
> (D 77–8)

The third and final figure of the politics of the philosophers, namely, metapolitics, will propose to undo this exorcism precisely in the name of the class struggle.

Indeed, in yet another instance of the capacity of politics to reclaim the subversive potential of political philosophies, the formulation of the problem of power in terms of sovereignty and individuality paradoxically opens a distance within each individual that is even more severe than the war between the part or party of the poor and that of the rich in Aristotle.

> In denouncing the compromise Aristotelian parapolitics makes with the sedition menacing the social body, and in breaking down the *demos* into individuals, the parapolitics of the social contract and of sovereign power opens up a more radical gap than the old political gap of the part taken for the whole. It sets out the distance of man from himself as the primary and final basis of the distance of the people from itself ... Hence the reopening of the gap in the modern people, this gap inscribed in the problematic conjunction of the terms man and the citizen: elements of a new

apparatus of political dispute whereby each term serves to reveal the noncount of the other, but also the basis for reopening the gap between archipolitics and politics and setting up this gap on the very stage of politics. (D 80–81)

This restaging of the revolutionary potential hidden within the conceptual apparatus of modern parapolitics then defines the program of metapolitics, which Rancière in *Disagreement* identifies with the figure of Marx and Marxism.

Metapolitics

Emblematized with particular force in "On the Jewish Question", the metapolitical answer to the scandalous paradox that is proper to politics as such typically oscillates between two contradictory extremes. All existing forms of politics, even revolutionary ones, on one hand, can be unmasked on the basis of the underlying truth of the social content that these forms cannot fail to cover up. Between man and citizen, there is always an element of a miscount, never a complete overlap, due to the purely formal nature of bourgeois democracy. On the other hand, all merely political emancipation can always be found wanting and subjected to criticism from the vantage point of a true, properly human or total emancipation yet to come, which would take us beyond politics.

For Rancière, in other words, metapolitics submits real political practices to a double verdict, either of being mere "appearances" that hide the infrapolitical "truth" of the class struggle beneath them or else of falling short of the realization of a "genuine" suprapolitics "beyond" politics, in which society would reach its true fulfilment that would also be its end. This double verdict applies in an exemplary manner to the Marxist concept of class, which socially can be seen as the true content of all political formations while politically class has no positive content whatsoever, being merely the empty operator of the withering away of all classes in the name of the proletarian non-class. Rancière writes:

> As the *truth* of the lie of politics, the concept of class thus becomes the central figure of a metapolitics conceived as a *beyond* of politics, in keeping with one of the two sense of the prefix. But metapolitics can be understood at the same time according to the other sense of the prefix, which indicates *a complement, an accompaniment*. ... So metapolitics becomes the scientific accompaniment

of politics, in which the reduction of political forms to the forces of the class struggle is initially equivalent to the *truth of the lie* or the truth of illusion. But it also becomes a "political" accompaniment of all forms of subjectivization, which posits as its hidden "political" truth the class struggle it underestimates and cannot not underestimate. Metapolitics can *seize* on any phenomenon as a demonstration of the truth of its falseness. (D 85, trans. mod.)

Now, in his book of the same title, Badiou also calls his philosophical approach to politics a "metapolitics". The obvious question, then, is whether this corresponds to what Rancière ascribes under this same name to Marx's treatment of politics. The answer to this question, it seems to me, is negative for at least two reasons. Badiou, first of all, has no intention to institute a recurrent set of operations with which to criticize the falseness of existing forms of political emancipation as falling short of true revolutionary politics. His aim is quite the opposite of anything resembling a Marxian critique of ideology. Instead, philosophy seeks to define a conceptual space in which the thought-practice of emancipatory politics actually becomes thinkable in the present. In this sense, and this is the second reason why the answer to the question above must be negative, Badiou's aim is really no different from Rancière's, since both seek to extricate the thinking of politics from the operations with which "political philosophy" attempts to obscure, displace or deny politics as such. For Badiou, metapolitics can become the exact opposite of those discourses bent on defining "the political" or even "the nonpolitical ground of politics", provided we accept that politics, as a truth procedure or militant form of emancipatory practice, is already in itself a mode of thinking:

> By "metapolitics" I understand the consequences that a philosophy can draw out in and for itself from the fact that true forms of politics are forms of thinking. Metapolitics is opposed to political philosophy, which claims that it belongs to the philosopher to think "the political," insofar as politics would not be a form of thinking in itself. (Badiou 2005a: xlix, trans. mod.)

Thus, ironically, while these two thinkers share a similar understanding of emancipatory politics as both egalitarian and universalist, Rancière sees metapolitics as an obstacle that covers up the play of liberty and equality inherent in all such politics, which Badiou with the very same concept proposes to think through and set free. What both thinkers rather wilfully seem to ignore, however, is the extent to which the history of this concept in the twentieth century has been steeped in right-wing ideology. Starting in 1968, with an international seminar on "What is Metapolitics?" organized by the conservative think-tank GRÉCE (Groupement de Recherche et d'Étude pour la Civilisation Européenne), metapolitics indeed has become an official watchword of the European New Right, led by the French writer Alain de Benoist (see Bosteels 2010).

In Rancière's treatment of metapolitics, finally, there occurs an interesting and in my eyes symptomatic slippage. Thus, in showing how categories such as "class", "the people" or "the social" in general hide an essential ambiguity in so far as they oscillate between a positive and a negative meaning, that is to say, between the true substance hidden behind political appearances, the real content behind the forms of ideology, and the empty operators with which those who have no part identify themselves with the whole of society, the author of *Disagreement* all of a sudden shifts his focus from a metapolitical interpretation of these terms to what he calls their political interpretation. There is thus a sense that Rancière's own discourse, which constantly distances itself from "the politics of the philosophers", somehow thrives on the suggestion that it coincides in a well-nigh tautological transparency with a "political interpretation of politics". The authority of this reading depends on the supposition of a discourse capable of erasing the traces of its own separateness.

Perhaps this is one more reason why Rancière is in fact always adamant in his refusal to name his own discourse – whether as philosophy, as history, as criticism, or as political or aesthetic theory. Far from merely connoting a playful resistance to disciplinary boundaries, the self-effacing gesture is also an intrinsic part of a peculiar discourse that requires this peculiarity to remain if not exactly silent then at least unmarked. Here, too, Badiou's approach provides us with a useful contrast, in the sense that here at least the lines of demarcation between politics and philosophy, between the condition and the conditioned, are clearly drawn. In the eyes of many readers, admittedly, this comes at the steep price of elevating philosophy once again to a higher-order discourse, never mind that Badiou's metapolitics openly submits itself to political–historical events that happen prior to and outside of it. Rancière, on the other hand, is capable of dwelling with great mastery and flair in a zone of indistinction in between politics and thought, provided that he never marks the separate status of his own discourse.

PART III

Poetics

SEVEN

"*Partage du sensible*": the distribution of the sensible
Davide Panagia

The specificity of any one concept in Jacques Rancière's *oeuvre* is difficult to grasp and impossible to localize because, as Rancière himself admits "I don't speak for members of a particular body or discipline. I write to shatter the boundaries that separate specialists – of philosophy, art, social sciences, etc." (Rancière 2007a: 257). This is especially true of Rancière's conceptual innovation of a *partage du sensible* (variously translated as "partition" or "distribution" of the sensible); – a term that refers at once to the conditions for sharing that establish the contours of a collectivity (i.e. "*partager*" as sharing) and to the sources of disruption or dissensus of that same order (i.e. "*partager*" as separating). In every respect, a *partage du sensible* is a liminal term that is at once central to Rancière's analyses of the aesthetics of politics but also requires an exploration of other conceptual specificities in his theoretical lexicon. In this chapter, I explore Rancière's notion of a *partage du sensible* by first addressing the multiple meanings of the French verb "*partager*"; I then outline how Rancière's *partage du sensible* is part of his critique of a poetics of knowledge, and especially of Louis Althusser's theoreticism. Finally, I elaborate the political dimensions of this concept by showing that politics involves, for Rancière, the rearticulation of a *partage du sensible* by the excluded or unaccounted-for elements in a political society.

The meanings of "*partager*"

Key to Rancière's understanding of a *partage du sensible* is the tension between a specific act of perception and its implicit reliance on preconstituted objects deemed worthy of perception. This tension is expressed through the related concept of dissensus, which is at once a dissent from inequality and an insensibility (i.e. an inability to be sensed, noticed or accounted for). Democratic politics occurs when certain elements in society that are deemed insensible are challenging the governing political order. The task of political action, therefore, is aesthetic in that it requires a reconfiguration of the conditions of sense perception so that the reigning configuration between perception and meaning is disrupted by those elements, groups or individuals in society that demand not only to exist but indeed to be perceived. A *partage du sensible* is thus the vulnerable dividing line that creates the perceptual conditions for a political community and its dissensus.

"This dividing line", Jacques Rancière tells us, "has been the object of my constant study" (PP 225). Indeed, the focus of Rancière's entire work is to examine the lines that divide and connect political allegiances, social organizations and aesthetic formations. Whether it is the rise of democratic revolutions in the eighteenth century and their polemical relationship to the writing of history (NH), or the appropriations of the time of night through the writing of poetry by nineteenth-century factory workers (NL), or his analyses of the thwarted trajectory between the mechanical art of cinema and its artistic vocations (FF), Rancière's work begins with the premise that our world is composed of lines in constant movement, alignment and realignment. "This dividing line", which Rancière considers the object of his attentions, is none other than the partition that establishes the forms of correspondence and disaggregation between collectivities, as well as between the collages of words and images, and between the assemblages of peoples and things. Rancière's dividing line is a basic unit of political analysis that he approaches from an aesthetic point of view: with a sensibility to the perceptual preconditions that make subjectivities at once visible, audible and available to our attentions.

As previously remarked, when reading Rancière's work it is important to keep in mind the multiple resonances of his terms: at one level, then, a *partage du sensible* refers to a sharing in the manner in which one might impart a piece of knowledge, an experience, or a morsel of food to someone else. The French verb "*partager*" further signifies an act of giving, of making something that is not common, common to all. In this respect a *partage* is a principle of aggregation that configures the forms of participation in a political community.

However, in order for something to be shared it must also be divided. Paradoxically, then, a *partage* is at once a sharing and a division, not unlike the "This is mine!" made famous in Part II of Jean-Jacques

"PARTAGE DU SENSIBLE": THE DISTRIBUTION OF THE SENSIBLE

Rousseau's *Discourse on the Origins of Inequality*. Rousseau's famous discussion of property begins with the image of putting up a fence, of dividing land into lots, and of making a noise (i.e. "this is mine") that also makes sense. The force of Rousseau's utterance exploits the shared conditions of possibility for sense perception and knowledge comprehension that make it so that the division of a piece of land actually signifies something (i.e. is meaningful) and that the assignment of territory to an individual through the poetic use of language (i.e. the invention of the speech utterance "this is mine") functions to create a line of correspondence and identification between lot and self. For Rancière too, lots, shares and parts that are at first common are cut up and assigned to individuals and groups according to their lot, that is, according to a proper order of society. Thus a *partage* not only refers to a sharing of goods but also to a division of property.

A *partage* is also a partition of propriety. In order to cut up lots and allocate goods there need to be criteria in place for the proper circulation of things, and it is this sense of the proper order of things that structures what Rancière refers to as "the order of distribution of bodies into functions corresponding to their 'nature'" (D 101). This order of distribution and correspondence (what Rancière will also call "the police") works equally effectively as a principle of organization for sense perception. The *partage* that is the division of propriety is thus also the partition that guarantees the division of the senses. The possibility for something to make sense is thus not the result of a rational agreement between participants in deliberation. It is, rather, the result of a correspondence between perception and meaning that dictates the terms of what will count as commonly sensible and what is, otherwise, mere noise, babble or insensible. The division between the sensible and the insensible is the locus of political struggle that is made manifest when those groups, individuals or collectivities whose modes of perception are deemed illegitimate (i.e. insensible) by a governing partition of the sensible demand to be taken into account. Rancière's *partage du sensible* is thus the site of political contestation directed at the subjugating criteria that impart propriety, property and perception and that structure a society's common order.

Althusser, theoreticism, and the critique of the proper

The critique of the proper and the sensible is thus crucial to Rancière's poetics of political thinking. This critique begins with his rejection of the theoreticist position endorsed by Althusser. Specifically, it is

Althusser's theory of ideology that is the source of Rancière's initial articulations of the relationship between perception and inequality. Although his extended treatise on this topic, *La Leçon d'Althusser*, is not translated into English, an essay written in 1969 and published in the 1974 spring issue of *Radical Philosophy* outlines Rancière's break with Althusser. The force of this break comes with his accusation that Althusser's theory of ideology creates and sustains a fundamental inequality by insisting that revolutionary movements cannot proceed without revolutionary theory. That is, Althusser's ideal of emancipation cannot work without a prior commitment to the authoritative knowledge of theory. On Rancière's reading of Althusser there is thus a shift in the ground of inequality – from that of class to that of knowledge – but not a dissolution of it.

Rancière's *partage du sensible* engages the principle of propriety – that there is a proper mode of understanding necessary for the project of emancipation – by introducing the possibility of dissensus as an interruption of the ways in which we establish the criteria of knowledge. Another way of stating this is to say that for Rancière dissensus is not an epistemological break but a break *of* epistemology as the qualifying perceptual criterion for political participation; that is, Rancière wants to wrest democratic political action from the demand that it correspond to a form of authoritative knowledge that will legitimate it. Thus, although Rancière has distanced himself substantially from Althusser's theoretical position, he has never abandoned the premises that sparked his initial critical break. Indeed, what Althusser's lesson taught Rancière is that the propriety of knowledge rests on conditions of perceptibility that establish an order of sharing (i.e. a *partage*) that sustains a fundamental inequality between those who know and those who do not, and that the possibility of designating what counts as knowledge further rests on specific perceptual criteria that draw a division (i.e. *partage*) between sensible and insensible objects of theoretical attention. Equality begins with a dis-composition of the dividing line between the sensible and the insensible in precisely the manner in which Rancière illustrates by introducing his readers to the figure of Joseph Jacotot – the nineteenth-century French professor – who asserted that an ignorant person could teach another ignorant person what he himself did not know, thus defending the idea of intellectual emancipation through an equality of intelligences (IS).

Thus the inequality of a *partage du sensible* that establishes a hierarchy between those who know and those who do not know, between those whose speech makes good sounds and those whose utterances are mere noise, holds the potential of its own dissolution. If the dividing line is the point of contact between commonality and divisiveness that structures the dynamics of a *partage du sensible*, then Rancière always holds open the possibility of a political part-taking by those excluded from the system of distributions that is the reigning *partage du sensible* (i.e. what Rancière otherwise calls "the police"). Politics emerges whenever the order of the police is disturbed by acts of dis-incorporation of the part of those who have no part. Political action is thus defined on the basis of this aesthetic part-taking: it is a reconfiguration of the perceptual disposition of sights and sounds. In short, the exclusiveness of a partition that divides legitimate and illegitimate modes of being always holds open the possibility of a dissensual part-taking by those deemed not to count as legitimate participants in the dominant political community.

"Uncertain communities"

In order for a collectivity like a social system or a political group to exist there needs to be in place a frame of equivalences that establishes the relations of commonality between things. Such a collectivity is at once a spatial and temporal composition that not only has a series of set dispositions that compose its structure but also an order to them that guarantees their proper functioning. The ability to share in this community of parts (i.e. to belong to it) is rooted in distinct conditions of perception that establish a correspondence between an object's impression and its meaning. We can thus speak of a collectivity as comprising the set of concrete correspondences between knowledge, awareness, sound, sight and so on – correspondences that count as the perceptual preconditions for counting. A political community thus holds its shape because these perceptual preconditions make some parts count as sensible and others as insensible.

The simultaneity of the sensible as what addresses the correspondence between the reasonable and the perceptible – or, better put, the idea that the sensible implies a condition of knowledge – is what Rancière means when he affirms that a *partage du sensible* "is the system of self-evident facts of sense perception that simultaneously discloses the existence of something in common and the delimitations that define the respective parts and positions within it" (PA 12). If, however, we were to limit our understanding of the *partage du sensible* to an external structural arrangement that imposes form and function upon heterogeneous elements, then we would be circumscribing this concept simply to an analysis of an external objective reality like a discursive formation or an ideological apparatus. However, the phenomenological, aesthetic and political challenge of Rancière's notion of a *partage du sensible* is to introduce the possibility of discomposing the inequalities that such structures produce.

"Politics", Rancière thus affirms, "is an activity of reconfiguration of that which is given to the sensible" (DW 115). That is, for Rancière the task of an aesthetics of politics is to engage the practices of disfiguration and reconfiguration of what is given to sense perception. Politics is always an aesthetic activity, then, not because there is a specific aesthetic to politics nor because there is a purposiveness to aesthetic objects that is political, but because within any specific social arrangement there are words and images in constant circulation and whose proper order is a perpetual source of disagreement. However, although a *partage du sensible* generates the conditions for circulation and for the production of meaning, these sensible intensities may disrupt that ordered configuration by introducing:

> lines of fracture and disincorporation into imaginary and collective bodies ... They form, in this way, uncertain communities that contribute to the formation of enunciative collectives that call into question the distribution of roles, territories, and languages. In short, they contribute to the formation of political subjects that challenge the given distribution of the sensible. (PA 39–40)

Thus the same force of circulation that gives words and images their proper meaning cannot prevent those words and meanings from falling into the wrong hands, or to be imparted to the wrong people, so to speak. Rancière specifies that "the concept of wrong is thus not linked to any theatre of 'victimization.' It belongs to the original structure of all politics. Wrong is simply the mode of subjectification in which the assertion of equality takes its political shape" (D 39). These "wrong people", who speak out of turn or incorrectly, are the agents of a dissensus whose modes of part-taking are illegitimate according to the reigning order of common sense. Thus what the conceptual specificity of a *partage du sensible* ultimately affords is the possibility of an illegitimate part-taking (*avoir-part*) that results in the dissensus of a pre-given sensible regime.

Equality is insensible

As Rancière has recently emphasized, this form of a dissensual calling into question of common sense is also what he means by emancipation. "Emancipation", he affirms:

"PARTAGE DU SENSIBLE": THE DISTRIBUTION OF THE SENSIBLE

begins when we dismiss the opposition between looking and acting and understand that the distribution of the visible itself is part of the configuration of domination and subjection. It starts when we realize that looking is also an action that confirms or modifies that distribution, and that "interpreting the world" is already a means of transforming it, of reconfiguring it. (ES 277)

In these passages, Rancière addresses the question of modern spectatorship and the assumption that the only account of viewing available to us is a passive one. The subjectivity of the passive spectator is the site of a fundamental inequality: the idea of passivity, in other words, presumes a smooth communication (or fluid circulation) of media and message. Emancipation from this inequality comes when we disfigure the subjectivity of spectatorship and reconfigure it as an attentive looking that actively observes, selects, compares and interprets. In other words, the passive spectator is not entitled to look, to interpret, to select; and yet there is nothing that prevents her from part-taking in all these activities. In doing so, she becomes active, thereby disfiguring the perceptual assumptions that configure a passive subjectivity.

Although Rancière's discussion of the emancipated spectator focuses on theories of viewing with regard to theatre, film and new media, it is difficult not to notice therein the kernel of his analysis of the relationship between aesthetics and politics; namely, his rejection of the assumption that an aesthetics of politics ensures the capacity for taste to give privileged access to political participation. Whether couched in attacks about the political hazards of the aestheticization of politics (e.g. Habermas), or formulations regarding the authoritarian ambitions of an ideology of aesthetics (e.g. Bourdieu), or even critiques of the reification and alienation perpetrated by the culture industry (e.g. Adorno), each of these formulated challenges assumes that taste is inextricably linked to privilege and that a commitment to an aesthetics of politics is implicitly a commitment to the inequality of privilege. From Rancière's perspective, however, such formulations inevitably rely on an antecedent inequality between those who know the truth of an image and those who passively absorb its transmission. Like Althusser's theoreticism implicit in his account of interpellation, each of these formulations is founded upon the Platonic assumption that images are collusive because they limit freedom, and the knowledge of the master critic is necessary to escape from their stultification. By introducing the figure of the emancipated spectator as an active participant in image-making, Rancière refutes the simple analogy between taste and privilege and affirms that the capacity to view is not linked to any intellectual qualification. Rather, the sensual intensities of everyday life are crucial to the agentic potential of human beings regardless of class or stature.

The inequality of a *partage du sensible* that establishes a hierarchy between those who know and those who do not know, between those whose viewing provides good interpretations and those who passively look, thus holds the potential for its own dissolution. If the line of partition is the point of contact between sharing and division that structures the dynamics of a *partage du sensible*, then Rancière always holds open the possibility of a political part-taking (*"avoir-part"*) by those who have no part in the established system of distribution. Politics thus emerges whenever a proper order is disturbed by the part-takings of the part of those who have no-part. Emancipation is thus defined on the basis of this aesthetic part-taking: it is a reconfiguration of the perceptual disposition of sights and sounds by those who are excluded from the fields of the visible and of the sayable.

Therein one also finds the prickly dimension – Rancière calls it the "polemical universal" (D 39) – of democratic politics: equality is insensible. It arises whenever a sensual intensity like a political subjectivity appears and when the conditions of perceptibility for that sensual intensity need to be created rather than derived. To revert to one of Rancière's own favourite examples – the tale told by Livy and interpreted by Pierre-Simon Ballanche of the plebian secession on Aventine Hill – the quarrel between the Roman patricians and the plebs is not one between competing interests, or even between differing conceptual accounts of equality. The contest, rather, is one over the conditions of a *partage*; that is, it is a polemical contention over whether there exists a common stage where the plebians and patricians might actually enter into debate. As Rancière states:

> there is no place for discussion with the plebs for the simple reason that plebs do not speak. They do not speak because they are beings without a name, deprived of logos – meaning, of symbolic enrollment in the city … whoever is nameless cannot speak.
> (D 23; see also DW 116)

In other words, the polemical universal of equality is not rooted in the pursuit of a consensual agreement over disputing interests but in the contest over the perceptual preconditions that make the noise coming out of one's mouth an utterance rather than a gutterance, speech rather than noise, language rather than blabber. The scandal of the plebs, ultimately, is that they part-take in a mode of action to which they are not entitled; that is, by talking they choose to act as if they had a name, as

"PARTAGE DU SENSIBLE": THE DISTRIBUTION OF THE SENSIBLE

if they had the right to speak, to make promises, to express themselves. In doing so, they disrupt the order of the city and, implicitly, the order of propriety that structures the city's *partage du sensible*. The perceptual, phenomenological, aesthetic and political dimensions of Rancière's analysis of a *partage du sensible* suggest that politics is an event of appearance. By "event of appearance" I refer to the power of monstrance or perspicuity that appearances have, and their capacity to disrupt conventional forms of looking, of hearing, of perceiving. An appearance's perspicuity refers to its ability to give explicitness to itself because it is insensible. In this respect, Rancière's insights offer us nothing less than an ethics of appearance by raising the question of equality and emancipation as a question of how to relate to the insensibility of an appearance's emergence. "Politics", Rancière affirms, "revolves around what is seen and what can be said about it, around who has the ability to see and the talent to speak, around the properties of spaces and the possibilities of time" (PA 13); he concludes that through this illegitimate part-taking in acts of appearance we have:

> the ground of political action: certain subjects that do not count create a common polemical scene where they put into contention the objective status of what is 'given' and impose an examination and discussion of those things that were not 'visible,' that were not accounted for. (DW 125)

In short, in the dividing line between a *partage du sensible* and its dissensus we find Rancière's subject of politics.

EIGHT

Heretical history and the poetics of knowledge

Philip Watts

After *The Nights of Labour* (1981, English translation 1989) Jacques Rancière published a long essay on what it means to write history from below. The main object of *The Names of History* (1992, English translation 1994) is to challenge the so-called scientific approach that came to dominate French historiography after the Second World War. Taking on the Annales school and then working back to Jules Michelet, Rancière seeks to understand what is at stake when historians attempt to replace "the primacy of events and proper names" (NH 1) with the study of demographics, economics, statistics and structures of thought. What to many historians and cultural critics may have seemed like a great leap forward in the human sciences turns out, on Rancière's reading, to be a deeply flawed approach to history. While the Annales school famously refused to study the lives of kings and diplomatic history, their approach nonetheless ended up overlooking the men and women who, for Rancière, are responsible for historical change. From his earliest texts through his more recent essays on literature and art, Rancière has argued that democratic politics comes not from institutions, disciplines or specialists, but from concrete individuals, often from the working classes, who are engaged in struggles and who remain conscious of their thoughts, words and deeds. Writing history from below means two things for Rancière. It means recovering the thoughts and speech and writings of these individuals and it means remaining aware of how the construction of knowledge can result in the silencing of democratic movements, aspirations for equality and new forms of thought.

Thinking history

The Names of History begins with the claim that history is a discipline in a sometimes contentious relation to science and to literature. What, Rancière asks, is the relation between the claims to science made by the Annales school and its reliance on the art of narrative? In order to answer this question, Rancière develops the concept of the "poetics of knowledge", defined as "the set of literary procedures by which a discourse escapes literature, gives itself the status of a science, and signifies this status" (NH 8). Rancière's "poetics of knowledge" is a way of analyzing how history produced what Michel Foucault called "truth effects" and what Rancière calls "the mode of truth" through which disciplines and forms of knowledge constitute themselves (*ibid.*). The modern age, writes Rancière, this "age of science" is also the "age of literature" and the "age of democracy", and the goal of *The Names of History* is to discover the relation between the three.

Rancière begins his investigation of modern historiography by quoting the famous passage from Fernand Braudel's *The Mediterranean and the World in the Age of Philip II* (1949) describing the death of the king. This scene is emblematic of Braudel's desire to move away from the history of great leaders to the history of what Braudel calls the "humble masses" of the Renaissance. In this regard, one could claim that Braudel's writings were democratic histories. At the same time, however, Rancière detects in Braudel a suspicion towards the masses that the new history claimed as one of its objects of study. For in his preface to *The Mediterranean and the World in the Age of Philip II* Braudel had also warned against putting too much stake in the writings and documents – the "masses of paper" – left by the poor, "eager to write" (*ibid.*: 17) but blind to their own actions and unconscious of what Braudel calls "the deeper realities of history" (*ibid.*). Rancière has always been a great practitioner of close reading and here he stops on a phrase Braudel uses to describe the poor: they were, Braudel tells us, *"acharnés à écrire"*. When Braudel calls their writing "masses of paper" – *"paperasses"* – when he describes the poor as blind to their own actions, when he says that they are *"acharnés à écrire"*, he is implicitly claiming that these masses are speaking and writing and thinking out of turn. *"Acharner"* is the verb of relentless and misguided effort, and Braudel's use of this term reveals, according to Rancière, the historian's suspicion towards the speaking poor, the writing people, the thinking masses. At work in Braudel's history is a "Renaissance of the poor" that denies that the poor had any sort of knowledge about the times in which they lived. This same historical approach repeatedly claims that the masses are un-knowing and that they act in ignorance and misrecognition. This leads Rancière to conclude that at the very moment that these humble masses are introduced onto the stage of history, they "immediately disappear from the scene" (*ibid*.). What Kristin Ross has called Rancière's "battle with strategies whose aim is the suppression of time" is also a battle with strategies whose aim is the suppression of the thought, will and reason of the poor (Ross 2009: 22).

The arguments in *The Names of History* were first developed in a series of lectures coinciding with the bicentennial of the French Revolution, and one suspects that beyond Braudel, the real object of Rancière's critique may have been François Furet and his famous premise in *Interpreting the French Revolution* (1975, English translation 1981) that the French Revolution was a non-event. At the core of Furet's book is this claim that individuals – in this case Revolutionaries – had no real understanding of their actions. Published after the author's own conversion from communism to a centrist neoliberalism, Furet's study is an attempt to remove the Revolution from the grips of what he called a *cartel des gauches* school of historiography. What Furet wanted was a "cooling off" of the interpretations of the Revolution (Furet 1981: 10) which meant, in effect, a move away from what he saw as leftist, progressive and sentimentalizing approaches to the history of France. To do this, Furet needed to separate the actions of the Revolutionaries from their own thoughts. "[A]ny conceptualisation of the history of the Revolution", Furet wrote, "must begin with a critique of the idea of revolution as experienced and perceived by its actors, and transmitted by their heirs, namely, the idea that it was a radical change and the origin of a new era" (*ibid.*: 14). To think the French Revolution, according to Furet, one must first reject the Revolutionaries' perception of their action. One must deny that they knew what they were doing. This is the sad revelation of Furet's title: his own interpretation starts by denying that the actors and their heirs could correctly interpret their own actions and words. And to buttress his claim, Furet turned to Tocqueville's *The Old Regime and the Revolution*, whose main thesis was that the Revolution had brought nothing new to France. The Jacobins may have thought they were creating a new society but they were actually completing the work of the state consolidation of power begun with Richelieu.

Certainly, Rancière has no interest in defending Albert Soboul and the official historiography of the French Communist Party, nor would he necessarily disagree with Tocqueville's claims that the Jacobins had consolidated state power. Rather, the poetics of knowledge he puts in place allows him to locate and question those moments when scholars and experts, those whom Rancière calls *savants*, erect boundaries between their understanding and the misunderstanding they attribute to others. For Rancière:

> No well-defined boundary separates the discourse of the woodworker who is the object of science from the discourse of science itself. After all is said and done, to trace these boundaries is to trace the boundary between those who have thought through this question and those who have not. (TBD 11)

The Names of History denounces a form of hermeneutic oppression in which the thought, words and actions of others, in particular the working poor, are turned into forms of non-thought, misconceptions and eventually silence.

Michelet's revolution

In all this, Jules Michelet stands as a paradoxical founding father. Michelet was the great Romantic historian, an indefatigable writer, an unrepentant literary stylist and a staunch advocate of the Republic. Still, according to Rancière, Michelet's histories have a difficult relation with the words and gestures of the people that they put on stage. Michelet's writing initiated "a revolution in the poetic structures of knowledge" (NH 42), but at the same time put in place the conditions that would allow later generations of historians, such as Braudel and Furet, to erase the thought and actions of the humble masses.

In order to reveal Michelet's paradoxical revolution, Rancière turns to the famous distinction proposed by the linguist Emile Benveniste between "story" (*histoire*) and "discourse" (*discours*). "Story" is an enunciation that relates past events, relies on the past tense, supposes the absence of the speaking subject and proclaims the truth about the past. "Discourse", for its part, is an enunciation that presupposes a speaking subject and an interlocutor, relies on first-person pronouns, readily uses the present tense, and is tied to persuasion and argumentation (Benveniste 1966: 237–50). For Rancière, the radical innovation of Michelet's history is that he combines these two forms of enunciation. Michelet writes history in the present tense; he gives to the present, and to his own voice as a historian, the truth usually reserved for the impersonal declarations of historical narrative. He "breaks the system of oppositions" (NH 48) between the "present of declarations" and the "narrative prestige" of the past tense that had dominated forms of writing throughout the *ancien régime*. There is no doubt that, for Rancière, Michelet is the historian of the new democratic age. Michelet made the archives speak and showed us the paperwork of the poor, the documents and traces left by the actors of the Revolution. In this, according to Rancière, Michelet writes as the voice of a new historical moment, what Rancière calls the age of literature and what he will very soon come to label the "aesthetic regime". This age of literature is defined by a new form of perception of the world in which laws of genre as well as social hierarchies have given way to the disorder of art and the arbitrariness of democracy. Rancière has spoken of this new age as characterized by the "reversal of the hierarchies of genre", that is, the breakdown of the rules that governed poetics from Aristotle to Voltaire and that fixed for each subject an appropriate mode of expression. After 1800, these rules give way to a poetic principle that dissolved the "necessary connection between a type of subject and a form of expression" (PA 53). This is the "poetic revolution" that Stendhal evokes in 1823 when he summoned his generation to write new tragedies, tragedies in prose whose subject could be anyone at all (Stendhal 1970: 51). Tragedies were no longer reserved for kings and princes, and history was no longer a genre reserved for rulers and diplomats. This is precisely what is going on in Michelet's histories, according to Rancière. By mixing "*histoire*" and "*discours*", Michelet mixes narrative genres and creates a new way of speaking the truth about history. The birth of the new subject of history – the people – corresponds precisely to the invention of new poetic forms. This is how Rancière can conclude that in "affirming itself in its absoluteness, in unbinding itself from *mimesis* and the division of genres, literature makes history possible as a discourse of the truth" (NH 51).

But as enthusiastic as Rancière seems to be about Michelet's "revolution", he remains cautious about the legacy. For when Michelet begins to speak about history in the present tense, he neutralizes what Rancière calls "the *appearance of the past*" (NH 49). By mixing "story" and "discourse", Michelet sets up what Rancière calls "an essential poetic structure of the new historical knowledge" (*ibid.*), the historian's claim that "all" is true. By speaking of past events in the present, Michelet erases the uncertainties of histories. By speaking in maxims, these grammatical bundles of truth, the historian is erasing the speech, the events – in a word the disturbances – of the past. Michelet shows the paperwork of the poor, but in his paraphrases he papers over "the democratic disturbance of speech" (NH 90). And, in a surprising turn of phrase, Rancière writes that Michelet, like Plato, has traded in "the dead letter in the name of living speech" (NH 50). The phrase is surprising in its evocation of Derrida's critique of logocentrism, and while Rancière has rarely commented upon Derrida's work, this one phrase points to momentary alliance in an investigation of the ways in which language participates both in the presence and in the disappearance of the past (Guerlac & Cheah 2009).

The production of silence

The Names of History raises far-reaching questions about how the production of knowledge is tied to the production of silence. Rancière's is a corrective voice, suspicious, like Roland Barthes, of "scientific arrogance", those moments when claims to authority become gestures of intimidation and domination (Barthes 2007: 152). What unites Rancière and the late Barthes is this kind of wariness towards claims of authority coming from the scientific community, especially in the humanities. This does not mean that Rancière is advocating a generalized indeterminacy, but rather that he is intent upon identifying the stultification that comes when the *savant* claims that there are those who know and those who do not know, those who understand and those who cannot, those who see the ideological domination and those who persist in acting in blindness, illusion or misrecognition.

The debate with the historians is thus a continuation of the founding principle of Rancière's work, that democracy and education come about only when we presuppose the equality of intelligence of everyone with everyone else. Along with books such as *The Nights of Labour* and *The Ignorant Schoolmaster*, in which Rancière works through this presumption of equality, he has also dedicated a sizeable amount of his scholarship to ferreting out forms of knowledge that explicitly or implicitly deny the thought of ordinary men and women. This work is at the heart of *The Philosopher and his Poor* (1983, English translation 1991), which begins with a critique of "Plato's lie", the philosopher's division of the world into those who can philosophize and those who cannot. One of Rancière's boldest claims is that the core of the Western philosophical tradition rests upon this initial gesture of intellectual arrogance in which philosophy claimed for itself the right to think and handed down to others the virtue of manual labour. This is what Rancière calls stultification, and this stultification is also at work in Pierre Bourdieu's sociology. In Bourdieu's *The Inheritors* (1964, English translation 1979) and *Reproduction* (1970, English translation 1990), his famous studies on the ways in which socially dominant classes maintain their domination through education and taste, Rancière identified what he called Bourdieu's "tautology" (SP 366). Here is how Rancière sums up Bourdieu's approach: children of the working class are excluded from the university because they ignore the real reasons for their exclusion. And this ignorance is the product of the very system that excludes them. Only the sociologist can reveal to the poor the rules that govern their exclusion from higher education. The triumph of the sociologist thus depends upon the continued ignorance of the poor.

Rancière's attacks on Bourdieu have been scathing at times, and Rancière enthusiasts run the risk of overlooking the real breakthroughs in Bourdieu's work. Any reflection on pedagogy would, it seems to me, be severely lacking if it rejected out of hand Bourdieu's attempts to expose the mechanisms of social domination. Still, Rancière's point is well taken: a premise in Bourdieu's thought is that society is governed by hidden forces that only the expert can detect, and that the poor, because they are poor, will never be able to see without the assistance of the scholar.

At the heart of Rancière's poetics of knowledge we thus find a critique of demystification, this hermeneutic process that claims to unveil hidden truths. Since the end of the Second World War, in France at least, demystification had been one of the most useful intellectual tools of the Left, allowing critics and scholars to reveal forms of power and ideological constructions that often operated by making themselves invisible. But this mechanism also served to maintain another form of power, that of the critics, scholars and intellectuals who deployed it and who, in deploying it, presupposed that the audience could not see the truth on its own. Demystification, whether coming from the public intellectual or the teacher, is part of what, at the end of a stunning essay on Roberto Rossellini's film *Europe 51*, Rancière calls the "stupefaction", the *abrutissement* of the public by "well-meaning souls" intent upon protecting us from the power of images and the excesses of language (SVLP 130).

Heretical histories

In *The Names of History* Rancière adopts the term "heretical history" to describe those writings, thoughts and actions that have been papered over and silenced by scholars working in the archives. The term is apt. Heresy is a dialogue with the invisible, with silenced voices and hidden bodies. It is invariably oppositional and dedicated to recovering the moments when what Rancière calls "a hitherto unknown subject of speech" (NH 92) makes itself heard.

In an illuminating essay, the historian Arlette Farge has written that Rancière's work is dedicated to teaching us how not to fear time, or language or even death (Farge 1997: 466). Rancière's work takes the form of an attempt to restore, to account for and to remain open to the "excesses of language" of "heretical history" that academic disciplines and forms of science have often silenced. From his earliest works, Rancière has attempted to construct a counter-history, a history that acknowledges the thinking of the working classes and that restores the possibility of progressive politics. *The Nights of Labour*, is a detailed demonstration of how certain workers around 1830 struggled for their emancipation not by making another Revolution, but by writing poetry, reading Goethe and Chateaubriand, imagining utopias, publishing pamphlets, dressing up as bourgeois and speaking in public. Take, for example, a passage about love. In one of the archives in which Rancière spent many years, he found a letter from a woodworker named Gauny to a friend who had helped him in a moment of despair: "'On my brow when you spilled the light of dawn, when the dew of your life spilled on my tempest-tossed ground, no, I was no longer from here, I had escaped from the revolts of my being ... I have become a flower'" (NL 122). This, for Rancière, is not a simple declaration of love and friendship from one worker to another; it is a reconfiguration of what can be said and done by individuals whom the institutions of society have attempted to turn into unthinking manual labourers. It is an uncalculating exchange where love is given freely. It is the creation of "a community of excess" in which Rancière locates what he calls the "overturning of a world" by workers who challenge the roles assigned to them by society's divisions of labour. Rancière's study is a magisterial work on emancipation as performance. Heretical history, as Rancière practises it, is a form of working with texts that remains open to how words and images can reshape our understanding of the world. This was Rancière's goal when he turned to the workers' archives to write *The Nights of Labour*, and this has guided Rancière's work from the archives through his current writings on contemporary art and forms of spectatorship.

In this journey, Rancière occasionally cites fellow travellers, and near the end of *The Names of History*, he calls forth British historian E. P. Thompson's 1966 work *The Making of the English Working Class*. With this book, Thompson produced a landmark study on how to retrieve the silent narratives of history from what he called "the enormous condescension of posterity" (Thompson 1966: 12). What Thompson described in his great book was a working class seizing language in order to constitute itself as a social and political entity, and individuals using speech in order to constitute themselves as thinking and voting subjects. In this history from below, the work of the historian consists in scouring the archives in order to restore to individuals their capacity for action, these moments of subjectivization in which the working class was "present at its own making" (*ibid.*: 9). For Thompson, as for Rancière a few years later, restoring to individuals their capacity to effect concrete historical change also meant taking seriously their capacity to think, to understand their situation in their own terms. One can imagine how sympathetic Rancière must have been to Thompson's description of a seemingly spontaneous riot in 1795: in this "mob" action Thompson located what he calls "unsuspected complexities" and a "legitimizing notion of right" that subtended and justified the workers' actions. Only a few years after the publication of Thompson's book, Rancière would begin his attacks on Louis Althusser's advocacy of theory over spontaneous action, and what Rancière saw as the transfer of power in Althusserian theory from the militant working classes to the public intellectual. For Rancière, as for E. P. Thompson, the lesson of Althusser was a cautionary tale about the poverty of theory.

There may be one more point in common between the English historian and the French philosopher, and that has to do with their insistence upon naming the actors of the history they are recounting. As we read Thompson, we encounter well-known figures of the time, Thomas Paine, for instance, and Mary Wollstonecraft, and Wordsworth as an early enthusiast of the French Revolution. But we also discover Thomas Spenser, a coiner, the Reverend William Winterbotham, the attorney John Frost, sent to the pillory for having publicly declared: "I believe in equality" (Thompson 1966: 124), Edward Marcus Despard, a Luddite and advocate of Irish independence, beheaded for treason in 1803, Gravener Henson, an early union leader, Citizen Lee, a vitriolic pamphleteer. These are precisely the names that have been silenced not only by the traditional history of kings and diplomacy but also by the structuralist analyses of later Marxist historians. These names stand as instances of an alternative history, a "heretical history" of political speech and struggles for "egalitarian and democratic values". The names of history are words in an archive, but they are also traces of action and of thought, a record of the action and the thought that is both most significant and most fleeting in the struggle for equality.

A defence of literature

Where does Rancière's polemic leave us today? To be sure, most historians have moved beyond the model of the *Annales* school. Historians and sociologists working today are certainly aware of the difficulties tied to uncovering the names, words and voices of the archive. British cultural studies, E. P. Thompson, Gayatri Chakravorty Spivak, feminist history, subaltern studies and the work of Ranajit Guha have, at least since the 1980s, shifted the humanities away from the structural and statistical history that was the object of Rancière's polemic. These approaches all coincide with Rancière's work in a number of ways, including their attempt to recover individuals as active and fully conscious participants in their own history. Ranajit Guha has written that in their studies of rebellions, historians have too often neglected the consciousness of the rebels themselves: "Historiography has been content to deal with the peasant rebel merely as an empirical person or member of a class, but not as an entity whose will and reason constituted the praxis called rebellion" (Guha 1994: 337). Readers of Rancière have been quick to pronounce on the radical innovation of his theories, but it seems to me that the real strength of Rancière's writing can be located in its alliances with scholars and artists working outside France and thinking, like Rancière, about the relation between the production of knowledge and egalitarian practices.

Still, there may be one aspect to Rancière's work that distinguishes it from that of the historians and philosophers with whom he is in dialogue. This has to do with what might be called his defence of literature. What Rancière has called the age of literature can be understood in two ways. In the first sense, Rancière is describing what he sees as an epistemological break situated around 1800 in which new forms of representation and new ways of perceiving the world (including the new definition of the word "literature" by Madame de Stael) were introduced. Shortly after writing *The Names of History*, Rancière would rebrand this "age of literature" the "aesthetic regime", a wider-reaching phrase used to describe a world in which laws of genre and social hierarchies have given way to the disorder of art and the arbitrariness of democracy. But when he speaks of literature, Rancière is also designating a phenomenon in which literary production – novels, poetry, speeches, philosophy, history – is accessible to all, to every citizen of the nation willing to put in the time and the effort of reading.

For Rancière, the defining characteristic of literature is what he calls its "availability". In *The Names of History*, after evoking Tacitus' description of an uprising of soldiers against their officers, Rancière describes a kind of reappropriation.

And when the language of Tacitus has, as a dead language, taken on a new life, when it has become the language of the other, the language whose appropriation procures a new identity, the overly talented students in the schools and seminaries will fashion, in their own language and in a direct style, new harangues; the self-taught will in their turn take these as models ... All who have no place to speak will take hold of those words and phrases, those argumentations and maxims, subversively constituting a new body of writing. (NH 30)

This is a precise description of the purpose of reading literature: talented students but also autodidacts and, in the end, all those who are not supposed to read these texts, will be able to seize their words and phrases in order to form new texts of their own. Rancière makes the bold, though somewhat speculative, conclusion that it is precisely in reading about the revolts of slaves and soldiers in Tacitus that the revolutionaries in 1789 were able to imagine their own revolution and put into words their claims for equality. Literature participates, and will continue to participate, in the democratic project not only because of the ideas it transmits, but because it is available to men and women who, in the standard distribution of social roles, have no business reading or writing. Literature is the site where anyone can read anything at all and anyone at all can write. The democracy of literature, writes Rancière in a more recent book, hinges on its availability to all (PL 21–2). The work of the teacher is to struggle for this availability.

To argue that the writing of Flaubert and Balzac is available to all and that anyone and everyone can "claim" literature is not without its dangers. This defence of literature depends upon specific local conditions – generalized literacy, availability of books, free and mandatory public education – that are fragile at best. What is more, several generations of critics in France and the USA have shown that canonical literature has the potential for being complicit with a nation's power structures, most specifically with an educational system bent on sorting out gifted students, and distinguishing a literary education from vocational training. To claim that Tacitus' "dead language" will necessarily end up in the hands of revolutionary autodidacts may be placing too much faith in the democratic potential of literature, not to mention the good will of librarians.

Rancière would, of course, admit that there are structural and institutional impediments to literacy, and that these are a measure of an unjust society. This said, his great innovation has been to refuse to stop at the observation that illiteracy exists. Rancière's entire career has been devoted to locating sites of equality precisely where others have claimed that equality does not, or could not, exist. After all, Joseph Jacotot discovered his universal method of education when he made the incongruous decision to ask his Flemish students to read Fénelon's

Télémaque. A worker thinking of equality when she should be sewing the queen's dress, a cabinetmaker reading Goethe, coiners dedicating themselves to learning "the secrets of versification" (NL 118), these are the instances of equality that Rancière has set himself the task of bringing to our eyes. And if Rancière's work has found such an enthusiastic reception among readers of all conditions, it is, perhaps, because of his assertion that literature is a common language, that we access freely, that we are all capable of understanding, that demands no specialized form of knowledge and requires from us nothing but effort and desire.

NINE

Regimes of the arts
Jean-Philippe Deranty

Rancière's notion of "regimes of the arts" appeared for the first time in *The Politics of Aesthetics* (2004; original French edition 2000). The term captured much of the substantial work of conceptual and historical analysis begun a few years earlier, notably in *La parole muette* (1998). In this book, Rancière spoke of "systems of representation" and of "poetic systems". Since then, his many aesthetic writings have greatly refined and enriched the content of that notion.

The notion of "regimes of the arts" is first a descriptive one. It is the gateway to Rancière's rich aesthetic thinking. At its heart, the notion serves to identify the specific features of the understanding of art characteristic of modern society, that is, the society that was ushered in by the political, economic and cultural revolutions of the late eighteenth and early nineteenth centuries. Crucially, the notion serves to contrast the modern understanding of art, summarized by the term "aesthetic", from a classical understanding, encapsulated in the terms "poetic" and "representative".

As always with Rancière, though, the notion also serves a polemical purpose. With its help, Rancière wants to contest some of the prominent approaches to art in the contemporary humanities. In particular, the notion is used by him to reject interpretations that frame artistic practices in linear, mono-causal historical narratives: for example, formalist accounts that read the history of an art form as a movement of purification towards the appropriation by that art form of the specificity of its own medium (like surface and colour for painting); or metaphysical interpretations that read modern art works against the background of a teleological vision of history, as the unfolding of some essential logic. The "regimes of the arts" by contrast define only the basic features of historical understandings of art and art forms. Within those broad frameworks, each artist creatively develops his or her own modes of expression.

Rancière lists three fundamental regimes of the arts: the ethical; the poetic or representative; and the aesthetic. After analysing the formal features shared by the different "regimes of the arts", we briefly delineate the content of those three historical instantiations. The "aesthetic" one is the most important, as it defines the parameters of artistic practice and aesthetic understanding for our time.

What is a regime of the arts?

A regime of the arts defines the specific ways in which a given epoch conceives of the nature and logic of artistic representation. As Rancière puts it succinctly in *La parole muette* in relation to literature, it is "the modalities of the relationship between thought, language and world" (PM 67, my trans.). A regime of the arts thus specifies how a given epoch thinks of the ways in which human expressions stand in relationship to the world, what words and other expressions capture from the world. A regime of the arts thus operates on the basis of a certain understanding of language and meaning, and their links to reality. A regime of the arts also specifies the ways in which these expressions take their place within society, what their functions are within social life in general and in relation to the other social activities in particular.

Rancière's fundamental intent with such an approach is first of all philosophical. He wants to emphasize the fact that conceptions of what artistic practices mean, or of who an artist is, are thoroughly historical, in the sense that they change over time. As Rancière puts it: "There is no art without eyes that see it as art" (FI 72). With this insistence on the historical nature of "ideas of art", Rancière is a direct heir of the great German philosophers of the nineteenth century (especially Hegel and Marx, despite all his criticisms of them), who emphasized the historical nature, and thus the temporal relativity, of the mental categories through which human beings make sense of the world, themselves and their society.

Rancière's intent is also political. He wants to insist on the fact that conceptions of what artistic representations are and achieve take place within a broader understanding of society. Regimes of the arts are intimately linked to the "*partage du sensible*", which points to the political underpinning of social perception (see Davide Panagia in Chapter 7). Artistic expressions are not defined in isolation from the rest of the social world. Their significance, that is, both their meaning and value, is characterized in relation to the respective significance given to other activities, but also in relation to the significance of the different elements making up social reality (for instance the home, the workplace, the market, the political institutions), as well as the significance of modes of being (for instance the qualities deemed to be attached to the conditions of worker or political leader), and of socially defined times and spaces.

With these preliminary remarks in mind, we can list the structural elements whose specific relationships define in each case a historical regime. There are different versions of such lists throughout Rancière's texts, depending on the dimension he wants to emphasize and the contexts of his interventions. Rancière's preferred mode of presentation tends to focus on three key elements. In *La parole muette*, for instance, the fundamental scheme revolves around the relations between thought, language and world. If we comb through Rancière's aesthetic writings, however, we find that there are five basic structural elements. Accordingly, a "regime of the arts" links together, each time in a specific way: the *world* itself, in its material and human dimensions; what in the world is *significant* (both meaningful and socially valuable), and thus worthy of representation; *language*, or *speech*, or *text*, as the discursive articulation of meaning; the artefacts in which meaning is expressed, in verbal, pictorial, bodily, cinematic or other forms, for which Rancière uses the generic term *image*; and finally the *community*, to which the artist addresses himself/herself, effectively as an actual audience, but also more loosely as a virtual addressee of the artistic message.

From the perspective of a historian of aesthetic ideas, dedicated to subtle conceptual shifts between historical periods, or for an anthropologist intent on showing the different cultural meanings attached to concepts that are only superficially similar across cultural spheres, the very broad historical and conceptual scope of Rancière's three regimes of the arts might sound naive and in need of refinement. For example, and most importantly, his main interest in the shifts between poetic systems regards the rupture that led from the classical regime, centred on the idea of the proper representation, to the modern regime, centred on the idea of expression. In analysing the demise of the representative regime, he seems highly indebted to Erich Auerbach's famous study of the shifts in the conceptions of *mimesis*, from Antiquity to modern times (Auerbach 1953). But compared with the detail and complexity of Auerbach's historical study, Rancière's very broad categories might seem to provide only a seriously truncated and impoverished treatment of the same matter.

A criticism of that kind would in fact be misplaced. Rancière is well aware of the constant evolution of those fundamental categorical frames through which societies make sense of themselves and of their world. Indeed, his work consists precisely in combining the analysis of the logic of practices with a painstaking attention to their historical specificities. His early work on the history of the labour movement, and his later writings on artistic movements in the nineteenth and twentieth centuries, are themselves detailed analyses of the subtle semantic shifts occurring within the modern paradigm. The distinction between different "ideas of art" and "regimes of the arts" in fact provides an indispensable analytical and conceptual language to make sense of these shifts beyond superficial biographical and merely factual data.

The impression that Rancière's "regimes" are too broad dissolves once we differentiate between two levels of analysis. The categories of the ethical, the representative and the aesthetic, which name the three main regimes of the arts, are not strictly speaking historical categories. They are in fact what we could call meta-historical categories. They point to three different fundamental "ideas of art", that is, to fundamental ways of linking the five structural elements listed above. It is true that these basic ideas of art can serve to differentiate large historical periods. Taken in order, they do constitute some sort of broad genealogy. But different regimes can also coexist in the same historical period. For example, Rancière's definition of cinema as a "thwarted fable" means that although cinema could be interpreted as the ultimate embodiment of the principles of the aesthetic regime, it also remains caught up in the logics of the ethical and representative regimes (see Hassan Melehy's analysis in Chapter 12).

Most importantly, Rancière shows that each regime entails its own central logical contradiction. A regime of the arts is defined almost as much by the way in which it links together the five elements listed above as by the internal contradiction resulting from this. Rancière's combination of conceptual and historical analysis consists in delineating the different historical attempts at resolving such contradictions. This links up with the previous point. If an art form like cinema remains under the sway of earlier poetic logics, this is like a "fate" (an accurate translation of the French title of *The Future of the Image* is "the fate of images") imposed by external circumstances (in particular political and economic imperatives) that prevent it from fulfilling its potential. And that potential is best defined as the attempt by each artist to deal with the specific contradiction of the regime to which that art form most eminently belongs.

The ethical regime of the arts

The purpose of the distinction between regimes of the arts is not that of historical instruction. Rancière does not aim to compete with Auerbach, for instance, and provide a full historical account of the many shifts in the meanings of "mimesis" or "representation". Rather, his interest lies in the specificity of the modern period, notably because it is the one in which democracy has become a real possibility. This theoretical agenda means that the two regimes to which Rancière has dedicated the most attention are the modern one, the one he calls the "aesthetic regime", and the one that preceded it, the "representative regime". In order to understand the specific potentialities and internal difficulties of the modern paradigm, Rancière consistently contrasts it with the paradigm from which the modern one emerged. As a result, the third regime of the arts, the "ethical" one, is rarely discussed. It was introduced in the writings around 2000, notably in *The Politics of Aesthetics*, when Rancière was still in the process of firming up his aesthetic thinking. We need to begin with this regime, however, because it is the one that comes first in the historical order.

The conceptual specificity of the ethical regime of the arts is for Rancière most precisely articulated in Plato's views on art. This regime is characterized by two fundamental features. First, it is a regime in which artistic representations are judged according to their ontological veracity, that is, the truthfulness with which they accurately represent an ideal model. This model can be a simple bed, as in the famous passage of Book X of the *Republic*, or the actions of heroes and noble characters, or indeed, as in later theological discussions about the status of images, the divine itself. Artistic artefacts are conceptualized according to their relative closeness and similitude to, or distance from, the model.

Secondly, this ontological veracity, or lack thereof, does not have significance only in terms of knowledge and truth, but also in moral and political terms. Famously, this is the reason behind the banishment of the poets and all artisans dealing in the art of mimesis in Plato's ideal city: their lies have a moral and political impact, they influence the *ethos*, the *mores* and spirit of the community. Hence the term *ethical*. The ethical regime of the arts is the one in which artistic practices and artefacts are judged according to their direct moral and political worth. It is clear that aspects of this regime remain valid today, notably for film. Many polemics concerning films, as the most popular of the art forms, revolve around their alleged nefarious impact on particular audiences.

The representative or poetic regime of the arts

The notion of a "representative" regime of the arts first arose in Rancière's work in relation to his study of literature, in *La parole muette*, published in 1998. This book is one of Rancière's key works, alongside *The Nights of Labour* and *Disagreement*. It is in *La parole muette* that we find the most detailed account of the defining principles of the "representative" and the "aesthetic" regimes. In the years that followed it, Rancière broadened the conclusions reached in it to apply them to the other art forms, in particular the visual arts and film.

The fact that Rancière's aesthetic thinking first crystallized around a study of literature reflects the special place literature holds within the regimes of the arts. In the representative or poetic regime, this special place is due to the reliance of all arts forms on a conception of the relationship between meaning and world that favours the verbal articulation of meaning. The name of the general system of representation, "poetics", is not by chance the same name as one of the art forms, poetry. And whilst Plato is the philosopher to whom one must return to define the conceptual apparatus of an "ethical" approach to art, Aristotle's *Poetics* is the philosophical work that gives key indications about the fundamental logic of the "representative" or "poetic" regime.

The classical system of representation, under the tutelage of Aristotle's theory of tragedy and classical rhetoric, made the intelligible, "conceptual" content the primordial part of all the aspects of the art work. The *"inventio"*, the choice of a right topic, was the foremost element, ahead of *"dispositio"*, the crafting of the narrative, and *"elocutio"*, the actual linguistic expression of the topic. In works of fiction, the *"inventio"* concerned above all the choice of the story, that is, the "actions of sufficient magnitude" performed by characters of sufficient relevance, as Aristotle famously argued in the first book of his *Poetics*. In this system, the specific sense of what constitutes "the poetic", of what is poetic in works of art, is thus primordially the value of the story, which is dependent on the standing of the characters and on what happens to them. This provides the standard that makes the art works and art forms commensurable: beyond their specific medium, all arts works tell stories; a story from one medium can always be retold in another (from a painting to a narrative, from tragedy to painting, and so on). We understand why such a conception makes "poetry" (taken in a broad sense that includes all fictional writings) paradigmatic among all the art forms. Rancière suggests that the famous sentence by Horace, *"ut pictura poesis"* (reading a poem is like watching a painting) was in fact also meant the other way around: "a picture is like a poem".

In *La parole muette*, Rancière makes this the first principle of the representative regime, and calls it the "fictional principle" (PM 21, my trans.). The first aspect of this principle is the one just mentioned, namely that "the essence of the poem is to be an imitation, the representation of actions" (*ibid.*), rather than being (as the aesthetic regime will say) a certain use of language. The second aspect of the principle is that it provides the fictional world with its own time and space. This allows the art work to escape the ontological and ethical judgements of the previous regime. This was Aristotle's key theoretical gesture to salvage tragedy from Plato's condemnation. Fictional works have their own rules, different from the rules applying to other forms of *techne* (the generic term for all techniques for the Greeks, including what we now call art). Unlike in Plato's construct, the arts are not judged according to their ontological veracity or technical efficiency.

The second principle is the "principle of genericity", a complicated term that simply points to the idea of "genre". Fiction is now separated from other realms, as obeying its own rules, but what are the rules of fiction? What rules should an artist or a writer follow, and according to what rules will their work be judged? "Once again, it is Aristotle who, in the first books of his *Poetics*, enunciated the key principle: the genre of a poem – epos or satire, tragedy or comedy – is dependent first and foremost on the nature of the object represented" (PM 21, my trans.). The subject of the story dictates the genre of the art work: noble characters performing actions of "magnitude" (gods, heroes, kings, noble souls) will have to be represented in the noble genres of tragedy in the theatre, historical painting and official portraits in painting, and so on. Low characters (folk people, sinners) will be represented in comedy and satire, and in the painting of everyday life.

The centrality of the genre dictates all the other aspects of the art work and thus leads to a third principle that Rancière calls the "principle of *convenance*", that is, the principle regarding "what is right and proper". The genre and the social and ethical standing of the characters dictate the kind of actions the writer will be able to put together in his or her narrative, and the language he or she will be able to use. Equally, the critics and the audience will be especially sensitive to breaches in the expected actions and discourses of the characters. A princess will not be expected to use certain words; certain actions are not allowed to be shown on stage. Four different kinds of criteria define the proper and the improper in artistic representation (PM 23): whether the actions depicted correspond to the nature of human passions in general; whether they conform to the spirit of the people or the main character as reported by the "good authors" (the classics of the canon); whether the current audience's sense of decency and taste is respected; and finally, whether action and speech follow a pattern commensurate with the logic that can be expected, and the logic of the particular character (Achilles and Ulysses would be expected to behave differently in the same situation). Altogether, although the work of art has been extracted from other forms of social activity, it has to obey strict norms defined by what is proper and what is improper in tight relation to a hierarchical scale.

Finally, the fourth principle is for Rancière the "principle of actuality". The representation of action is guided by an underlying norm, that of the actuality of speech. This corresponds to the translation in the domain of expression of the hierarchy between the high and the low that structures the entire classical system. The ultimate demonstration of the superiority of the intelligible is in a form of speech that is live and efficient, the speech of important men commanding or converting, or counselling, or convincing other men: a god enunciating a fiat; a king whose decision is final; a general commanding his army; a noble individual winning his opponents to his arguments or counselling the prince; a barrister winning his cause or a priest saving a soul. The ideal case that regulates the whole system is one in which there is adequation of an ideal kind between author, character and audience: the artist's superior spirit allows him to depict the speech and actions of noble characters for an audience of educated and tasteful people. All along, the norm is that of the power of speech and the speech of power: the audience, composed ideally of powerful men, whose power is demonstrated in the efficacy of their own speech in real life, marvels at the power with which an author has represented a powerful speech in the fictional world. Unlike in the ethical regime, the two systems of norms (in the real and the fictional worlds) are allowed to be different in their content. It is fine to portray on stage the travails of suffering souls and imperfect heroes (Oedipus, or the terrible fate of the Atrides family). But the hierarchy of the high and the low (relating to genre, style, actions, feelings and so on), and the general rule of the power of speech, must be respected.

As mentioned earlier, a regime of the arts is defined as much by its constitutive rules as by the specific contradiction that emerges from these rules. What is, according to Rancière, the peculiar contradiction of the representative regime? The clearest account of it appears in later texts, when the initial analyses dedicated to literature are broadened to the field of the visual arts (in particular in FI 113–23: "What representation means"). The primacy of speech means the primacy of the textual over the visual; or, to refer to the five key elements above, of language and text (the discursive articulation of meaning) over image (the forms created by artistic practice, which can also be verbal images). The power of speech is to "make visible", to name and explain what is invisible, either because it is distant (in space or time), or hidden (like the inner motives of characters, or some invisible forces at play). But because of all the constraints operating in the representative system, notably on the narrative level, this "making-visible" must be gradual and can never be complete. The logic of action demands that the story be organized on the logic of cause and effect, with an appropriate presentation of all key logical relations. This necessarily entails delaying the presentation of some aspects of the narrative, and remaining silent over others, those that would get in the way of the most efficient presentation of action. Similarly the need to be true to characters' and audience's "passions" demands that some things be shown and explained while others remain unsaid (for instance, the gouging of Oedipus' eyes must never be shown on stage). Accordingly, "speech makes visible, but only in accordance with a regime of under-determination, by not 'really' making visible" (FI 113). Or: "This system adjusts the relations between what can be seen and what can be said, between the unfolding of schemas of intelligibility [language, text] and the unfolding of material manifestations [image]" (FI 117). It is clear that such a poetic system is highly unstable. The system has built into it the temptation to present images that are not already or fully justified in terms of their integration in the plot or by the logics of morality or affects; or to disrupt the accepted logic of story-telling and to reorganize the narrative according to a logic different from the cause–effect relations or the logic of discovery enunciated by Aristotle in the *Poetics*. The exploration of such breaches in the representative logic is precisely what the shift from the representative to the aesthetic regime makes possible.

The aesthetic regime

The aesthetic regime is Rancière's name for artistic modernity. This new regime is ushered in along with the political revolutions. The representative regime was based, as we have just outlined, on the commensurability of the structures and norms organizing the social and the fictional worlds: like the real world, the fictional had to abide by its own hierarchy of topics, genres and styles. Similarly, a series of imperatives commanded the relationship between meaning and expression, duplicating in the fictional world the ideal relationship between the intelligible and the material in the real world. Underneath these similarities operated the basic principle that the noble, the powerful and the knowing are naturally destined to rule over the low, the poor and the ignorant.

But the advent of democracy and with it the rise of the principle of equality challenge this hierarchical worldview and the aesthetic system that duplicated it in the fictional realm. Of course the emergence of the principle of equality does not magically erase hierarchical structures in real societies. Indeed, one of Rancière's most famous pairs of concepts describes the intertwining of structures of hierarchy (the police) with the egalitarian challenge to these structures (politics proper), which is inherently built into hierarchy (see Chapters 4 and 5). Translated into aesthetics, this means that even in the new regime, modern art remains partially under the sway of the representative logic, despite the possibilities opened up by the new regime. Cinema is the best example of an art of modernity returning to a classical, representative format in the majority of its productions.

But political equality does create the conditions for an entirely new regime of the arts. The simplest way to describe the basic features of the new regime is by showing how it performs the systematic inversion of the four principles of the previous one (PM 28–9).

The primacy of fiction (of *inventio* over *elocutio*, of the narrative over expression) is replaced by the primacy of language. Poeticity, what is "poetic" in the art work, what distinguishes it from other artefacts and makes it a special, spiritual entity, now stems from the powers of language itself, not from the arrangement of actions. Language is no longer seen as a medium in which a truth external to it comes to be represented, as a means to an end. Expression itself is the end now. This shift affecting the art work relies on a more fundamental shift, one that concerns the way in which meaning and world are seen to relate. In the aesthetic regime, the world itself, at all levels, including the material ones, is seen to entail meaning. Even the pre-human is symbolic. The exemplary thread Rancière follows in the beginning of *La parole muette* is that of Hugo's novel, *Notre-Dame de Paris*. Hugo's book is built like a cathedral, not because the author has randomly decided to build his book on the model of its central building, but because the cathedral is itself already like "a book of stone", that is, something that is more than just brick and mortar, a spiritual entity full of meaning. The artist's job then is to rearticulate in a human way the expression already present in the stone, the statues and the architecture. More broadly, what is true of a man-made monument in this particular example is also true, within the new regime, for natural entities (as in British romanticism but also Hugo's or Baudelaire's poetry), for historical forces (in the realist novels of Balzac, Dickens or Tolstoy) or social realities (as in the novels of Zola).

What made the arts comparable in the previous regime were the stories they were all to represent. Now the common element is that all arts are a form of language, bringing to a kind of superior form and reflexivity the discursivity inherent in the world itself. The change from one regime to the other corresponds to the change from a poetic system where representation (mimesis) is the guiding principle to one where it is expression.

The second and third principles, that fictional works must belong to a specific genre dictating the type of discourse and of actions depicted, now become void. If every entity potentially holds a deep meaning waiting to be rearticulated, it no longer makes sense to categorize topics and characters into genres organized along a high–low axis. Every subject, any action, from the most heroic to the most trivial, can be treated in any genre, with the use of any style. One of Rancière's favourite examples is Flaubert, who uses the same sublimely poetic style to narrate the spiritual torments of Saint Anthony's temptations in the desert, the epic revolt of the mercenaries against Carthage in *Salammbô* or the drab world of provincial life in *Madame Bovary*.

Finally, the fourth principle (live, efficient speech, the speech of power as ideal model) also gives way. Language is now the norm, but language is present in different forms everywhere. It is not the preserve of men of power.

At first the universal scope of the notion of language (captured in the Romantic motto that "everything speaks") seems to overlook the simple fact that there are two fundamentally different forms of language: the metaphorical "language" of nature and things can only be an implicit or indirect one, not to be confused with language in the strict and proper sense, human language. In the new regime, however, these two types of language are intimately related, simply because the human world is now conceived as an inherent part of the world as a whole. Human language is now seen to reflect in a higher order of awareness the indirect language of the world itself. But the expressivity of human language would not be possible without the general expressivity of the world. And this logic of reciprocal exchange and belonging, which views the smaller part as participating in but also rearticulating the reality of the larger part, is also at play between the language of the singular artist and the language of the community. In the end, the regime is premised on the model of a circle uniting in one phenomenon of general inter-expressivity the artist, his or her community, and the world itself:

the representative circle defined in a specific way the society in which the act of speech took place, as a set of legitimate relations and criteria of legitimacy between the author, his "subject" and the audience. The rupture of this circle makes the sphere of literature coextensive with social relations. It brings together in one direct relation of inter-expression the singularity of the work of art and the community that the latter manifests. Each expresses the other. (PM 51, my trans.)

What is the contradiction that lies at the heart of this new regime? Rancière formulates it by focusing on the Romantic paradigm and its unravelling at the hand of Hegel in the *Lectures on Aesthetics*. Inspired by Schiller's seminal lectures on poetry, the young Romantics had fashioned a consistent vision of the poem as a "fragment" re-expressing in the realm of human discourse the poetry inherent in the world, thus proposing a new model of community in touch with its deep forces and the forces of the world. In the poem, the unity of individuality and collectivity, world and society, language and matter, nature and spirit could be pointed to in anticipatory fashion. In particular, the famous "Oldest System Programme of German Idealism", the utopian project devised by the young Hegel, Schelling and Hölderlin, linking poetry, philosophy and politics, became the paradigmatic example of avant-garde political–aesthetic projects for the next two centuries (Critchley 2001).

But this utopia contained a major contradiction. On an immediate level, the contradiction is between the first expressive principle (that the poetic is a dimension of the world itself) and the second (that any subject can be represented in any genre, using any style). The "indifference" of style in relation to its subject would appear to equate with the ruin of the principle that was supposed to define the new status of poetry: that it would capture in the right human words the implicit meaning of the world. If style is indifferent, then what could secure the necessity of poetic expression?

The Romantic theory of the fragment seemed capable of dealing with this contradiction, because it emphasized strongly the subjectivistic, voluntaristic aspects of poetic practice. The poem was not supposed merely to reflect an already-existing meaning present in the world, nor an already existing community, but actively to anticipate and indeed help bring about a unity to come. As a result, the poem could both be utterly subjectivistic and yet, as announcement of a future world of meaning, an objective mirroring of the world itself. The two principles remained in tension in the present but could be united in the projected utopia. Hegel's critique undercuts this construct. Hegel accepts the model of a full adequacy between the artist's singular voice, the "spirit" of a historical community and the material world. But, as he argues, this model does not capture the essence of modernity. Rather, it corresponds to classical times, a time when Homer could be seen both as a unique voice of genius and the mouthpiece of an entire culture. Hegel's "operation consists in transforming romantic poetry into a theory of classicism" (PM 65, my trans.). Ulysses, the archetypal character of the classical age, made his own bed: this symbolized the lack of radical gap between the human, the material and the natural worlds. His virtues pointed to the entire value system of his culture. His dealings with the gods also demonstrated a relation of familiarity between the human and the superhuman. In the Greek character was thus captured the perfect circularity between the levels of reality, from the natural to the human and the divine, which the Homeric poem recaptured a second time again in poetic expression. By contrast with the epic world, in the age of the division of labour, material objects can no longer be taken as expressions of their owners; modern science makes it impossible to view nature as an expressive realm mirrored in human spiritual powers; and complex societies make the dream of a unity of individual and community impossible. The utopian dream expressed in the "Oldest System Programme of German Idealism" was thus only a description of the past. Famously for Hegel, the power of art to capture a whole epoch is a dream gone by, which today is replaced by the prosaic languages of the positive sciences and philosophy.

Through his emphasis on the dreary "prosa" of the modern world (the term that captures the impossibility of universal poeticity) and the impossibility of the Romantic programme, Hegel unveils a second, deeper contradiction, which for Rancière structures the whole modern aesthetic regime. This second contradiction is between the ideal of writing the language of things themselves, and the lack of a necessary link between signifiers and their referents. This lack prevents expressions from fully capturing the meaning of the world, either because the latter remains reticent to expression, or because it overflows it. The contemporary paradigm of the arts for Rancière is one in which, on the one hand, artists strive to develop expressive means that would be commensurate with the meanings of the world itself, and in tune with a state of the community (present or future); while on the other, any attempt to link meaning and expression in some necessary way is doomed.

This feature of the modern paradigm makes any attempt to signify and express inherently incomplete and hazardous. In the terms listed earlier, image takes precedence over text: the figurative expressions created by language use (not just verbal images but also those of all the other media) are not exhausted by their intended meanings. The representative paradigm put images under the sway of the story (the intelligible, "conceptual" aspect): the "sayable" was to regulate the "visible"; logical connections gave an order to the successions of figures. In the aesthetic regime, the inverse takes place:

> contrasting with the representative scene of the visibility of speech is an equality of the visible that invades discourse and paralyses action. For what is newly visible has very specific properties. It does not make visible; it imposes presence ... (and possesses an) inertia that comes to paralyse action and absorb meaning.
>
> (FI 121)

In the new regime, meaning can be found at all levels of reality (principles of expressivity and symbolicity), but no expression can fully capture this meaning. Rancière summarizes this as the twofold identity of *logos* (meaning, the intelligible) and *pathos* (passivity, brute presence of things that "absorbs meaning"): "the immanence of logos within pathos, of thought within non-thought", and "of pathos within logos, of non-thought within thought" (IE 31). Against Ulysses, the archetypal figure of the classical regime, Oedipus is the symbol of the aesthetic age: a hero who knows and does not know, who is fully active yet utterly passive (IE 27; FI 112–19).

Such insistence on the excess of the signifier over the signified could make it sound as though Rancière shared the views of famous poststructuralist authors like Lyotard or Derrida. But Rancière's aesthetics is not based on a deconstruction of the metaphysics of truth and language. Rather, his purpose is to underline the contradiction operating at the heart of the new poetic system. That contradiction is a direct consequence of the principle of symbolicity: if the things themselves contain meanings that overreach the narrow scope of socially constrained interpretations (beyond the representative logic), how could any language, as a form of social convention, even literary language, ever fully capture these meanings? The idea of an expressivity of the world liberates language and expression to such an extent that it can no longer be brought back under control.

The contradiction, however, does not lead to a literature or to an art of the un-sayable and the un-representable. Rather, the contradiction is for Rancière a productive one: each writer and artist faces its challenge and invents his or her own ways to try to circumvent it. Indeed, this is the mark of all genuine artistic projects: they have faced and attempted to do something with the overwhelming possibilities opened up by the demise of the constraining representative logic. Rancière's concern in aesthetics is the same as that in politics: to establish, on the basis of a productive contradiction at the heart of the modern world, the possibility of free, creative action.

PART IV
Aesthetics

TEN

Expressivity, literarity, mute speech
Alison Ross

A provisional description of the concept of "literarity" needs to bring out Rancière's distinctive intermeshing of the fields of aesthetics and politics. As we shall see in the first section, the concept of "literarity" is what the political term "equality" would do were it to become an aesthetic principle of analysis. It is not that "literarity" transposes a set of political concerns into aesthetics, but that if one were to ask what "equality" could mean in aesthetics, then one would answer: "literarity".

How, we might ask, are we supposed to understand the political value of "equality" in the context of literature; how are we supposed to understand what "equality" does in the case of literature? In Rancière's telling, the modern age is the age of equality. One of the features of this age, as we shall see, is the ways words and things are separated and united (FW 13–14; NH 57, 93). It is these relations between words and things that reconfigure the sensory field of experience and most especially *social* experience. It is important to emphasize, however, that the modern poetic revolutions are just one part of a broader revolution of societies' frameworks. In so far as literature uses words to endow things with meaning and in so far as anything at all is able to bear expressive meaning, "equality" is germane to understanding the significance and effects of the modern poetic revolution. The events, the status of words and the institutions of modern literary production can all be analysed under the concept of "literarity" precisely because they are not a "simple matter of words" (NH 7). Modern literature disregards the hierarchies of the old representational systems. As such its "aesthetic" functions are immediately "political" because its use of words points in particularly powerful fashion to the possibility of setting

133

up new relations to things that promise to reconfigure the sense data of experience. But then, if we look outside the field of "literature", "literarity" in turn extends into politics as a specific structural feature of political speech, namely, as a condition of its democratization. A different cluster of questions intervenes from this angle: who can be heard and understood? Under what conditions does the democratization of speech extend effective audibility to a speaker? One may look at Rancière's notion of *parole muette* (mute speech) as a snapshot of this dynamic movement between politics and aesthetics. Mute speech is his way of critically marking the factors involved in the democratization of words as well as the consequences of the inclusion of "equality" into the literary field.

"Literarity" brings with it layers of meaning from a number of different traditions and gathers nuances from the specific contexts in which Rancière deploys it, such as the analysis of the status of words in historical narratives, literature, philosophy and politics. The function of the term is inherently critical. As we shall see in the second section, "literarity" has a diagnostic function in Rancière's discussion of the innovations and legacies of nineteenth-century and modernist literature. When he discusses Balzac, Melville, Flaubert, Mallarmé, Proust, Woolf or Blanchot, Rancière wishes to identify the shared assumptions that distinguish modern literature as a field. He wants to make intelligible in a pointed way the new conditions under which literature occurs with the rise of modernity. Specifically, he wants to highlight the interactions between modern literature and modern democracy, on the one hand, and the new social and political modes of democratic suppression, on the other. His discussion of literature, like his discussions of the other arts, has the status of a counsel that calls for vigilance regarding the modern constitution of supposedly autonomous aesthetic fields. In the case of literature he wishes to underline the fragility, but also the political potentialities, of the distinction between the literary use of words in depicting the prosaic and "merely" prosaic, that is, non-literary, "common" words.

From his perspective, the practice of modern literature is a knot. Untangling the strands that literature ties together is also a new way of diagnosing the stakes and consequences of its practice. "Expressivity" and "mute speech" are two different ways of naming the knots that compose the literary field. The first critically evokes the Romantic assumption that the world is full of meaning. According to this assumption, the bodies of things are saturated, like hieroglyphs, with meaning and significance (PoL 17). The second underlines the paradox of this assumption. It is otherwise silent, prosaic things that literature makes eloquent; but literature also discovers how obstinately silent these things can be, how, in other words, any attempt at giving a literary rendering of them remains problematic, contingent, fraught and self-contradictory. The obstinate silence of things is productive: it demands of each writer and also in the exchanges between different writers constantly new efforts to make things speak (*La parole muette*). Above all, "mute speech" is used to articulate a critical perspective on pretensions to mastery. The expression of the plenitude of meaning in things is "mute" because it always escapes the posture of authority of the supposed masters of language, those such as the consecrated writers and experts who are presumed to own the "means" of expression (NH 54).

Rancière uses this critical perspective to defend his ontology as well as to characterize the functioning of discursive protocols in diverse fields of knowledge. His position appeals to two different sources of evidence: first, the obstinate silence of things to expressivity means that they exceed the power of words to name or evoke them in any absolute way; and secondly, words themselves are, in a way, "silent", that is, they exceed the authority of those who speak the meaning of the meaningful things. Words are incapable of placing things and bodies in fully determined positions. This is because there is no necessary structural link between "ways of doing, ways of being and ways of speaking". Rather, Rancière's ontology holds that the relations between ways of doing, being and speaking "are" malleable and democratic. Words, accordingly, bear a political potency to alter the relations between the order of bodies and the order of words: it is when those who had been rendered inaudible by the socially authorized distribution of roles effectively communicate their claims that the social hierarchy is altered and new ways of doing, being and saying come into view.

In addition to its role in the discussions of the prospects and conditions of modern literature, the vocabulary of literarity is also used to identify the work of discursive protocols in knowledge fields like historiography (Michelet) and philosophy (Deleuze). As we shall see in the third section, in these cases too the diagnostic function of the term "literarity" carries an explicitly critical aim. This latter is elaborated in different ways in Rancière's discussion of literature and discursive knowledge protocols, on one hand, and in his work on politics, on the other. Further, because he intends to fuse aesthetics with politics the critical function of literarity in these respective contexts needs to be carefully specified. Above all, it is important to be alert to the effects of these different contexts so that the critical edge of Rancière's commentaries on literary procedures is not obscured. I will briefly describe the different functions of literarity in light of his fusion of aesthetics and politics in the fourth section.

From politics to aesthetics

The term "literariness" is used by Rancière in his 1992 book, *Les noms de l'histoire* (1992, English translation 1994 as *The Names of History*). This book develops the critical import of what he terms the "excess of words" and refers, as well, to the status of the human being "as a literary animal" (NH 52). However, the concept of "literarity" first appears in the 1995 book – *La Mésentente: Politique et philosophie* (1995, English translation 1998 as *Disagreement*). This is striking given that this book is a book of political theory. Its place here indicates that the term cannot be successfully contained to the context of his studies in literature. Rather, it is the orientation of Rancière's political theory that frames the use and even motivates his commentaries on the topic of literarity in the case of modern literature. In *Disagreement*, Rancière defines literarity as a threefold excess of words (i) over what they name, (ii) over the requirements for the production of the necessities of life, and (iii) over the modes of communication, which legitimate and reinforce a given social order. With this definition Rancière develops a structural analysis of the relation between word-use and social order. In particular, he aims to show that it is the structural excess of words over their actual use (production of necessities) and meaning (communication and naming) that disrupts hierarchical social orders. It is because words exceed their function of naming that the distribution or positioning of things in social space is always provisional. Similarly, words exceed needs and thus have disposition over the social hierarchies that govern the division of labour. Finally, words are not fully identified with the patterns of established communication, and this means that they may be a resource for the redistribution of the social roles and positions of other patterns of social order. More precisely, words are able to effectively communicate new redistributions of roles and positions and to do so on account of their structural excess over prevailing distributions. Rancière links these three types of literary excess to his "ontological" characterization of "ways of doing, ways of being and ways of saying" as the fabric of social order. In his view, the sharing out of the sensible and the apportioning of positions within the sensible are the hierarchical function of the police. Words are ways of rendering effective the redistribution of the order of sensibility.

Rancière reformulates Aristotle's dictum regarding "man's" status as an animal with the additional capacity for politics in order to argue that "[t]he modern political animal is first a literary animal, caught in the circuit of a literariness that undoes the relationships between the order of words and the order of bodies that determine the place of each" (D 37). His understanding of words as able to effect "a disidentification" from "the naturalness of a place" supports a perspective on politics that takes "words" in the expansive sense of contributing to and shaping places and sites of intelligibility (D 36). In the context of politics Rancière thus focuses on the relation between the structural features of words and bodies. But he also wishes to mark the specifically modern democratic "circuit of a literariness that undoes the relationships between the order of words and the order of bodies". Thus, in *Disagreement*, Rancière gives the example of the Aventine Hill succession when the plebs carry out a "series of speech acts linking the life of their bodies to words and word use" (D 25). This scene, in which the Aventine plebs establish "another partition of the perceptible" in constituting themselves "as speaking beings sharing the same properties as those who deny them these" (D 24) is retold by the nineteenth-century French thinker, Pierre-Simon Ballanche. Ballanche reprimands the Latin historian Livy for failing to understand this event as "anything other than a revolt". Ballanche restages the *modern* significance of the event of the Aventine succession in terms of the pivotal status of speech in reconstituting social order (D 23). From this example we can see that Rancière understands the political to be the exercise of a particular kind of speech. More specifically, Rancière cites Ballanche's modern retelling of the Aventine event in order to show that

> politics exists because the logos is never simply speech, because it is always indissolubly the *account* that is made of this speech: the account by which a sonorous emission is understood as speech, capable of enunciating what is just, whereas some other emission is merely perceived as a noise signalling pleasure or pain, consent or revolt. (D 22–3, original emphasis)

In contrast to his examination of the structural features of words in their capacity to enable individuals to transcend their social place, the use of "literarity" in his discussions of modern literature accentuates the historical frame of reference that gives literarity its modern political significance. Rancière understands modern literature to inaugurate what he calls the "aesthetic regime of the arts". This regime installs a particular conception of sensibility in which any and all things are saturated with aesthetic significance or meaning. Rancière has an ambivalent attitude towards this regime. From one perspective, the equality it installs regarding what can have aesthetic significance means that the line separating aesthetic from non-aesthetic objects can now be seen to be tenuous. According to Rancière, this insight comes into view first in modern literature in the frailty of the distinctions between poetic and prosaic words, as well as that of worthy and unworthy objects for literary treatment. One feature of this insight is the generalized status of the poetic, which extends, for instance, to Kant's account of nature's "cipher language", which Kant had used to defend the idea that nature "communicates" moral ideas (PM 58).

In particular, Rancière details the way that the aesthetic regime of the arts expresses the life of a people, and in this respect markedly departs from the classical, Aristotelian rules regarding the representation of the lives of gods and heroes in terms of the form and style appropriate to noble lives (PM 62). It is important to keep in mind that he supposes that there is an intimate parallel between the social system of order and the order of genres and styles in classical aesthetics. Rancière's analysis dovetails with Erich Auerbach's position in *Mimesis* (Auerbach 1953). The aesthetic regime of the arts is important to him because it refuses the distinction between the poetic depiction of noble action and merely prosaic life, and thus expresses the structural features of "equality".

From another perspective, however, the aesthetic regime suppresses the consequences of its democratic conception of aesthetic significance. The crux of the contradiction of this regime lies in its very principle of aesthetic equality. According to this principle, the regime sweeps away the hierarchy of genres and aesthetic styles, and yet the aesthetic regime replaces the hierarchies pertaining to aesthetic treatment with the defence of a singular concept of art. Thus one of the ways Rancière characterizes modern literature is in terms of this contradiction between the equality of words and the idea of literature as a discrete field of writing. He uses the same insight regarding the frailty of the distinction between art and non-art to characterize the visual arts and cinema. In each of these contexts he also specifically makes the point that an art is first of all an "idea" of art (FF; FI). His discussion of the knots and contradictions of modern literature clearly has the status of a critical commentary on the uneven features of the aesthetic regime of the arts. For instance, "literarity" is used to mark out the paradoxical limit at which "literature" is indistinguishable from other forms of discourse. Thus conceived, the term identifies the discursive procedures that establish the scientific credentials of modern academic discourses like history, sociology and political science. In literature, as in these latter discourses, it is the excess of words over what they name and communicate that renders their meanings malleable and susceptible to being reshaped.

We can understand the force of such commentaries in relation to Rancière's view that literature, like the political practice of literary dis-incorporation, carves out new conditions for sensory perception. This position is also the source for his criticisms of the aesthetic regime of the arts: the political significance of such a reframing of perceptual conditions is lost when literature is deprived of its connections to the field of the prosaic, or non-literary. It is in this context that Rancière draws on Hegel's articulation of the features of Romantic art (PM 62, 65–7). Hegel describes many of the features of what Rancière terms the "aesthetic regime of the arts" under the category of (the dissolution of) Romantic art (Hegel 1998: 81). Art no longer has to be fine art; among the signs of this alteration in what and how a work is classified is the incorporation of the everyday into works of art. In the case of literature Hegel refers specifically to the incorporation of ugly things as topics for writing and notes as well the lack of proportion in the way such things are treated. Heinrich von Kleist is his favourite example of this phenomenon. Hegel also describes a similar disregard for "what" is an appropriate object for art and "how" it may be represented in the case of painting (Hegel 1998: 593–602).

We see that there is an intimate connection between the use of literarity as a tool of criticism in literature and politics. This intimacy follows from Rancière's original thesis regarding the establishment of equality as a structural feature of social life in modernity, which, however, emerges only with revolutions. This thesis underpins the relation between literarity in the contexts of literature and politics as well as his tendency to focus on post-revolutionary French literature, although he is also interested in its legacies in modernist writers such as Virginia Woolf. The convergences due to the way he uses the concept in these contexts show that "literarity" cannot be fully or satisfactorily defined in either context. Thus Rancière describes "literarity" both as the "contradiction" and the "essential link" between politics and literature (FW 108). To elucidate this claim, I would now like to look in more detail at Rancière's treatment of the concept of literarity in the context of his discussion of modern literature.

From aesthetics to politics: the case of modern literature

The main theme in Rancière's discussion of the paradoxes of literature is the fragility of the very concept of "literature". This fragility has to do with the difficulty in finding criteria able to adequately distinguish between the words of literature and non-literary words. Rancière explains this difficulty as the outcome of the passing of the classical and normative belles-lettres. This passing inaugurates the modern literary field. Instead of the classical rules of genre that determine appropriate subjects for poetic treatment as well as the style in which they are to be treated, modern literature is "democratic" in the sense that it speaks about prosaic matters in styles that are indifferent to what they treat; anything may be a topic for literature. This democratic attitude to topic and style mirrors the post-revolutionary shift in the hierarchical distribution of roles and capacities within the social body. Noble action belonged to the realm of the poetical, and prosaic life had its own territory. After the Revolution:

> The traditional expressive relationships between words, feeling, and positions collapsed ... There were no longer noble words and ignoble words, just as there was no longer noble subject matter and ignoble subject matter. The arrangement of words was no longer guaranteed by an ordered system of appropriateness between words and bodies. (PA 57)

Rancière's favourite example of this "democratic literarity" is the consummate French stylist Gustave Flaubert, who was in fact apolitical (PoL 21). Rancière makes frequent mention of how Flaubert's *Madame Bovary* treats the mediocre affairs of a farm girl according to Flaubert's dictum that "style is an absolute way of seeing things". Against the hierarchical rules of belles-lettres, Emma Bovary's love affairs are a worthy subject matter; but this is the case not because Flaubert's style dignifies them, as if they could be beautified and adorned in the manner of a kind of "literary" redemption of mediocrity. Instead, for Flaubert, the absolute manner of seeing things refers specifically to "the manner of enjoying sensations as pure sensations, disconnected from the sensorium of ordinary experience" (WHY 241). Flaubert's writing thus belongs to the constellation of the "aesthetic regime of the arts" on account of the way he describes what "happens" at the micro-level of sensations. Whenever something "happens" in the novel, "the real content of the event" is the sensory details, which Flaubert meticulously describes, such as the "'draught beneath the door'" that blows "'a little dust over the flagstones, and [Charles] watched it creep along'"; this, for instance, is the "content" of the event that occurs "when Charles first falls for Emma":

> When Emma falls for Rodolphe, she perceives little gleams of gold about his pupils, smells a perfume of lemon and vanilla, and looks at the long plume of dust raised by the stagecoach. And when she first falls for Leon, "weeds streamed out in the limpid water like

green wigs tossed away. Now and then some fine-legged insects alighted on the tip of a reed or crawled over a water-lily leaf. The sunshine darted its rays through the little blue bubbles on the wavelets that kept forming and breaking." This is what happens: "little blue bubbles" on wavelets in the sunshine, or swirls of dust raised by the wind. This is what the characters feel and what makes them happy: a pure flood of sensations
(WHY 242, translation from Flaubert is Rancière's own)

In this attention to micro-sensation Flaubert "follows the principle that constitutes literature as such": "there are no noble subjects or ignoble subjects ... there is no border separating poetic matters from prosaic matters, no border between what belongs to the poetical realm of noble action and what belongs to the territory of prosaic life" (WHY 237). But he also radicalizes this principle in so far as he makes it the task of "literature" to detail the register of micro-sensations. As a consequence, his novels may be characterized in terms of the schism between the failings of characters "who are still trapped in the old poetics with its combinations of actions, its characters envisioning great ends, its feelings related to the qualities of persons, its noble passions opposed to everyday experience, and so on", and the structuring perspective of the writing that places these characters in the new regime of the arts. This regime is a way of characterizing things in fundamental terms, of framing the experience of things within a new ontology of sensibility. And the principle of this ontology is that "life has no purpose. It is an eternal flood of atoms that keeps doing and undoing in new configurations" (WHY 243). Flaubert's idiosyncratic Spinozism (which attempts the dissolution of the world into atoms) is one of the possible ways of implementing the general condition of modernity, which in Rancière's account is favourably disposed to the destruction of social–political hierarchies. Thus he uses "literarity" as a new grammar for "the politics of literature", which he specifically understands as the questioning of established ways of organizing in advance the perception of the sensible world (PM 108).

We can see that Rancière uses the example of Flaubert to make a number of points about the nature of words. He wishes to emphasize, for instance, that the politics of writing has nothing to do with the political commitments of writers, but concerns the way words partition the sensible, in this case making visible and audible a new way of experiencing things. For this reason, Flaubert's aesthetic stands apart from the types of politically motivated criticisms it attracts. The negative reaction of his conservative contemporaries to his shunning of the hicrarchies of belles lettres and the censure of his indifference to politics by writers like Sartre who speak in favour of politically committed literature are then both irrelevant to Rancière's way of assessing things (PoL 11–12). What Rancière emphasizes in his treatment of Flaubert are the paradoxes that condition Flaubert's conception of writing. Rancière thus does not argue against Flaubert's aesthetic commitment to the writing of micro-sensations. Rather, he holds up to scrutiny Flaubert's suppression of the consequences of literarity, which he did so much, at the same time, to pursue as faithfully as possible.

Ultimately, this leads to the provocative thesis that Flaubert had the well-known suicide, Emma Bovary, "killed" on account of her insubordinate desire to "decorate" her life and furnishings, as if "life" were under her "aesthetic" discretion, as if she too had disposition over "style" and, most crucially, as if "style" could be realized, against the features of the new aesthetic regime, in purchased "things". Rancière phrases her punishment as a censure directed, before the fact, against what we now know as *kitsch*:

> literature means to her a nice blotting pad and an artistic writing case. Art in her life means nice curtains on her windows, paper sconces for the candles, trinkets for her watch, a pair of blue vases on the mantelpiece, an ivory work box with a silver gilt thimble, and so on.
>
> Such is the disease that the pure artist wants to display as the contrary of his art. We can give it its name: the aestheticization of everyday life. The expression does not yet exist at that time for sure. But the concern does. ... Flaubert already deals with what Adorno will spell out as the problem of kitsch. Kitsch does not mean bad art, outmoded art. It is true that the kind of art which is available to the poor people is in general the one that the aesthetes have already rejected. But the problem lies deeper. Kitsch in fact means art incorporated into anybody's life, art become part of the scenery and the furnishings of everyday life. In that respect, *Madame Bovary* is the first antikitsch manifesto. (WHY 239–40)

For Rancière, Flaubert is representative of the stylistic disposition of a whole cohort of nineteenth-century authors like Victor Hugo whose writing about "the people" coexists with the wish that they remain enclosed in their beautiful silence (NL xxx). The people who do not understand the meaning of words are characterized as being in possession of a "mute eloquence" (*ibid.*). He makes a similar point about enclosing people in silence in the case of Jules Michelet who, he writes, substitutes the prolix words of the village scholars for the "picture of a silent people" (NH 45). In each of these cases the "chattering" of the mute letter is emphasized. This chattering is a consequence of the democratic status of the written word, which emancipates meaning from the ownership of any expert class and also encourages as well their expression of the wish for silence.

Flaubert wishes to protect Art: "if the future of Art lies in the equivalence of Art and nonartistic life, and if that equivalence is available to anybody, what remains specific to Art?" (WHY 238). In other words, Flaubert aims to disentangle two equalities: the equality of Art and non-artistic life from the equality that would make this latter available to just anybody. Against Flaubert: one of the functions of the concept of "literarity" is to show that this democracy of art and non-art *is* available to just anybody and this is so on account of the orphan status, the "muteness", of words. It is worth noting the parallel with the case of Jacotot (see Chapter 2). Words can be appropriated by anyone (they do not require the authority of a mediator) and for this reason democracy is shown to be at work in education as much as it is in politics. Rancière also names "mute speech" *"trop bavarde"*, by which he means to underline the "indifferent chatter" of too many words (IE 34). This position draws on the ambiguity of Plato's position in which the book is "at once silent and too loquacious" (IS 38). In his *Phaedrus* Plato compares the "solemn silence" of writing with the mute presence of a "painting". In the same breath he objects to the way that "once it is written, every composition trundles about everywhere in the same way, in the presence both of those who know about the subject and of those who have nothing at all to do with it", and he insists that this democracy of the written word requires "its father to help it; for it is incapable of either defending or helping itself" (Plato, *Phaedrus*, 275d5–e5).

Rancière's use of the phrase *"parole muette"* emphasizes the reversibility of the position of "things" and "words" in modern literature. If the "things" that words name and poeticize are "mute", then "words" too are "silent"; that is, they always stand ready for further elaboration or adaptation, and they do so, in no small measure, on account of the fact that they are "orphans" and hence without any authorizing figure able to police the ways by which, nor by whom, they are used and understood (PM; FW). Rancière often casts the words of literature in terms of Plato's pejorative designation of "writing" as "silent", by which he means that they are silent in the face of how they are used and understood. Words do not of themselves furnish any clarifying commentary or reproach (FW 3–4; PA 15).

Rancière, furthermore, is interested in the narrative consequences of Flaubert's attempt to suppress this feature of words in the modern regime. Rancière describes how, for Flaubert, the "temptation" to put art in "real" life needs to be "singled out in one character and sentenced to death in the figure of that character, the character of the bad artist or the mistaken artist. Emma's death is a literary death" (WHY 240). Similarly, the eponymous clerks *Bouvard and Pécuchet* find themselves unable to use the words of the books of medicine, philosophy, pedagogy, agronomy, geology and so on in their lives and end up returning to their old job of copying the words in books. This is Flaubert's medicine "for the disease of literariness and its political disorder"; it quashes the aspiration for just anybody to use words in life and also dismisses its corollary, namely, that there is a continuity between the words of literature and life (PoL 22). Flaubert may quash the presumption that art could be in life (and thus open to anybody), but he writes precisely on the premise that life itself is already art. For this reason, his "treatment" of the disease of literature is also

> the self-suppression of literature. The novelist himself has nothing more to do than to copy the books that his characters are supposed to copy. In the end he has to undo his plot and blur the boundary separating the prose of "art for art's sake" from the prose of the commonplace. When "art for art's sake" wants to undo its link to the prose of democracy, it has to undo itself.
> *(Ibid.)*

In his account of political equality Rancière draws attention to the structural contradiction of modern politics: the axiom of equality is the necessary presupposition of modern politics, but this axiom is constantly suppressed by the institutional organizations of social and political life. A similar contradiction provides the context for his pointed analyses of modern literature. Flaubert, for instance, rejects the consequences of literarity, but these consequences are also the condition of possibility for literature. Moreover, one of the chief consequences of literarity is the untenability of the distinction between literature and the commonplace, so that the condition of possibility for literature is also the mark of its fragility as a practice and category.

Rancière addresses the topic of this fragility in a number of places. For our purposes what is important is the critical perspective that this point opens up on the aesthetic regime of the arts – of which Flaubert is exemplary. The case of Flaubert shows that words have a structural excess over the modes of communication that legitimate what is "proper", such as the distinction between "art" and "life" and, just as importantly, the policing of the hierarchy between who should speak and who should remain silent. In this respect, the new field of sensibility that the works of modern literature configure communicates a new distribution of the sensible. The excess of words refers in this case to the way that words exceed Flaubert's attempt to retract the features of the field he depicts.

In general, Rancière's terminology of "mute speech" designates the fundamental character of the different species of literature in the modern age of equality and democracy, from the sacralization of literature in Mallarmé to the privations of Blanchot, from the committed literature or conception of literature in Zola or Sartre to the indifference of Flaubert. Rancière wants to make these different forms and conceptions of writing intelligible aspects of the same constellation, namely, the contradictions that arise from the political project of speaking the egalitarian axiom of the modern age.

One of the key corollaries of this position is the way it opens a new perspective on the full variety of the different authors of the modern literary canon. Each writer responds in different ways to the contradictory specifications of the new regime of the art of writing that is literature. The fact that different writers respond in unique, locally specific ways to the exigencies of the literary regime shows that Rancière understands mute speech as a productive contradiction, and one, we might add, that is not confined to literature. Modern literature, it is true, inaugurates a new conception of the mute things of the world as forces able to speak. But this inauguration, in turn, installs new practices that are susceptible to analysis from the perspective of "literarity".

Literarity and the poetics of knowledge

Rancière's theses regarding literature cannot be confined to the "new regime of writing" that literature constitutes, when one of the defining characteristics of this field is that it is unable to adequately differentiate itself from the field of non-literary words, and this as a direct consequence of the "new regime" it installs. Two examples of this paradox may be given here to show how Rancière's formulation of the contradictions of literature, and especially his account of the absence of a border to separate poetic matters from prosaic matters, opens up an array of topics to the critical perspective of "literarity".

(1) His work on the "poetics" of knowledge is especially instructive regarding the scope of this perspective. As Rancière tells it, the shift

from the "representative" to the "aesthetic regime of the arts" is first and foremost a rejection of Aristotle's hierarchy between poetry and history. Aristotle famously described poetry as "more philosophical" than history because "it deals with combinations of actions, while history deals with 'life', where things just happen without necessity, one after the other. Action *versus* life: the formula tied poetical hierarchy to social and political hierarchy" (WHY 237).

Now, it is clear that the core principle of the aesthetic regime – the refusal of the distinction between noble action and prosaic life – is both the principle that constitutes literature and a rehabilitation of the vocation of modern history *vis-à-vis* the hierarchy of Aristotelian poetics. This is true in the sense that Rancière explains: modern history is the discipline that finds meaning in the prosaic. We can cite as examples of the assumption of the meaning-laden status of the ordinary the histories that are written of *mores* and everyday practices (especially in the French Annales school), as well as the attempts to chart otherwise invisible social and economic changes through the use of statistical studies able to identify and track them (NH 100–101). But Rancière also wants to draw attention to the literary protocols that shape and enable such meaning and that also credential history, under these new conditions of meaning, as a science (see Chapter 8). He pursues a poetics of knowledge through literary resources, where the suppression of the contribution of these resources is the counterpart to Flaubert's suppression of the consequences of literarity in the figure of the character of Emma Bovary. In particular, Rancière takes the example of Michelet's practice of bringing the silent, mute subjects of history to voice. Michelet is used as the representative figure of the practices of modern historiography in much the same way that Flaubert was taken to be representative of the paradigms of modern literature. In the case of Michelet, the double reference to muteness as the condition under which things are brought to speech, and to the orphan status of speech, that is, the muteness of writing in the face of how and by whom it is circulated and understood, is emphatic.

Michelet's narration of the "new subjects" of history belongs to the aesthetic regime of the arts and comports the constitutive contradictions of this regime: it attempts to speak the events, things and persons it describes and to suture thereby the gap between the past and its narration. Michelet endorses the Romantic idea of the expressivity, the plenitude of meaning that belongs to the world. He thereby commits the contradictions of "mute speech" because when he makes the past speak, he also encounters the difficulties of redeeming silent things in speech. Rancière argues that Michelet makes the silent voice of the meaning of things the voice of the figure of the conditional in order to give "a logical structure" to his images:

> The only one who speaks is *the only one who would be able to speak*. The silent voice of the conditional is that which can come back to us only through the tombstone or the cries of the rocks: a voice without paper, a meaning indelibly inscribed in things, which one may read, which one *would be able* to read endlessly in the materiality of the objects of everyday life. (NH 57)

But the narrative that wishes to "gather everything" is, in Rancière's words, a "utopia ... that does not know the emptiness of words" (SVLP 100). Further:

> Beneath his pen the historian's utopia becomes one with the end of literature. Literary excess is entirely absorbed into the ability to express a world in which there are only the living and the dead – none of those quasi beings produced by fiction – where all speech is the murmur of a well or the voice of a grave and makes manifest the configuration of a place or the state of a subject.
> (SVLP 99–100)

Like Flaubert, Michelet brings into visibility a new register of experience that an older distribution of the sensible had obscured from view (NH 45). He inaugurates a practice of history that shows us the mute subjects of history (not just women and children, but also the "silence" of the elements and quotidian things like mud) (PoL 18); but, as such, his practice does not just utilize the features of literary excess but it also disowns them in the last instance, since it undermines the capacity of the dispossessed and silent to author their own speech (NH 54).

Here again it is possible to see Rancière criticize the way that the aesthetic regime that frames the practice of modern historiography effects a dis-placement, but stops short of fully embracing the principle of "literarity" that enshrines dis-placement as a feature of words. Again, Rancière interprets this shortfall in terms of the suppression of the political implications of radical equality: historians, like the poets and writers of his analyses of modern literature, shy away from the equality that their work does so much to uncover.

This analysis of words in the new aesthetic regime, especially if we consider the insistent pattern it forms in his work, raises the question as to the status of this "principle". How is one faithful to "literarity"? What use of words or literary practice could keep in mind the structural excess Rancière finds in them? These questions bring up the topics of Rancière's style, voice and approach: is his writing "faithful" to "literarity"? In some of his other writing on the use of literary procedures to procure credence for knowledge claims (which entails in the case of Althusser's science/ideology distinction a furious denial of "literary dereliction"), it is clear that sensitivity to "literarity" is seen to entail modesty regarding the scope of the claims made for superior knowledge (FW 138). In this way the concept of "literarity" is used, among other things, to assert the need for intellectual modesty. This modesty takes the form of adhering to the guidance of hermeneutic methodological principles, such as treating each discursive object in terms of its own aesthetic qualities, and within its specific historical context, thus leaving room for new ways of reinterpreting and reusing these objects. Rancière practises such modesty in the careful way he treats each discursive case as uniquely crafted machinery, designed to deal with the potentialities and contradictions of mute speech.

(2) As a final example, we may look at Rancière's account of Gilles Deleuze's ontology. Deleuze puts in words the conception of sensibility as a pre-personal logic of sensation without direction or purpose. He thus renders into a fundamental ontology the perspective on sensation that Rancière describes as that of the "aesthetic regime of the arts". In a series of important essays on Deleuze, Rancière argues that Deleuze suppresses the discursive mode in which this ontology is presented, and that this suppression characterizes too his treatment of the literary corroboration he seeks for his work. Deleuze uses literary features like "plot" (in Kafka's novels) and "character" (in the stories of Herman Melville) to elucidate his ontology of pre-personal singularities in which these very features are seen as a false carapace over the primary field of sensation (ITDA; FW). The presence of these literary contradictions in Deleuze shows how Rancière's "literarity" may be used critically for identifying and analysing the utopian impulse that confuses what is described in words with the fundamental way things "are". The "literariness" of words means that they are expressive, but they are also mute: the words themselves do not speak, they do not bind a thing or idea to a relation of final meaning. As such, as the very condition of their functioning, words exceed Deleuze's aspiration to incorporate, to place in bodies, the ideas of his ontology. Deleuze uses Kafka's story *Metamorphosis* to defend the thesis that words encode and also transform experience; he charges that literary critics misunderstand the pragmatic efficacy of words when they describe Kafka as a "metaphorical" writer (Deleuze & Guattari 1986, 1987). In contrast, Rancière points out that Gregor

Samsor's "transformation is indeed literal, and at the same time it is not so" (FW 153). He argues that Deleuze shuts down the prospects of words redistributing meanings by virtue of his utopian view that meanings are somehow embodied in particular literary operations. As a consequence, Deleuze leaves himself open to the charge that the ontology he describes is "only" words precisely because he fails to consider the ways literary meanings may be reshaped and redirected.

In each of these cases the concept of "literarity" thus has a function of criticism: it helps to elaborate a genealogy of the contradictions of the aesthetic regime that literature inaugurates, but it does so primarily to show that literary displacement works against attempts to finalize the meanings and references of words. It remains to ask how such treatments of the topic of literarity in literature, historiography and philosophy have any necessary connection with the political question of the disruption of the "relation between an order of discourse and its social function" (DW 115).

Literarity: aesthetics and politics

At the beginning of this chapter, I suggested that it was possible to identify the main threads of the knot that Rancière's "aesthetic politics" presents to us in order to analyse the constituents and functions of "literarity" as they are treated in relation to the specific features of modern literature. Identifying these features helps to distinguish the significance of his use of "literarity" in the context of literature, from the political significance the term has in his work as the conditions under which the relations between words and bodies may be altered. In the case of literature (and its progeny) Rancière refines his account of the contradictory elements of the "aesthetic regime of the arts" to make legible the scope and efficacy of literary operations in this regime. In this context it is clear that "literarity" becomes a tool of analysis able to establish terms for the critical reflection on the use of literary–discursive protocols in literature, history and philosophy. The constituents of "literarity" may be described in terms of the contesting forces of the aesthetic regime: at once literature inhabits the landscape inherited from Romanticism in which the expressivity of things and persons is pressing for literary articulation; but at the same time this articulation, like the things that call for speech, is mute. Words are indifferent to who uses them and how they are used; crucially, they are indifferent to the ideas and things they "express". Rancière thus understands modern literature to be constituted out of a series of fundamental contradictions regarding the power and effects of words. In the face of these contradictions, Rancière states that "literarity" is more than the condition of literature; it is also the "contradiction" and "essential link between politics and literature" (FW 108). The conception of literature "as a historical mode of visibility of writing, a specific link between a system of meaning of words and a system of visibility of things" (PoL 12) is the core of his conception of literature as political. Literature earns its link to politics on account of its participation in the ontological partition of the perceptible. The way words are used is effective in partitioning space and dividing and apportioning capacities. "Literarity" thus nominates a new poetics of knowledge. It describes the mechanisms of a new aesthetic of perception and proposes too a new thesis regarding the politics of literature.

Literarity, however, is not just about the political background of aesthetics (in the axiom of equality), the politics of poetics (as this relates to knowledge protocols) and the politics of literature (in the ontological partition of the perceptible). Literarity crucially points to the literary condition of modern politics. Rancière had first articulated this literary condition in *La Mésentente*. It is only with the full explication of the literary paradigm in the contexts of aesthetics, poetics and literature that this condition of modern politics becomes fully intelligible.

ELEVEN

Image, montage
Toni Ross

Jacques Rancière's writings on aesthetics and politics are currently provoking much interest in international art-world circles and art-historical scholarship. A large part of the appeal of his work may be attributed to his novel articulation of links between art and democratic politics, which, in turn, revises established narratives of modernism and postmodernism. Rancière's summation of his contribution to art theory speaks of "reframing the temporal categories by means of which modern and contemporary artistic practices are generally grasped" (PtA 19). The specific orientation of this reframing emerges as a concern to "construct a paradigm of 'historicity' equally opposed to the symmetrical one-way narratives of progress or decadence" (PtA 21). As such claims suggest, the deconstructive approach adopted by Rancière seeks to modify essentialist or teleological premises regarding modern art's identity or destiny. Moreover, he combines attentiveness to the philosophical implications of specific art practices with a sense of the historical contingency of what have been accepted as the central premises of artistic modernity. Considering the abject condition of aesthetic theory in art history and criticism of recent decades, Rancière's weaving together of post-Kantian continental aesthetics with analyses of historical developments in modern art offers those working in the visual arts much food for thought.

The following explication of Rancièrean concepts of visual art examines how they overlap with and differ from conventional theories and historical accounts of artistic modernity. The chapter will also address what might be considered Rancière's most notable and controversial contribution to art discourse. I refer to his central argument that ideas

151

of aesthetic autonomy and art's involvement in socio-political life need to be thought as co-implicated rather than distinct inclinations of the modern art tradition.

Rancière's engagement with the visual arts, encompassing painting, photography, design and the moving image, has emerged relatively recently. Many of the concepts he brings to these fields are gathered together in a small volume of essays titled *The Future of the Image* (2007), first published as *Le Destin des images* in 2003. But the ideas essayed in this text are strongly inflected by earlier publications, which bring Rancière's specific conception of democratic politics to studies of nineteenth-century literature. More recently, however, Rancière identifies a parallel between the visual arts and literature of modernity. He contends that both "share a kind of common political programming, if we understand *politics* in a broad sense as the reframing of the sensory community" (AaI 180). Such comments indicate the necessity of grasping some of the basics of Rancière's socially disruptive conception of politics, and his understanding of aesthetics, so as to illuminate the ideas he brings to the visual arts.

Democratic politics and modern aesthetics

In the first instance, Rancière conceives of aesthetics beyond the realm of art as the multiple ways in which any social order establishes, manages, privileges or marginalizes different modes of perception. As Gabriel Rockhill translates Rancière's terminology, this "distribution of the sensible" refers to communal forms of naturalized perception based on what is allowed to be "visible or audible, as well as what can be said, made or done" within a particular social order (PA 85). Given that Rancière casts social formations as incorrigibly oligarchic, he conceptualizes both politics and artistic operations as capable of reconfiguring hegemonic perceptions of reality. In other words, art and politics share a potential to dispute any sense that existing meanings of sociocultural life are unassailable or inevitable.

At the heart of Rancière's characterization of democratic politics lies the supposition of the *equality* of all. This premise is situated as a guiding thread of practices that struggle against institutionalized patterns of domination in all their forms. However, in keeping with the anti-essentialist tenor of Rancièrean theory, the egalitarian maxim is neither construed as a pre-established ontological principle, nor as a fully perfectible goal of political praxis. Rather, in order to generate politics, the axiom of equality is said to require an ongoing process of testing and verification via localized acts of dissent. Rancière reiterates this idea in his critical analysis of a *hatred of democracy* that has crystallized in sectors of French intellectual life in recent decades, where he writes, democracy "is not based on any nature of things nor guaranteed by any institutional form. It is not borne along by any historical necessity and does not bear any. It is only entrusted to the constancy of its specific acts" (HD 92). The contingent and unpredictable gestures of politics are typically directed towards prevailing ways in which a society defines and manages the capabilities and functions of its population. As Jean-Philippe Deranty has proposed, Rancière's conception of democratic politics may be equated with a kind of "ontological disorder", where fixed hierarchies and categories of identity are both disputed and transformed (Deranty 2007: 245–6).

The attention Rancière devotes to disassembling hierarchical systems and fixed ontological premises recalls aspects of Derridean deconstruction. However, Rancière's writings tend to focus on the specifics of art works and the historical valences of different aesthetic philosophies to a greater degree than Jacques Derrida's reflections on art and aesthetics. Another distinctive feature of Rancière's approach to aesthetics is signalled by his willingness to investigate and intervene in debates about contemporary art.

Rancière's extensive writings on art from the nineteenth century to the present sustain that alliance between democracy and the making contentious of prevailing realities that he proposes. Importantly, however, his discussion of artistic instances typically references different "regimes" or paradigms of art, which provide collective conditions of possibility for individual practices. Contrary to great men (or great women) approaches to art history, Rancière insists that a single artist's inventiveness is not on its own sufficient "to open the doors of artistic visibility ..." (FI 75). Rather, artistic cases are rendered salient and intelligible within specific "regimes of art", or different systems of making, conceptualizing and assessing artistic activity. Therefore the second meaning of the aesthetic Rancière deploys includes both art practices and their framing theories of production and reception.

Much of this aspect of Rancièrean aesthetics has entailed reinterpreting given narratives of artistic modernity by tracing the historical emergence of what he names the "aesthetic regime of art". Like many commentators before him, Rancière locates the philosophical seeds of modern art in writings on aesthetics by Kant and Hegel, as well as those of the poets and philosophers of German Romanticism. In fact, he insists that we continue today to "engage with art according to the modes of attention forged in the Age of Romanticism" (Guénoun *et al*.

2000: 10). At the same time, his writings link artistic movements such as Romanticism and Realism with political upheavals and sociological shifts that in the nineteenth century challenged the oligarchic worldview of the European *ancien régimes*.

One of the key revisions of conceptions of modernism ventured in Rancière's writings deposes the technical features of different media as constitutive of the identity of art works. An oft-cited example of this kind of thinking is Clement Greenberg's thesis that each sphere of fine art self-referentially explores the technical properties unique to its medium. Although Greenbergian doctrine may have retreated since the 1980s, the reification of the medium's technical properties remains as strong as ever in sectors of contemporary art discourse, whether focused on established art forms or various "new media". An example of this continuity may be found in current theories of photography.

The first chapter of *The Future of the Image* addresses the widespread influence of Roland Barthes' argument in *Camera Lucida* that bestows ontological priority on the indexical nature of the photographic medium: its mechanical registration of a past reality untouched by artistic manipulation (FI 10). According to Barthes's well-known formula, the *punctum* effect of the photograph arises from details that are unintended or uncontrolled by the photographer. Photography may thus be distinguished from painting or drawing in that its apparatus visualizes the world automatically, rather than being wholly formed by the interventions of the photographer/artist. As Rancière paraphrases it, the aesthetic impact of the *punctum* effect for Barthes stems from its assertion of "the wordless, senseless materiality of the visible" that eludes or resists discursive domination (FI 9). In *Camera Lucida* the cognitive alterity of the *punctum* is counterposed with the informational axis, or *studium* of photographs. The *studium* designates historical, social or cultural meanings extracted via semiotic analysis of photographs. As Rancière implies, the privilege Barthes assigns to the photographic *punctum* suggests an exaggerated form of realism (defined by Rancière as *hyper-resemblance*), where the essence of the medium derives from its purported capacity to directly register the wordless, senseless being of things prior to representation. Rancière's deconstructive redirection of this argument detaches Barthes' ontology of photography from any unique technical features of the medium, linking it instead to the aesthetic regime of art, which has informed art practice and theory for at least two centuries. Specifically, he argues that the polarities of *punctum* and *studium* express a "double poetics" of the "*aesthetic image*" as it came to be conceived and manifested within the aesthetic regime (FI 11).

The aesthetic image

The important concept of the "*aesthetic* image" (or artistic image) in Rancière's writings is not confined to the visual arts, but bears on the productions of modern art more broadly. Like other concepts of art that Rancière revises or invents (*phrase-image*, *montage*, *collage*), "aesthetic image" comprises a portmanteau category that combines contradictory principles. In *The Future of the Image*, the twofold potential of the "*aesthetic* image" is articulated as an interplay between "the image as raw, material presence and the image as discourse encoding a history", or as "the unfolding of inscriptions carried by bodies and the interruptive function of their naked, non-signifying presence" (FI 11, 14).

Added to this dialectical phrasing of the "aesthetic image" is a broader conception of artistic operations in keeping with Rancière's account of the anarchic, routine interrupting gestures of politics. Here artistic images are described as creating "discrepancies" within a given order of expectation or reality (FI 7). This emphasis on the disruptive operations of modern art upon naturalized convention has been a staple of art-historical discourse and art institutions for some time, so much so that it has become an avant-gardist cliché. Although it should be acknowledged that Rancière has recently cautioned against a tendency in the contemporary art world to pre-emptively assume the efficacy of art's transformative powers (AaI 181). But, perhaps more intriguing from the perspective of art history is the contradictory logic he imputes to the new way of thinking and making art introduced by the aesthetic regime. Early signs of this historical shift emerge in Romantic and Realist art.

Rancière traces how both art movements set about dismantling the normalized standards of a previously hegemonic artistic paradigm that he names the "representative" or "poetic" regime. This disordering activity is directed towards certain features of the "representative" regime that codified art according to a conception of *mimesis* conveyed by Aristotelian poetics. While roughly synonymous with what Michel Foucault called the European Classical Age, the representative regime of art does not function as a simple epochal category in Rancière's discourse. Rather, his studies suggest that while different paradigms of Western art may predominate during particular historical periods, they may also recur historically or operate in combination within individual practices. Having said this, Rancière's reading of Romanticism and Realism as inaugurating moments of modern art traces three primary ways in which the aesthetic regime registers a waning of influence of the "representative" paradigm.

The key changes in art practice that register a collapse of the representative regime's norms of artistic excellence may be summarized as follows. First, Romanticism and Realism dismantle the hierarchical system of artistic subject matter, styles and genres consolidated in the representative system. Secondly, art of the aesthetic regime, according to Rancière, breaches ontological divisions between fine and applied art, or between art and non-art categories that subtend the representative framework. The third shift instituted by the aesthetic regime repeals the privilege assigned to the written word and art's story-telling function in Aristotelian poetics.

Regarding the third displacement of the representative regime's framing of art, Rancière emphasizes that Aristotelian mimesis refers to the representation of actions, with actions being conceived as logical sequences of words and deeds normally undertaken by human agents, and governed by the ends at which they aim (PtA 14). Consequently, for painting to attain fine-art status in the representative regime, "it first had to demonstrate its capacity for poetry – its ability to tell stories, to represent speaking, acting bodies" (MSDC 75). In this context, the imagistic or visually descriptive capacities of painting are subordinated to the directives of established "poetic" narratives. Rancière reiterates this point in a number of his analyses of the visual arts of modernity, where the visual image, without being entirely cut off from textual operations, no longer occupies a servile relation to narrative intelligibility (FI 39). The relatively uncontroversial art-historical point being made here is that painting of the aesthetic regime no longer acts simply as a vehicle for giving visual form to mythological, religious or historical stories.

Echoing the findings of literary and art-historical studies, Rancière casts Romanticism and Realism as democratizing movements that rejected the hierarchies of the representative order by making visible themes and experiences previously unseen, unspoken or marginalized within the higher echelons of art. The hierarchical logic of the representative regime is expressed by history painting owning a higher status that genre painting, or tragedy being placed above comedy, or the deeds of kings or religious notables above those of commoners, as the proper subject matter of art. On the basis of such gradations of subject matter and genre, Rancière draws an analogy between the representative regime and an oligarchic vision of social arrangements, a vision that naturalizes inequalities between social groupings, as well as divisions between different human capacities and functions (PA 22).

In a number of publications Rancière examines how the novelistic realism of writers such as Gustave Flaubert, Honoré de Balzac and

Victor Hugo attends to a world of insignificant actors and everyday objects, which acquire a new level of social visibility and symbolic worth (PA 36). In the nineteenth century, works by Gustave Courbet, Edouard Manet, Adolph von Menzel and many other realist painters likewise register a new alertness to the anonymous poetry of undramatic, trivial and commonplace aspects of modern life. Rancière therefore reminds us that far from being an invention of Pop Art or postmodernism, the retraction of strict boundaries between high and low subject matter has been on art's agenda at least since Romanticism. As Chapter 9 has shown, Rancière's political analysis of emergent tendencies of nineteenth-century art recalls Hegel's observation in his *Lectures on Fine Art* that "the more art becomes secular, the more it makes itself at home in the finite things of the world, is satisfied with them, and grants them complete validity" (Hegel 1998: 294).

The "everything speaks" principle that Rancière attributes to the aesthetic regime revokes the hierarchies of the representative system by presuming a capacity for expression inscribed in the world, in all of its manifestations and dimensions. More specifically, according to Rancière, the artist, somewhat like the new figure of the nineteenth-century social scientist, becomes an interpreter of signs impressed "on the very body of mute objects", signs that express the "ciphered meaning of an age, a history or a society" (PtA 17). This idea, which Rancière casts as one side of the twofold aspect of the aesthetic image, recurs in Barthes' conception of the photographic *studium*.

However, the other incline of the aesthetic regime identified by Rancière disrupts the idea that art channels social and historical meanings inscribed in the material world in all of its manifestations. Instead, the second arm of the poetics of the aesthetic image attests to the suspension or disempowerment of symbolizing procedures. Barthes' *punctum* concept may be considered in this light, since it brackets the communicative function of photography to impose the senseless presence of things that find themselves imprinted by the photographic image. But, rather than attributing this vision of the real as non-signifying presence (or chaos) to any technical specifics of photography, Rancière refers to the disordering of established artistic standards perpetrated by the aesthetic regime. Here, he again invokes Hegel when he asserts that the aesthetic regime is caught up in "a new idea of thought itself: an idea of the power of thought outside itself, a power of thought in its opposite" (PtA 17). Hegel, of course, conceived of consciousness as an encounter with and recognition of otherness, and Rancière implies that aesthetic modernity assimilates this dialectical conception of thought.

One indication of the disorder of modern aesthetics traced by Rancière is an increased propensity for art to stage promiscuous exchanges between images, words, discourses and disciplines. Since in the aesthetic regime any and everything may lend itself to artistic creation, strict boundaries between art and non-categories become shifting and unstable. This development is amply demonstrated by many twentieth-century practices, where "art is turned to kitsch; or, on the contrary, disused commodities enter the realm of art" (MSDC 105). Moreover, the intermingling of different categories that Rancière views as a hallmark of the aesthetic regime, undoes any stable referential transmission or clear ontological separation between empirical reality and artistic expression. Thus "all the common terms of measurement that opinions and histories lived on have been abolished in favour of a great chaotic juxtaposition, a great indifferent melange of significations and materialities" (MSDC 43). Rancière describes the collapse of the representative regime as ushering in "the great parataxis" of modern aesthetics, where: "It is the common factor of dis-measure or chaos that now gives art its power" (MSDC 45).

In philosophical, specifically Hegelian, or perhaps Nietzschean terms, the dialectic that Rancière assigns to the aesthetic regime co-implicates the rationalizing schemes of thought with that which exceeds, resists or disrupts such procedures. His quarrel with the version of this dialectic expressed in *Camera Lucida*, arises from Barthes' privileging of one side of the equation, which, for Rancière, consolidates an entrenched conception of modernism that proponents of postmodernism also accept without question. This is the idea that modernism by definition means the progressive achievement of each art's autonomy. Just as Barthes seeks to isolate the quintessence of the photographic medium, the familiar idea of modernist autonomy endorses ontological distinctions between different arts so that each may express the fundamentals of their given medium. As Rancière argues, this one-sided thinking of modernism operates in poststructuralist aesthetic theories that locate the truth of modern literature in its staging of the "intransitivity" of language, where linguistic forms are freed of any communicative purpose. In the case of modernist painting, autonomy traditionally designates the historical advance of abstraction, and the self-enclosure of painting from the impingements of society at large. In *The Flesh of Words*, Rancière characterizes such accounts of artistic modernity as reducing each art to "the exercise of its own autonomous power" (FW 108).

Rancière has traced the continuity of such thinking in the quarantining of artistic images from those circulated by the Society of the Spectacle that recurs in discourses of late modern art. From the

Situationists through to contemporary art prognostics of the dissent-deadening effects of mass media on passive audiences, art is defined by its isolation from the products of capitalist spectacle and commodity culture (PL 71–80). In a catalogue essay on the mixed-media works of Alfredo Jaar, Rancière wonders about the continuing critical purchase of art incessantly negating the pernicious effects of a world awash with images spewed out by the global capitalist machine (TI 71–80). Against this rhetoric of catastrophe, Rancière maintains an optimistic attitude towards art's creative potentials. He argues that in the context of globalization, governmental and capitalist interests devote substantial energy to managing how media images are staged and circulated. Citing Jaar's work as an exemplary response to this situation, Rancière suggests that rather than restating the sordid truth behind capitalist spectacle, contemporary political art might be better engaged in combining materials from art and media culture in order to create alternative configurations of the visible to those that currently predominate.

The medium as a "surface of conversion"

As previously indicated, Rancière tends to focus on the various ways in which modern art activates slippages between different ontological categories, and normally separated levels of experience. In the chapter of *The Future of the Image* entitled "Painting in the Text", for example, he disputes the consensus that modernist painting be defined by its expulsion of words or representation through the purely painterly assertion of its own nature. The arguments proffered in this text engage in critical dialogue, not only with Greenberg, and French formalist Maurice Denis, but also the particular view of (modern) art's mission proposed by Gilles Deleuze.

Deleuze's thinking of modernist painting is put forward in his book on artist Francis Bacon. Here he proposes that by projecting the material tangibility of its basic means (colour and line), pictorial modernism offers immediate access to a sensory stratum of experience normally repressed or disavowed by rationalizing procedures. By evacuating representational forms, modernist painting registers the existence of an orderless, non-synthesizable world of sensational life that reason both arises from, and regularly denies. Rancière shifts this argument by insisting again that the logic of the aesthetic regime need not be characterized by a strict separation between the mute pathos of material life and art's signifying operations. He also makes the rather obvious, but easily overlooked, point that what modernist painting made newly visible has from the beginning required the mediation of words, just as Deleuze's privileging of painterly presence depends on his discursive eloquence.

"Painting in the Text" exhibits Rancière's own articulacy in a concrete analysis of the "plaiting" together of words and visual forms, presence and representation that, for him, characterizes the bivalent logic of the aesthetic image (FI 79). Here he cites a fragment of nineteenth-century art criticism by brothers Edmond and Jules Goncourt. Published in 1864, this text interprets a still-life painting by the eighteenth-century artist Jean Siméon Chardin. Rancière focuses in particular on the "matterism" of the Goncourts' metaphorically rich chronicle of Chardin's painting of dessert fruits, which at times transmutes the precise depiction of natural objects into an assertion of the tactile palpability of pigment and traces of the painter's brush. The Goncourts write, for example: "In one corner there is apparently nothing more than a mud-coloured texture, the marks of a dry brush, then, suddenly a walnut appears curling up in its shell, showing its sinews, revealing itself with all the details of its form and colour" (FI 80).

This passage reminds us that art history, since the nineteenth century, has viewed realist painting as adopting techniques of intrusive *impasto* that intensify the physical qualities of painted pigment, thereby obscuring or muting the representational efficacy of the picture. Pictorial realism has thus been channelled into that narrative of modern painting, continued by Deleuze, that locates painting's essence in an assertion of the painted matter's independence of representational operations. As Rancière observes, the Goncourts' reading of Chardin not only prefigures the future of Impressionism and the action painting heuristic of Abstract Expression, but also recent art-theory appropriations of Georges Bataille's concept of the *informe* and Deleuzean aesthetics. However, contrary to the advocacy of a perceptual immediacy specific to modernist painting, Rancière stresses the active role played by the Goncourts' discourse in enhancing features of Chardin's art previously unnoticed by eyes not guided to see them. In this example of creative art criticism: "Linguistic tropes change the status of the pictorial elements. They transform representations of fruits into tropes of matter" (FI 81). Rancière therefore concludes that the recognition of novelty in art practice is necessarily related to shifts in the discourses of art criticism and art history. In this respect, the visibility of a modern preoccupation with the materiality of paint arises from *particular linkages* between visual forms and discursive operations, rather than their isolation from each other. Rancière contends that instead of separating linguistic and visual forms, the aesthetic regime introduces a different "regime of imageness" to that of the representative system.

The "regime of imageness" concept refers to particular ways in which words and images interact within a particular regime of art (FI 11). By undoing the hierarchical relation between visual and narrative forms sustained by the representative regime, modern aesthetics instigates situations where:

> Words no longer prescribe, as story or doctrine, what images should be. They make themselves images so as to shift the figures of the painting, to construct this surface of conversion, this surface of forms-signs which is the real medium of painting – a medium that is not identified with the propriety of any support or any material. (FI 87)

To describe the medium of modern painting as a surface of transformation, or departure from self-same identity, gives equal credence to different tendencies of modern painting. It may encompass the "purity" of some forms of abstraction, as well as the mixing of visual, linguistic and object forms in Cubist collage, or Conceptual Art's interjection of bureaucratic language formats into the field of visual art (FI 87–8). Rancière's conception of the medium of painting as a surface of conversion, where visual and discursive forms, different media and disciplines exchange places, overlaps with aspects of his political theory. It recalls his conception of egalitarian politics as disruptive of stratified partitions of identity, of social roles and capacities calculated and managed according to socially authorized badges of identity.

"The Surface of Design"

Another salient example of Rancière's revision of official accounts of modern art history occurs in the chapter of *The Future of the Image* titled "The Surface of Design". This essay questions a longstanding and ongoing polarity in art history between two divergent political gestures of modern art. The first involves the assertion of aesthetic autonomy, and a view of art as disconnected from normalized modes of perception. This roughly Kantian idea of aesthetic experience as resistant to instrumental assimilation has traditionally located art's critical powers in its autarkical isolation from everyday patterns of experience. In the opposed camp are the projects of various avant-gardes, which turned artistic practice towards the creation of new symbols and designs of collective life. Here art loses any separate status on account of its incorporation into the aims of social or political transformation. As Rancière notes, this ambition co-ordinates not only the programmes of Russian Constructivism and the Bauhaus, but also earlier applied arts movements such as the German Werkbund, founded in 1907, and the British Arts and Crafts Movement of the mid nineteenth century.

The two cultural practices discussed in "The Surface of Design", those of symbolist poet Stéphane Mallarmé and modernist designer Peter Behrens, are normally placed on opposite sides of modern cultural tradition. In literary history, the art of Mallarmé is often treated as the apotheosis of modernist aestheticism. While Behrens, as a founding member of the Werkbund and a design consultant for the German electrical company AEG, is commonly situated within a lineage of modernist design movements that sought to transform the spaces and objects of collective life. However, Rancière's unorthodox reading of these practices proposes that Mallarmé and Behrens have something in common. They share a "spiritual" mission to create artistic forms or "types" that "outline the image of a certain physical community", that "define a new texture of communal existence" (FI 95, 97).

This argument involves positing a link between Mallarmé's poetic experiments and Behrens's application of reduced geometric forms to designs for household goods, advertising formats and buildings he created for AEG. At first glance, Mallarmé's art would seem to be more difficult to characterize in these terms. However, on Rancière's reading, this exemplar of symbolic obscurity activates exchanges between different artistic fields, as well as activities extracted from popular culture and everyday life, an obvious example being the poet's famous late production, *Un coup de dés*. Here abstract forms and signs of poetic language, graphic design, the spatial choreographies of dance, and the unpredictable resting places of dice share the planar surface of the page. By enacting that cancellation of hierarchical division that Rancière associates with the aesthetic regime, Mallarmé's art is recast as inventing a mode of writing that seeks to express symbolically, formally and materially an egalitarian vision of social arrangements. In Rancière's words, Mallarmé sought to compose the "shape of a world without hierarchy where functions slide into one another" (FI 107).

Peter Behrens, by Rancière's account, also seeks to develop a vocabulary of simplified design forms that symbolize an egalitarian vision of common life. Like other theorists and practitioners of modernist design who formed the Werkbund, Behrens considered an overabundance of decorative featurism then being applied to household commodities to be the aesthetic counterpart of social stratification, and a hangover from aristocratic culture (Schwartz 1996). In this respect, Behrens, according to Rancière:

thinks of himself as an artist, inasmuch as he attempts to create a culture of everyday life in keeping with the progress of industrial production and artistic design, rather than the routines of commerce and petty bourgeois consumption. His [design] types are symbols of common life. (AR 140)

Rancière's discussion of Behrens and Mallarmé together suggests that ideas of aesthetic autonomy and of artistic practice symbolizing new forms of life are not as antagonistic as normally assumed. Rather, they comprise two sides of the aesthetic regime that emerge historically in tandem and tension with each other. The "surface of design" incorporates symbolic expressions of art's independence from predetermined expectations, as well as instrumental applications of cultural practice.

Phrase-image (or sentence-image) and montage

While Rancière undoubtedly sustains an avant-gardist view of art as inventing new forms of collective life, he does not subscribe to any idea of art becoming indistinguishable from the social field, as popular accounts of the art–life nexus might suppose. His reticence towards this perspective may be clarified by examining two other concepts he formulates: *phrase-image* (sentence-image) and montage.

In *The Future of the Image*, the "sentence-image" and its analogous term, "montage", are understood as responses to the disorder unleashed by the aesthetic regime. They denominate devices of artistic reasoning that acknowledge the heterogeneity of art's resources, while drawing art back from collapse into sheer nonsense or full submission to communal consensus (FI 46). As this precarious engagement with contending forces suggests, the sentence-image does not entail a simple blending of images and linguistic sequences. Rather, Rancière speaks of the sentence-image as combining visual and textual elements differently to their interaction in the representative system, where the image occupies the secondary role of enhancing narrative plausibility. The sentence-image overturns this hierarchical relation in two ways. First, while textual forms still maintain rational linkages between different elements, they simultaneously assert their material palpability, a process that impedes conceptual transparency, disturbing the smooth sequencing of cause and effect. Secondly, the visual image assumes a newly active power, that of disrupting rather than fleshing out textual directives (FI 46).

Put simply, Rancière's concepts of sentence-image and montage refer to practices, ranging across literature, theatre, film and the visual arts, that link heterogeneous elements in ways that maintain some tension between and within the combinatory components. In this respect, the sentence-image tempers the "chaotic force of the great parataxis" by bringing together the incompatibles of "phrasal continuity" and the "imaging power of rupture" (*ibid*.). Instead of blending harmoniously together, the disordered materials that "hang together" in the sentence-image manufacture effects of disturbance, while maintaining some semblance of meaningful connectivity or "measure" between the different elements. Rancière analyses montage operations in numerous examples of modern art. However, before turning to these cases, it may be useful to consider how the sentence-image concept departs from another influential post-structuralist theory of modern art.

The dialectical articulation of the sentence-image as an encounter between sense-making and the disruption of homogeneous meaning may be contrasted with Jean Francois Lyotard's concept of the *affect-phrase*, which ties modern art to an aesthetic of the sublime. A number of Rancière's publications set up a critical dialogue with the modernist sublime formulated by Lyotard, where the *affect-phrase* concept signals a materialist radicalization of Immanuel Kant's account of sublime experience. For Kant, sublime feeling has little to do with art, since it ultimately authorizes the active power of reason and moral judgement over the phenomenal world. Lyotard, similarly to Deleuze, reverses this conclusion, accenting the mind's indebtedness to a sensuous, corporeal or unconscious dimension of experience that is ungraspable by concepts, measures or forms (Lyotard 1991: 142–3). Lyotard therefore characterizes the specific task of modern art as bearing witness to the mind's powerlessness when confronted with the unrepresentable: as staging material events that resist conceptual or representational capture. For Lyotard, the *affect-phrases* of sublime art suspend exchanges and linkages between elements that normally sustain discursive procedures, or indeed the qualitatively indifferent economic transactions of capitalist culture.

In a number of contexts, Rancière has identified the theological implications of Lyotard's aesthetic theory. In his view, Lyotard, responding to various ethical catastrophes of the twentieth century, subtracts all emancipatory aspiration from the avant-garde tradition. Instead, art's task is to betoken what Rancière phrases as humanity's "inescapable enslavement to the Other", whether this figure of transcendental determination recalls "the Thing" of Freudian psychoanalysis or the Jewish god that proscribes graven images (SLS 15). Rancière clearly considers Lyotard's assertion of an unbridgeable gap between the sensorial signs of art and the ideational universe to be in keeping with those theorizations that make aesthetic autonomy definitive of artistic modernity. Alternatively, his concepts of the sentence-image and montage propose a paradoxical linking of art's separation from and engagement with other spheres of experience.

Dialectical and symbolic montage

The particular conceptualization of the modernist technique of montage proposed by Rancière nominates two primary ways in which art creates some sense of intelligibility ("common measure") out of the disorder inaugurated by the aesthetic regime. These two modalities of montage are named *dialectical* and *symbolic* (FI 56–7).

Dialectical montage operates in art forms that choreograph *clashes* between incompatible elements in order to set forth conflicting visions of reality – in particular, to present alternative realities to those purveyed by hegemonic constructions of communal life. In a recent essay titled "Contemporary Art and the Politics of Aesthetics", Rancière writes that with dialectical montage: "The clash of heterogeneous elements is supposed to provoke a break in perception, to disclose some secret connection of things hidden behind everyday reality" (CAPA 41). Historical examples of dialectical montage include bizarre encounters between objects (umbrella, sewing machine, ironing board) proposed by Surrealist method, which upgraded the unconscious of dreams and desire as the repressed counterparts of bourgeois morality and social convention.

Rancière also associates dialectical montage with twentieth-century activist photomontage that includes the work of John Heartfield and Martha Rosler. According to his reading, each of these artists appropriates mass media and advertising materials to expose a social reality riven by political conflict rather than buttressed by consensual homogeneity. Rancière mentions Rosler's "Bringing the War Home" series in particular, which was produced in the USA during the latter years of the Vietnam War. Here Rosler montages advertising imagery, resonant with ideas of American affluence and domestic complacency, with press images of the brutal conflict in Vietnam (FI 56).

More recent examples of art contoured by dialectical montage cited by Rancière include the mixed-media installations produced by Hans Haacke over many decades. These works typically bring into view a second order of economic rapaciousness and hidden violence covered over by idealized or therapeutic constructs of art's cultural value. In all of these cases, according to Rancière, the mixing of heterogeneous elements produces a discernible political message that denounces the verities of a given socio-political order, while creating "a vision of history as a locus of conflict" (FI 60).

The other category of montage (symbolic) denominated by Rancière also gathers together disparate elements from art and non-art fields, but it produces a different perception of history. When discussing symbolist montage, Rancière regularly invokes the late productions of Jean-Luc Godard, in particular, the filmmaker's eight-part video work *Histoire(s) du cinéma* (1988–98). In the last episode of this monumental project a title insert provides Godard's definition of montage: "To bring together things which have never been brought together and don't seem disposed to being so". In *Histoire(s)* Godard puts this definition into practice to a hyperbolic degree, by creating an elaborate paratactic fabric out of extant cultural materials from multiple historical sources. These materials include film images, sounds, titles or dialogues, news photographs, the spoken and written words of philosophers and art historians, passages from novels and poems, fragments of paintings, songs and advertising signs. Rancière argues that while Godard's cinema has traditionally been, and may continue to be, viewed through the prism of dialectical montage, symbolic montage provides the keynote of the *Histoire(s)* project (FI 62). Contrary to the dissensual logic of dialectical montage, symbolic montage connects disparate elements to create affinities and analogical connections between divergent categories. As stated in *The Future of the Image*:

> Between elements that are foreign to one another it [symbolic montage] works to establish a familiarity, an occasional analogy, attesting to a more fundamental relationship of co-belonging, a shared world where heterogeneous elements are caught up in the same essential fabric, and are therefore always open to being assembled in accordance with the fraternity of a new metaphor.
>
> (FI 57)

Rancière then proceeds to articulate a certain historical continuity between the fraternal logic of symbolic montage operative in Godard's late work, and the aesthetic category of *mystery* formulated by Mallarmé. Mallarméan mystery, however, has little to do with an idea of art manufacturing effects of mystical inscrutability. Rather this term relates to the previously mentioned socio-political reading of Mallarmé's art developed by Rancière. Mystery here refers to the staging of convergences between heteroclite levels of experience that gesture to the possibility of a shared human world. While Rancière analyses a number of segments of *Histoire(s) du cinema* to convince us that Godard's late works tend towards symbolic montage, the aforementioned idea of *mystery* is expressed especially succinctly in a line from Godard's film *Nouvelle vague* (1990): "The past and the present that they felt above them were waves of one and the same ocean." Thus, while dialectical montage constructs a vision of community as susceptible to dissent and contention, symbolic montage, according to Rancière, creates a "redemptive" image of communal connectedness (FI 63).

The "neo-humanist tendency of contemporary art"

Although Rancière refuses to allocate any singular direction to modern art, his recent publications do trace shifts of emphasis in contemporary practice, as well as various curatorial tendencies. Extending his analysis of symbolic montage in Godard's late work, Rancière perceives an increasing departure from dialectical montage in favour of art works that exhibit "a new sensitivity to the signs and traces that testify to a common history and a common world" (FI 66–7).

The widely circulated theory of "relational aesthetics" developed by art curator Nicolas Bourriaud to describe 1990s art provides one indication of the alteration Rancière refers to. Bourriaud declares that relational art is inclined by a democratic ethos since it stages real-time events that foster social interaction and dialogue. In this respect, relational art creates situations where temporary communities might be formed. He also surmises that artists of today are less likely to adopt an antagonistic perspective towards the status quo, since, while the "imaginary of modernism was based on conflict, the imaginary of our day and age is concerned with negotiations, bonds, and co-existences" (Bourriaud 2002: 31). Such claims echo the fraternal logic of symbolic montage outlined by Rancière, who in a number of publications cites Bourriaud's account of relational art restitching the broken threads of community (MSDC 67). Rancière, however, has expressed certain reservations about a "shift from dialectics to symbolism" in contemporary art. He suggests that this trend arguably participates in a contraction of spaces of political dispute that he associates with consensus-based models of politics that currently overdetermine thinking on democracy (CAPA 48).

In *The Future of the Image* and elsewhere, Rancière implies that art that continues the political legacy of the aesthetic regime navigates the logics of *both* dialectical and symbolic montage. On this basis, art drawn to dialectical montage falls short if it posits a deeper truth behind present realities without sustaining a sense of the social realm being open to contested meanings. Alternatively, art of symbolic montage loses political energy if it privileges some foundation of human community insulated from political dissent. In a recent essay, Rancière proposes that critical art needs to "keep something of the tension that pushes aesthetic experience toward the reconfiguration of collective life and something of the tension that withdraws the power of aesthetic sensoriality from other spheres of experience" (CAPA 41). This twofold formulation suggests that Rancière's approach to modern art seeks to plot a path between Kantian and Hegelian aesthetic philosophies. One of the lessons of his analyses of art practice is that these philosophies continue to impinge on how we perceive and respond to art of modern times.

TWELVE

The film fable

Hassan Melehy

With the publication of *Film Fables* in 2001 (English translation 2006), Rancière added cinema to the broad array of subjects to which he had devoted major works. Before that, by writing extensively on film in articles and shorter sections of books, he had already shown that cinema was an important component in his thinking on aesthetics. Film turns out for Rancière to present a special case, highlighting a problem that stems from a basic contradiction of art in the modern era that he develops in many of his writings. This problem has to do with the relationship between art and reality during what he terms "the aesthetic age", the period following the creation of the branch of philosophy called aesthetics in the late eighteenth and early nineteenth centuries, among whose principal theorists are F. W. J. Schelling and G. W. F. Hegel. During this period, art claims an autonomy by freeing itself from its representational or mimetic function. According to Rancière, this development in the theory and practice of art lead them to run up against impasses. As a result of these impasses, cinema especially among the arts is involved in what Rancière terms a "thwarted fable", an idea that I shall examine further in the first section below.

Closely related to this problem, since the relationship of art to reality has to do with the role of art in the social world, is the inevitable confrontation between aesthetics and politics, which Rancière sees played out very strongly in cinema. For Rancière, cinema is both an artistic and a popular medium, and it must be viewed in its constant contact with everyday life. In his account, some of the impasses of art come to the fore in the transition from cinema to video and digital media. In order to illustrate Rancière's understanding of how the relationship between cinema and television affects the contradictions of art, in the second section of this chapter I shall examine the chapter from *Film Fables* on Fritz Lang. At the same time that such developments occur in art, they occur in the philosophy of art, which according to Rancière must look at cinema in its continually unfolding manifestations in order to work through the contradictions of the aesthetic age. In the third section below, I shall present Rancière's reading of the philosopher who in his view confronts these contradictions while remaining caught in or thwarted by them, Gilles Deleuze. In the fourth section, I shall consider Rancière's interpretation of the filmmaker whom he regards as having understood most effectively the aesthetic powers and pitfalls of cinema, Jean-Luc Godard.

The thwarted fable

In the prologue to *Film Fables*, Rancière situates the cinema with respect to the major conflict of the aesthetic age, that between the conception of art as, on the one hand, representational and, on the other hand, expressive. A principal characteristic of cinema, its unprecedented capacity to record reality, enables it to capture and present myriad details of things in the world; cinema thus offers images that evade subordination to the causal linkages of narrative and thereby become expressive. Rancière opens *Film Fables* with a commentary on Jean Epstein's 1921 essay entitled *Bonjour cinéma*: cinema "records things as the human eye cannot see them, as they come into being, in a state of waves and vibrations, before they can be qualified as intelligible objects, people, or events due to their descriptive or narrative properties" (FF 2). That is, cinema presents the world such that it may continually exceed the determinations of narrative, cognition and ideology.

Such expressivity is the defining characteristic of what Rancière terms "cinematographic modernity", the two principal thinkers of which, later in the book, he identifies as André Bazin and Gilles Deleuze (FF 107). For Bazin, who wrote mainly in the 1950s as editor of *Cahiers du cinéma*, cinema brings out aspects of reality more challenging and revealing to the intellect than any offered by painting, photography or unaided vision. According to Bazin, this realism is actualized when cinema moves away from the narratively ordering techniques of montage and relies mainly on long shots in deep focus; such filmmaking invites the spectator to a much greater independence of thought than he or she can have in being required to follow the imposing hand of the director (Bazin 1967: 35–6).

Rancière's starting point in *Film Fables* is the modernist account of cinema that Epstein's *Bonjour cinéma* exemplifies for him; according to this account, the seventh art presents the greatest challenge to one of the oldest conventions of Western poetics, that of the "Aristotelian hierarchy that privileged *muthos* – the coherence of plot – and devalued *opsis* – the spectacle's sensitive effect" (FF 2). (Rancière is here referring to chapter 6 of Aristotle's *Poetics*.) Rancière explains that it is the Aristotelian definition of *muthos* (translated into Latin as *fabula*) or fable that interests him: this definition is at the heart of the "representative regime", which Rancière elaborates in his writings on aesthetics and which has been described at length in previous chapters of this book. For Rancière, the fable is the main dimension of artistic representation: it is "the arrangement of necessary and verisimilar actions that lead the characters from fortune to misfortune or vice versa, through the careful construction of the intrigue [*noeud*]" (FF 1). He begins his book with Epstein in order to examine the latter's theses on the essential opposition between cinema and storytelling or the fable. Rancière remarks on Epstein's modernism, "Cinema seems to accomplish naturally the writing of *opsis* that reverses Aristotle's privileging of *muthos*" (*ibid.*).

However, Rancière immediately announces that, although such expressivity is indeed a property of cinema, the claim to reverse the Aristotelian hierarchy is untenable because it simply sets aside the intimate connections between cinema and the representative regime that has dominated Western art. Epstein enthusiastically takes up modernism's challenge to representation and overlooks the contradictions and unresolved problems that Rancière finds lingering in it. Epstein presents cinema as the culmination of the art of the aesthetic age, as the fulfilment of the modernist dream of a total aestheticization or pure expressivity of art. Rancière sees a decisive movement in this direction in Gustave Flaubert's technique of saturating novelistic narrative with descriptive detail; Flaubert depicts the pathos of static moments in the life of Emma Bovary, a practice that foregrounds the modernism of literature and painting. But Epstein, according to Rancière, obscures a good part of the aesthetic functioning of cinema by omitting any consideration of the links between representation and the modernist project of a full artistic apprehension of the unordered details of the world (FF 9).

In treating cinema as a development of the aesthetic age, Rancière underscores his understanding that the technology of cinema was a response to developments in the theory and practice of art, not the other way around (Guénoun 2000: 252–3). Here Rancière takes strong issue with a longstanding interpretation of cinema as developing, unlike the other arts, from a technological innovation, an understanding exemplified by the opening premise of Erwin Panofsky's famous essay on motion-picture style in 1934 (Panofsky 1995: 93). Because it entails a mechanics, which can in principle operate independently of the artist's hand, cinema may have appeared to furnish an undirected or passive vision of reality. But it is precisely this technology that, as a consequence of developments in aesthetics, allows cinema to offer itself spontaneously as passive – in contrast to the other plastic arts, which their practitioners must push to be such. Authorial agency then harnesses the passivity of cinema in procedures that, even when they de-emphasize montage, necessitate wilful decisions about camera placement and exposure. In its subordination to the guiding intelligence of an artist, cinematic expressivity is once again rendered representational, through a disposition of its material according to an authorial logic.

In his extended commentary on Epstein in *Film Fables*, Rancière situates him with respect to the triumph of modernist art in the twentieth century and also cinema's place among the arts. The result is that Epstein's reasoning is caught in shortcomings. To sum these up, Rancière offers "the very simple reason that cinema, being by nature what the arts of the aesthetic age strive to be, invariably reverts their movement" (FF 1). That is, because cinema is a development of the aesthetic age, it reveals the limitations of this age while fulfilling its dream. Hence cinema presents its central problem, to which Rancière devotes the analyses of his book – that of the "thwarted fable".

Rancière concludes this part of his argument by characterizing the thwarted fable as stemming directly from the basic contradiction of the aesthetic age, played out in the novelistic narratives that succeeded Flaubert and accompanying phenomena in the other plastic arts: "In the age of Joyce and Virginia Woolf, of Malevich and Schönberg, cinema arrives as if expressly designed to thwart a simple teleology of artistic modernity, to counter art's aesthetic autonomy with its old submission to the representative regime" (FF 10). That is, by the very fact that it is the fulfilment of the modernist dream, functioning as a medium capable of rendering panoramas made up of small and variegated details of reality, cinema turns against modern art in so far as it is a technology in the hands of an authorial agency that brings it to serve the logic of the fable – and hence, ultimately, commercial interests. However, the fable of cinema, by its nature involving the unruly expressivity of the image, also thwarts the fable as a pure disposition of narrative events. Rancière explores those moments in cinema when the representational and the expresive fables of cinema run into each other.

Fritz Lang, between mimesis and expressivity

Engaging in close analyses of a number of directors' work in *Film Fables*, Rancière extensively develops the notion of the thwarted fable. He finds in the films of Fritz Lang a measured negotiation of the relationship between the two contradictory fables of cinema, manifested as the tension between screenplay and *mise en scène*. But it is also at the juxtaposition of these two aesthetic functions in Lang's movies that Rancière sees a staging of the relationship between art and social and political reality. In the progression between Lang's *M* (1931) and the film that Rancière terms "in some ways, [its] American remake" (FF 48), *While the City Sleeps* (1956), Rancière explains, Lang shows an increased pessimism with regard to the powers of cinema to offer social mimesis, or an image of a society by which its members may apprehend and understand it. *While the City Sleeps* has often been understood as an expression of the director's disillusionment with American democracy; he manifests his pessimism, in Rancière's account, in the role he accords to the televisual image as the rising form of social mimesis. For Rancière, the most important question in this transition from the 1930s to the 1950s and from Europe to America is the fate of democracy as social representation under the consolidating reign of the televisual image. This image, bearing its fable of complete social mimesis, thwarts the poetics of expressivity that would effect a breach in the overextended narrative of the determination of social roles and destinies.

Rancière's reading of these two movies provides an excellent example of his concrete analysis of cinema from the perspective of the thwarted fable. Both movies tell the story of a serial killer and the mechanisms by which he is brought to justice. In this chapter of *Film Fables*, Rancière juxtaposes two sequences in which, in each film, the murderer is in effect apprehended. In *While the City Sleeps*, the striking image is that of journalist Ed Mobley appearing on television to trick the murderer into revealing himself by indicating that his identity is already known. The film stages the ubiquity of the televisual image, able to reach the murderer because it reaches all citizens; citizenship has become equivalent to spectatorship. Rancière notes an inversion of the common conception of the televisual image as a picture transmitted from a distance to spectators that the broadcasting agency cannot see or know. Television instead targets the spectator, putting an image of him or her on screen; the person represented on television then becomes, in fact, the one watching. In this technological set-up, the spectator sees him- or herself designated from a distance. According to a second meaning of the French word *télévisé* ("televised"), then, this person is the *télé-visé*, the one aimed at or seen from a distance (FF 46). This polysemy suggests the power of television to dominate social mimesis. In detailing a composite description in which the murderer, Robert Manners (John Barrymore Jr), recognizes himself, Mobley is able to present an image of omniscience:

> That requires an apparatus that institutes a face to face with someone who is closer to you than any policeman can ever be, precisely because he is farthest away, because he only sees you from far away; a face to face with someone who is instantly on intimate terms with you, who speaks to you while speaking to everyone else, and to you just as to anyone else. (FF 47)

In this face to face enabled by the mimetic powers of television, Manners has no choice but to feel enveloped by the approaching discovery of his identity. Rancière describes John Barrymore's face in this moment of identification, the very limited expressiveness of which tells the fable of the encroachment of television into all realms of social mimesis. Rancière contrasts Barrymore's facial expressions, which indicate stereotypical reactions of, first, satisfaction at his accomplishments and, secondly, panic at being discovered, with the much greater range of Peter Lorre's performance in *M*, twenty-five years earlier, at moments when his character comes under pressure of accusation. Lorre's expressiveness contributes to the expressivity of the sequence, which thwarts the fable of the apprehension of the criminal in an inflexible social role.

Rancière comments on the sequence in Lang's *M* (1931) that cuts from the police, who find damning evidence in the apartment of the murderer, to the latter standing with a little girl whom the narrative marks as probably his next victim; both of them are happy, and Lorre's character appears to have forgotten his narrative role. Rancière characterizes this interaction as a "moment of grace" (FF 49), an interval during which the screenplay pauses and "the *mise-en-scène* grants him his chance at being human" (*ibid.*). That is, against the film's narrative fable in which Lorre is a mass murderer who will be hunted down, the *mise en scène* offers a contrary fable of humanity in the moment in which the shot shows Lorre and the little girl, smiling, looking through the window of a toy store. Rancière explains this moment as marking the conflict between a representational or mimetic poetics and an expressive one:

> Aristotle's requirement that the narrative must lead the criminal to the point where he'll be caught and unmasked runs into a new, and conflicting, requirement: the *aesthetic* requirement for suspended

shots, for a counter-logic that at every turn interrupts the progression of the plot and the revelation of the secret. In these moments, we experience the power of empty time ... (FF 49–50)

This "empty time", Rancière explains, is not simply a pause in the narrative; it is a basic change in the nature of the incident, such that a transformation in character occurs, allowing the murderer to live a humanity that is not subordinate to the persecution to which the narrative will bring him. "The new action, the aesthetic plot, breaks with the old narrative plot by its treatment of time" (FF 50).

M stages the key problem of aesthetics in modernity, which is one of producing moments in a work of art that exceed the mimetic determinations of narrative time. Rancière here returns to his analyses of the close relationship between cinematic and literary expressivity: "Literature came upon this pure power of the sensible between Flaubert and Virginia Woolf, and Jean Epstein, along with a handful of others, dreamed of making this power the very fabric of the language of images" (ibid.). But Lang is striking in that he never wholly accepted a modernist aesthetics. Rancière points out that the director never liked the label of expressionist that film history placed on him – that is, that he was quite aware of the problem of the thwarted fable (FF 59). In maintaining a foothold in mimesis, in understanding cinema as a necessarily representational art even as it embodies an immense expressive power, Lang negotiated the tension between two contrary artistic fables that the aesthetic age tried to surmount by suppressing one of them:

> True, the allures of this language never fully seduced Fritz Lang, nor did he ever embrace the notion that cinema was the new art of *aisthesis* that would supplant the old arts of *mimesis*. Lang understood very early on that cinema was an art insofar as it was the combination of two logics: the logic of the narrative structuring the episodes and the logic of the image that interrupts and regenerates the narrative. (FF 50)

Closely related to Lang's understanding of the necessary interdependence of these two logics in the conception of the relationship between cinema and reality is the relationship between art and politics. For Rancière, one of the great values of Lang's work is its examination of the socially representative function of the cinematic image that stems from its mimetic function: "Lang also noticed early on that the combined logic of cinematographic *mimesis* bore close ties to a *social* logic of *mimesis*, that it developed as much in reaction to the social logic as under its shelter" (*ibid.*). The outcome is the televisual mimesis that Lang stages in *While the City Sleeps*, which Rancière underscores through another comparison between the two movies. In *M*, the murderer faces a trial put on as theatre by the criminal element of the city, in which prostitutes and thieves assume the roles of grieving mothers and purposeful attorneys. Rancière characterizes this scene as one of broad social mimesis, one that dramatizes the interchangeability of roles that is basic to a democratic society, in which representation of particular interests occurs in a public forum. Not only can a prostitute imitate a mother's cry to the point of effectively representing it, but the serial murderer can in turn mimic this cry in order to signal his own distress. That is, the mimesis at the heart of democratic social functioning can give place to a narrative that defies the strict determination of social roles; this mimesis can bring into public vision alternative accounts of a person's place, such as in the criminal's happiness at the very moment he is discovered (FF 51–2).

To mark changes in the process of bringing a malleability of social roles into the realm of knowledge, Rancière considers Mobley, a quarter-century later, in a televisual image able to control social functions through a newly far-reaching knowledge.

> This is, essentially, the knowledge of the actor, and it is as an actor that the journalist combines in himself all these roles. Mobley confiscates the power of *mimesis* and its performance and identifies them with the position of the one who knows. He chains this power down to the place filled by his image, the place of the one who sees and knows. (FF 53)

The fable told by the *mise en scène* of *While the City Sleeps*, then, is that of "democracy's identification with the tele-visual" (FF 57), of the variety of social roles becoming, through the extended mimesis that television offers, subordinate to the authoritarian agency of the talking head. It is through his continued adherence to mimesis in the aesthetics of cinema, in his sceptical disposition toward the pure expressivity of cinematographic modernity, that Lang is able to show the shortcomings of the emerging form of televisual mimesis through a fable that counters it.

Deleuze and cinematographic modernity

By enlisting the work of Lang and a number of other classical filmmakers, such as Sergei Eisenstein, F. W. Murnau, Anthony Mann, Nicholas

Ray and Roberto Rossellini, Rancière builds his account of cinematographic modernity in *Film Fables*, an important thrust of which is his critique of Deleuze. Rancière presents Deleuze as the major philosopher of cinematographic modernity, who offered a "solid foundation" to Bazin's often unfinished, intuitive formulations (FF 107). At the outset of his chapter on Deleuze, Rancière restates the challenge to representation that the expressive image posed: cinematographic modernity "confronted the classical cinema of the link between images for the purposes of narrative continuity and meaning with an autonomous power of the image whose two defining characteristics are its autonomous temporality and the void that separates it from other images" (*ibid.*).

In this phrasing, Rancière alludes to the main concepts that Deleuze introduces in his two monumental books on cinema, *Cinema 1: The Movement-Image* (1983; English translation 1986) and *Cinema 2: The Time-Image* (1985; English translation 1989). Over the course of these two volumes Deleuze analyses a vast number of films from the entire history of cinema: he devises a complex system of image classification that boils down to two major categories, corresponding to the subtitles of the books. The movement-image is the image that captures movement and operates in it, taking shape in sequences produced by narratively inflected montage. Over the course of film history, in about the middle of the twentieth century, this mimetic image gives way to the cinematographic manifestation of modernism, the image that captures time and is autonomous with respect to the temporal progression of narrative, not subordinate to its requirements. The time-image, then, is more closely linked with reality, and its expressivity is a furthering of the expressivity of things themselves: in its most accomplished form (for Deleuze, the cinema of Godard) it thus presents an "outside" to human thought, radically challenging any perceptual or conceptual unity that human beings might experience with the world (Deleuze 1989: 173–88). However, Deleuze is not hard and fast in this taxonomy: Rancière points out that his predecessor analyses the work of Robert Bresson in both books, treating the latter's films as offering examples first of the movement-image and then of the time-image. Deleuze does the same with the work of a number of other directors. This dual status of many cinematographic images is a principal basis on which Rancière, always interested in the interaction of these two versons of the poetics of the image, is able to launch his critique of Deleuze.

The difference between the movement-image and the time-image, Rancière explains, might then be understood as two points of view on images: the movement-image would stress the relations among images, their sense as produced in the motion from one to the next and in a series; the time-image would involve their autonomous expressive power, even if they are still situated by montage. "Tenable as this perspective is," writes Rancière after citing a number of directors whose work is analysable according to both perspectives, "Deleuze won't allow it" (FF 114). Deleuze continues to insist on their separation, which turns on a historical breach that occurs in the aftermath of the Second World War. Like many philosophers and cultural critics, Deleuze sees a crisis of artistic and media representation in its failure to convey the horrors of the war. The immensity of these horrors produced unfamiliar types of spaces that eluded the narrative of the progress of history, and hence also eluded representation; a new kind of image was necessary for an apprehension of these spaces, one that was not subordinate to the conventions of representation for which the war presented unfathomable events. Deleuze sees cinema as broadly responding with its valorization of the time-image (Deleuze 1989: 11–12).

In the work of Alfred Hitchcock, Deleuze finds a concentration of the crisis of the cinematographic image. Hitchcock's cinema sums up prior technical and expressive developments of the art; relentlessly dramatic, his movies are heavily dependent on montage. Yet the effectiveness of the montage stems from the quality of the "opsigns" (optical signs – the word is conveniently close to *opsis*) or purely expressive images, such as the white intensity of a glass of milk in *Suspicion* and that of snow in *Spellbound* (FF 114). That is, the expressivity of Hitchcock's images wrests them out of the movement in which his exacting montage places them. Rancière explores Deleuze's interest in two Hitchcock films involving immobilization, both with James Stewart: *Rear Window* (1954), in which Stewart is a photographer (a maker of images) handicapped by a broken leg, and *Vertigo* (1958), in which the actor plays a detective (or discerning observer, another producer of images) immobilized by acrophobia. Rancière characterizes Deleuze's analysis as an allegory of the paralysis of the movement-image such that it may be transformed into the time-image. But Rancière raises the problem of Deleuze's reliance on the narrative dimension of these films in order to make a case for the expressivity of their images, in a philosophical treatment that overtly opposes the narrative emphasis in cinema. Rancière wonders if Deleuze's allegory is necessary: the paralysis, after all, does not move beyond its fictional status as an element of an otherwise undisturbed narrative – it does not extend to the Hitchcockian images themselves, and the latter continue to function as both time-images and movement-images (FF 115–16).

Here Rancière makes his most scathing statement about Deleuze's cinematographic fable: "The movement-image is 'in crisis' because the thinker needs it to be in crisis" (FF 116). This is the case because Deleuze's attempt at transforming the movement-image into the time-image is a story or fable of the redemption of the image, of the restoration of its function as an expression of things themselves, away from the subordination of the image to the cinematographic fable or *muthos*. Deleuze's own cinematographic fable, Rancière remarks, is itself a thwarted fable: in order to accomplish its redemption of images, it must tear them out of their material disposition in montage, a gesture of philosophical subordination. "The gesture of restitution is always also a new gesture of capture" (*ibid.*). Rancière thus discovers that Deleuze himself is effecting the paralysis he slyly attributes to Hitchcock's "manipulative thought" (*ibid.*) – that Deleuze rather than Hitchcock is responsible for the manipulation.

Godard's film fables

Through this treatment of Deleuze, Rancière arrives at what he sees as the most accomplished set of cinematographic fables, Godard's *Histoire(s) du cinéma*, an eight-part television programme the director made between 1988 and 1998. In much of his work on aesthetics and politics, Rancière continually returns to *Histoire(s) du cinéma*. In the title, Godard makes the pun usually rendered in English as "(hi)story," taking advantage of the fact that the French word *histoire* betrays the rootedness in storytelling of the practice of history. Godard further emphasizes the intermingling of history and story by suggesting, through the use of parentheses in his spelling, that each may spill over into plurality. In the 1994 book that Rancière devoted to historiography, *The Names of History*, he mentions this hackneyed but telling pun in order to signal just this close connection between the writing and even the occurrence of historical events and the narrative organization of their telling (NH 3–4). In other words, in that book he also examines the narrative ordering of events, or their placement in a *muthos* or fable.

In the case of *The Names of History*, the valorization of the story and stories of history contributes to a retelling of history such that a greater democratization might be possible, for example in the works of nineteenth-century French historian Jules Michelet, who shifted the subject of history from royalty to the people (NH 42–60). In similar fashion, Godard tells one or several *histoire(s)* or story(ies) of cinema in order to rewrite the history and histories of cinema, with precisely the aim of pointing out the failure of cinema to apprehend history. Godard accomplishes this rewriting by emphasizing the expressive power of images initially placed in narrative montage; like Deleuze, Godard is very interested in Hitchcock. As Rancière describes Godard's project in *The Future of the Image*, "To Alfred Hitchcock's obsolete stories [Godard's words] oppose the pure pictorial presence represented by the bottles of Pommard in *Notorious*, the windmill's sails in *Foreign Correspondent*, the bag in *Marnie*, or the glass of milk in *Suspicion*" (FI 30).

In *Film Fables* Rancière focuses more pointedly on the relationship of Godard's project to history: "[T]he history of cinema is that of a missed date with the history of its century" (FF 171). The expressive power of images, wrested in Godard's presentation from the narrativity of montage, enables an apprehension of the complex realities of history, which elude classical film narrative. Godard's prime example, similar to Deleuze's complaint, is the failure of cinema to represent the death camps between 1939 and 1945, other than in a few very notable exceptions such as Ernst Lubitsch's *To Be or Not to Be* (1942). In this final chapter of *Film Fables*, Rancière is able to further explore many of the issues he raises in *The Names of History* on the apprehension of history in words and images. (In "L'Inoubliable," his essay in *Arrêt sur histoire*, Rancière more explicitly takes up the capacity of cinema to apprehend history.)

Just as Rancière sees cinema as a result of the development of art in the aesthetic age, Godard is interested in pointing out that the images of cinema form a series with the images of prior epochs in the history of art, that a rigorous understanding of aesthetics demands a view of art in which cinema is part of that history. Segments of *Histoire(s) du cinéma* are devoted to demonstrating the affinity between a certain cinematographic image and in particular a painting with religious power, such as in the superimposition of Elizabeth Taylor in George Stevens's *A Place in the Sun* over Giotto's painting of the resurrection of Christ (FF 184). Godard's aim is to show that cinema has largely failed to recognize the power of its own image, "its inheritance from the pictorial tradition", and that it has done so by subordinating its images to its stories, "heirs of the literary tradition of plot and characters" (FF 171). In what qualifies as a commonplace in his comments on cinema, Godard continually faults the majority of filmmakers for not recognizing the difference between an image and a text. Rancière assesses the story of cinema that Godard tells as follows:

> The thesis thus counterposes two types of "(hi)stories": the stories the film industry illustrated with its images with an eye to cashing in on the collective imaginary, and the virtual history told by

these same images. The style of montage Godard develops for *Histoire(s) du cinéma* is designed to show the history announced by a century of films, whose power slipped through the fingers of their filmmakers, who subjected the "life" of images to the immanent "death" of the text. (*Ibid.*)

Godard goes about this restitution of the redemptive capacity of the cinematographic image – here its power to make contact with historical reality and be effective in it – by a practical version of the reading Deleuze effects on Hitchcock, a montage of many different images that wrests them from their narrative imprisonment. Rancière considers a part of Godard's justification for doing so, which is that despite the density of Hitchcock's suspenseful narratives, such images as the illuminated glass of milk in *Suspicion* (in which Hitchcock put a light bulb in order to shoot Cary Grant carrying it to Joan Fontaine) make a far more powerful impression on viewers than the narrative motivations for their placement in Hitchcock's movies. "Hitchcock's cinema, Godard is saying, is made of images whose power is indifferent to the stories into which they've been arranged" (FF 172). But Rancière raises an obvious objection to Godard's observations, which is that the images derive their power precisely from their narrative placement – from the suspense they carry in the movement of Hitchcock's stories, which every viewer recognizes (*ibid.*). What Godard does with them, then, far from simply freeing them from narrative determination in order to show the power of their involvement with reality, is to situate them according to the fable of the necessity of recognizing the redemptive power of the cinematographic image.

But Rancière is not saying that, through montage and voice-over narration, Godard is telling a merely fictional or imaginative fable that gives to the images something they do not already have. Hitchcock's images, and those of many other directors whose work Godard shows in *Histoire(s) du cinéma*, do indeed have the relationship with things in the world that Godard claims for them; it is Godard's particular situating of them that shows it. Borrowing a text from Elie Faure on Rembrandt and the "new painting", through a montage that involves both sound and image tracks, Godard underscores how cinema records the small details of everyday life that bring to history the pathos and meaning of its events. Rancière reprises here some of his observations from *The Names of History* on nineteenth-century historiography as a democratization of history in its attention to "the essential gestures and emotions of everyday life that succeed the pomp that normally surrounded exalted subject matter and memorable exploits" (FF 176–7).

181

Just as Rembrandt was viewed retrospectively in the nineteenth century as having made available to vision a reorientation of history, Rancière understands in Godard's resituating of Elie Faure's observations on Rembrandt a furthering in cinema of the same movement of the democratization of art.

In assessing the effectiveness of *Histoire(s) du cinéma*, Rancière signals that Godard's dazzling montage of short clips from thousands of films is possible only through video technology. One of the fables that Godard's project tells, then, is that of the progress of the cinematographic image through the video image; Godard uses the latter to advance a redemption of real things in the artistic image. Here Rancière's treatment of the video image contrasts wth his characterization of its function in the work of Fritz Lang, in that it may contribute to the extension and complication of cinematographic vision. Rancière mentions that Godard thus overturns reigning dogma concerning the video image as the play of the simulacrum and the complete loss of any connection with the real (as the work of Jean Baudrillard has it) (FF 185). Rancière sees Godard as furthering the major problems of the aesthetic age involving the autonomy of the work of art with respect to its representational function, the creation of a purely expressive form that was the wish of Romantic aesthetics. In its valorization of the redemptive capacity of the image, in its placement of the image in contact with historical reality, Godard's cinema provides Rancière with an episode in his own fable, that of the efforts of art to engage the details, feelings and systems of everyday life, which amounts to art's democratization.

Afterword

Jean-Philippe Deranty

Read in order, the different chapters of this book retrace the intellectual journey accomplished by Jacques Rancière, from the early affirmation of his commitment to radical equality, to the application of this fundamental "axiom" in many areas of the social sciences (the history and sociology of the labour movement, historiography, education, politics), culminating in the seminal books of the last decade (*Disagreement, Film Fables, The Future of the Image*). As we look back on the rich and complex work this journey in radical equality has produced, five important threads become visible, the texture of which gives this work its amazing consistency. These are Rancière's distinctive conceptualization of equality and freedom, his humanistic concern, his hermeneutic approach and his materialism. Identifying these threads helps us to better understand where the originality of Rancière's thought lies, and the reasons that explain why his key concepts and arguments have become attractive to many theorists and practitioners.

Obviously, the major thread running through Rancière's writings is the principle of *equality*. With Badiou, Rancière calls this an "axiom", to indicate the fact that equality between individuals must be postulated because it can never be definitively proven. Indeed, many factual aspects of modern societies seem to run counter to this axiom. However, once postulated, the principle transforms the way in which individuals, society, politics and even the arts are seen. For Rancière a true theory of emancipation not only takes political emancipation as its object of study but aims to participate practically in emancipation. Such a theory must rely on this axiom of equality. Otherwise, it denies in its theoretical apparatus, in its assumptions and conclusions, the practical goals it sets out to support.

The emphasis on equality could seem trivial. The principle has been identified for a very long time as an achievement of modernity; it is one of the fundamental principles underpinning national and international constitutional and legal documents in modernity. As such, the principle has been taken up as a key assumption and commented upon by innumerable social and political thinkers, from the early nineteenth century onwards. The originality of Rancière, as the book has shown, lies in the scope of the principle's application. Equality for him is not just a normative principle in law and politics, or a moral obligation. It is an overarching principle that elicits not just moral rules but leads to radically altered visions of entire fields: the social, the political, the historical, the literary, the aesthetic and so on. It is fair to say that equality in Rancière has not just a normative but also an ontological reach. Apart from Alain Badiou, no one in contemporary philosophy has propounded such an extensive theory of equality. As a result, Rancière has become an author of choice for all those, in social and political theory, who want to hold on to the idea of equality against all the methodologies, concepts and arguments that tend to limit its reach.

The second thread in Rancière's work, closely linked to his commitment to radical equality, is his unwavering defence of *freedom*, and in particular, the *freedom of action*. His fundamental assumption, in all the debates in which he has taken part, is that people are always more free than the social scientists and external observers give them credit for. People should always be assumed to be capable of thinking and acting. We should avoid descriptions of the social realm and politics, analyses of domination and oppression, that lead to the conclusion that those suffering from them are fated to be crushed by them and are forced to accept them. Put negatively: the structures of inequality can always be denounced and struggled against. In positive terms: the unexpected can always occur. The task of theory for Rancière is to transform categories of thought and language so that we can be receptive to, and participate in, the emergence of new configurations, whether in social and political relations, in educational organizations or in artistic practices.

Given his commitment to equality and affirmation of the possibility and creativity of individual and social action, we must conclude that, in the end, Rancière's thinking is deeply *humanistic*. This is a surprising conclusion to reach given the strong anti-humanistic tone of postwar French philosophy. What complicates the matter is that, undeniably, Rancière's thinking and writing share many of the key moves and assumptions of that tradition. How credible then is the claim that his philosophy, in the end, is humanistic? The claim is not credible on a traditional conception of humanism, based on the assumption of essential traits of human nature. But this is not the only way to articulate a humanist concern. Rancière's humanism is a paradoxical one, based on the positing of an axiom and enquiring into its effects in different fields, not on a general theory of human nature. Despite all the stylistic and conceptual overlaps with the other thinkers of his generation, Rancière is unique among them for his insistence on the irreducible freedom and capacity for action of individuals and groups. We might say that the paradoxical result of his embrace of the radical egalitarian motto, following the break of 1968, is a mediated return to a form of existentialist freedom.

Readers can easily recognize in Rancière's writings echoes of the key concepts and methods of postwar French philosophy. His historical approach to social and political phenomena bears strong resemblance to Foucauldian genealogy. His insistence on the productivity of contradictions inherent in historical paradigms looks like a materialist version of deconstruction. The notion of political subjectivation underpinning his theory of democracy leans heavily on Badiou's logic. His other central political concept, "disagreement", sounds quite similar to Lyotard's "*différend*". Many other examples could be cited. Despite all the undeniable family resemblances, however, the humanistic and praxeological dimensions in Rancière's work make it unique in postwar continental philosophy. Indeed, these dimensions are precisely the ones Rancière himself has emphasized in developing his critical responses to the main authors of that tradition.

The fourth main thread in Rancière's work is also connected with the focus on the creativity of action. This thread relates to the importance of the *historical perspective*. In every one of the areas to which Rancière has contributed, his key arguments and concepts have been gleaned from an approach to the problems at hand in terms of key semantic and material shifts. But Rancière's historicism is highly idiosyncratic. The comparison with Foucault has paradigmatic value in that it is representative of his relationship of simultaneous sympathy and critical distance with the main thinkers of his generation. Rancière's historical method aims to undercut any form of essentialism in the approach to social and political phenomena. In this respect, it is close in spirit to Foucault's genealogy. But Rancière's historical reconstructions are also antithetical to it in other respects. Instead of attempting to unveil the epistemic categories through which specific historical worlds construct reality, Rancière's histories are reconstructions of concrete practices (in politics, at work, in schools, in the arts) from within.

The productive contradictions of the movements he studies (of the nineteenth-century Saint-Simonian utopians, of twentieth-century trade unionists, of modernist writers and painters, to name just a few examples) are not observed from an external position, but emerge from the logic of practice itself. This is a form of hermeneutics. It lets discourses and actions speak for themselves. This means first of all that the voices of the subjects studied are not covered by that of the theorist, beginning very simply by quoting at length the words and acts of those one studies, and making sure one does not squash them under the weight of theoretical references and abstract language. And secondly, letting discourse and action speak directly means that their inherent logic and contradictions are not teased out from an external position, but out of their own unfolding. One of Rancière's favoured modes of enunciation is free indirect style, that is, a presentation of thoughts and actions that is in the third person but formulated from the perspective of the agents themselves.

This method is unique in contemporary philosophy and the social sciences. It gives the Rancièrean texts their unmistakable tone, which an increasing number of readers find productive and attractive. In all the areas in which Rancière has written, this method has produced original results and allowed him to develop productive critical stances towards established paradigms. In general terms, it has focused the interest on the agency of the actors, and undercut the disempowering effect of grand narratives. In the history of the labour movement, Rancière's historical hermeneutic has uncovered the richness, complexity and contradictions of working-class experiences and expressions. This explains why he was taken up with great interest by those in the 1970s who were attempting to develop new forms of materialist critique outside the orthodoxy of the time. In political philosophy, Rancière's hermeneutic stance leads to a robust defence of democracy, one however that is not grounded in unverifiable theoretical claims (extrapolations from psychoanalysis or set theory) or derived from some abstract normative principles, but arises from the trust in the efficacy and intelligence of the democratic struggles themselves. The conceptual path Rancière's method thus prepares towards a recovery of democratic agency, one however that does not overlook the pitfalls and difficulties of real democratic movements, explains why so many political theorists today refer positively to him. Rancière's method seems particularly well placed to account for the irreducible necessity yet tremendous difficulty of holding firm to the democratic ideal in contemporary challenges. Finally, Rancière's hermeneutic stance leads to an approach to artistic practices and art works that does not pre-empt their meanings by framing them in large historical or metaphysical narratives. Rather, it is open to their unique modes of structuration, as well as their creative contradictions. This explains why so many in the art world today, in particular art practitioners, are drawn to Rancière's difficult aesthetic texts. In them, they find a sophisticated account of the historical conditions under which arts are performed, but one that puts the focus squarely on the artist's, and the audiences', practical engagements.

One last strand remains to be mentioned, one that the secondary literature has not fully explored so far, but which undeniably runs throughout Rancière's work, namely Rancière's *materialism*. As in the case of his historicism and egalitarianism, Rancière's materialism is highly idiosyncratic and paradoxical. It is starkly different from classical historical materialism, or contemporary philosophical enquiries exploring the relationships between the mental and the material. Rancière's materialism relates to his continued insistence on the material embeddedness of discursive practices. Rancière does not propound a simple, one-dimensional dependence of human productions on material conditions. Rather, his historical enquiries, in politics and in aesthetics, often highlight how ideas about the social (a given "*partage du sensible*", see Chapter 6), or "ideas of art" (Chapter 9), are materialized in ideas about social spaces, the media in which expressions are manifested, and so on. These materializations in turn affect the discursive and the conceptual. Discursive, conceptual realities, by informing the views of material realities, determine the types and forms of practice, and thus indirectly shape the material, while the material, being the only plane in which practical meanings can be realized, determines thoughts and discourses. It is as though Rancière's radical extension of the axiom of equality reached all the way into the material. This extension becomes quite explicit in his aesthetics, since its central assumption is the fluidity of the boundaries separating different expressive media (in particular the visual and the intelligible, image and text), and more generally the discursive and the material. This materialism is paradoxical in that it is not premised upon a single, firmly defended metaphysical option, but emerges rather from a mode of thinking and writing that is sensitive to the constant exchanges and blurrings between mental and material realities.

As in the case of the other strands, this conceptual direction affects the very style of Rancière's writing. One of its most striking features is its high level of sophistication, making his texts difficult to read, even as he avoids academic references and abstract concepts. His analyses display a dialectical subtlety equal to any philosophical classic, yet all the while using the prose of the everyday. No "-isms", no big concepts, simple concrete words (the "nights" of labour, the "names" of history, the "barriers" around Paris to denote the people's cultural world, the everyday term of "*mésentente*" as core political concept, and so on), which however entail complex critiques of theoretical assumptions and models. The enigmatic poetry of Rancière's prose that arises from this combination of the arcane and the everyday, the philosophical and the material, probably explains in no small part the seduction exerted by his texts on so many readers today.

Chronology

1940 Born in Algiers.
1954 Beginning of the Algerian War.
1960 Enters the École Normale Supérieure. Certificate of Higher Studies (Masters degree), thesis on Marx's early writings.
1961 Althusser seminar on the young Marx.
17 October: massacre of Algerian protesters by French police in the streets of Paris.
1962 Althusser seminar on "the origins of structuralism".
Evian accords; end of the Algerian War.
1963 Althusser seminar on Lacan.
Student revolt, occupation of the Sorbonne.
1965 Co-organizes Althusser seminar, "Reading *Capital*", and gives paper on Marx's concept of critique. Publication of first French version of *Reading Capital* in November.
1967 First factory occupations by workers.
1968 General strike following student revolt in May. In the following years, Rancière takes active part in the radical movement born of the 1968 uprising.
1969 Long article, "Sur la théorie de l'idéologie" ("On the Theory of Ideology"), following the rupture with Althusser.
Lecturer in Philosophy at the newly founded Université de Paris Vincennes (Paris VIII). Begins a research group on the history of the labour movement.
1973 New edition of *Reading Capital*, in which Rancière's contribution is to be re-included (it was not in the 2nd, 1968 edition). Rancière's self-critical foreword is rejected. The text appears in *Les Temps modernes*, 328, 1973 (HOW).
Occupation of the Lip factory by its workers.
1974 *La Leçon d'Althusser*.

1975 *La parole ouvrière, 1830–1851*, anthology of workers' writings edited and presented with Alain Faure.
First issue of *Révoltes logiques*, subtitled: "Notebooks of the Centre for Research into Ideologies of Revolt".

1977 "Portrait du vieil intellectuel en jeune dissident", *Le Nouvel Observateur* (663, 25 July).

1978 Special issue of *Révoltes logiques*, "Les lauriers de Mai" ("May's laurels"), on the decade following May 1968.

1981 *The Nights of Labour* (English trans. 1989), Rancière's "doctorat d'Etat".
Election of the Socialist candidate, François Mitterrand, at French presidential elections.

1982 Participation in the seminar of the Centre for Philosophical Research on the Political of Lacoue-Labarthe and Nancy (with Derrida, Lyotard); publication in *Le Retrait du politique*.

1983 *The Philosopher and his Poor* (English trans. 2004).

1985 *Louis-Gabriel Gauny, le philosophe plébien*.
Last issue of *Révoltes logiques*.

1986 Director of programmes at the Collège International de Philosophie, Paris (until 1992).
Massive student mobilization against university reforms. Rancière supports the movement.

1987 *The Ignorant Schoolmaster* (English trans. 1991), Rancière's intervention in the debate on education reform.

1990 Professor of Aesthetics and Politics at Paris VIII.
First edition of *On the Shores of Politics*.
Short Voyages to the Land of the People (English trans. 2003).

1992 *The Names of History* (English trans. 1994).

1995 *Disagreement* (English trans. 1998).
Protracted social movement initiated by nurses; in December, general public sector strike. Bourdieu gives spectacular support to the movement.

1996 *Mallarmé: La politique de la sirène*.

1997 *Arrêt sur histoire* (with Jean-Louis Comolli).
Signs a petition, alongside other French intellectuals, for the liberation of Italian philosopher Toni Negri from incarceration in Italy.
Support for the "*sans-papiers*" movement ("undocumented", or "illegal" immigrants).

1998 *La parole muette*.
The Flesh of Words (English trans. 2004).
Second, enlarged edition of *On the Shores of Politics* (English trans. 2007).

2000 *The Politics of Aesthetics* (English trans. 2004).

2001 *The Aesthetic Unconscious* (English trans. 2009).
Film Fables (English trans. 2006), mostly articles published in film journals, *Trafic* and *Cahiers du cinéma*.

2002 Retires from Paris VIII.

"Prisoners of the Infinite", in *Counterpunch* (30 April), in reaction to the campaign for "Infinite Justice" (the initial name of the "war on terror").

2003 *The Future of the Image* (English trans. 2007).
Les scènes du peuple (Rancière's contributions to *Révoltes logiques*).
Petition on the Chechen elections.

2004 *Aesthetics and its Discontents* (English trans. 2009).

2005 Cerisy colloquium dedicated to Rancière's work. Proceedings published in *La philosophie déplacée*, 2006.
Invited speaker at the Frieze Foundation, London. One of numerous invitations around the world, increasingly by art institutions.
The Hatred of Democracy (English trans. 2007).
Chronique des temps consensuels (collection of articles published in Brazilian newspapers).
L'espace des mots.

2007 *Politique de la littérature*.
At the presidential elections, the Socialist candidate, Ségolène Royal, cites Rancière as a key reference.

2008 *The Emancipated Spectator* (English trans. 2009).

2009 *Et tant pis pour les gens fatigués* (collection of interviews).
Moments politiques (collection of political texts, 1977–2009).

Bibliography

Works by Rancière

Rancière, J. 1974a. *La Leçon d'Althusser*. Paris: Gallimard.
Rancière, J. 1974b. "On the Theory of Ideology (the Politics of Althusser)". *Radical Philosophy* 7: 2–15.
Rancière, J. 1975. *La parole ouvrière, 1830/1851*. Paris: Editions 10/18.
Rancière, J. 1988a. "Going to the Expo: The Worker, his Wife and Machines". In *Voices of the People: The Politics and Life of "La Sociale" at the End of the Second Empire*, A. Rifkin (ed.), 23–44. London: Routledge. Reprinted in *Les scènes du peuple*, 63–84.
Rancière, J. 1988b. "Good Times, Or, Pleasure at the Barriers". In *Voices of the People: The Politics and Life of "La Sociale" at the End of the Second Empire*, A. Rifkin (ed.), 45–95. London: Routledge. Reprinted in *Les scènes du peuple*, 203–52.
Rancière, J. 1989a. "How to use *Lire le Capital*". In *Ideology, Method and Marx*, A. Rattansi (ed.), 181–9. London: Routledge.
Rancière, J. 1989b. *The Nights of Labour: The Workers' Dream in Nineteenth Century France*, J. Drury (trans.). Philadelphia, PA: Temple University Press. Originally published as *La Nuit des prolétaires: Archives du rêve ouvrier* (Paris: Fayard, 1981).
Rancière, J. 1991a. *The Ignorant Schoolmaster: Five Lessons in Intellectual Emancipation*, K. Ross (trans.). Stanford, CA: Stanford University Press. Originally published as *Le Maître ignorant: Cinq leçons sur l'émancipation intellectuelle* (Paris: Fayard, 1987).
Rancière, J. 1991b. *The Philosopher and his Poor*, A. Parker, C. Oster & J. Drury (trans.). Philadelphia, PA: Temple University Press. Originally published as *Le philosophe et ses pauvres* (Paris: Fayard, 1983).
Rancière, J. 1991c. *Short Voyages to the Land of the People*, J. Swenson (trans.). Stanford, CA: Stanford University Press. Originally published as *Courts voyages au pays du peuple* (Paris: Seuil, 1990).
Rancière, J. 1994. *The Names of History: On the Poetics of Knowledge*, H. White & H. Melehy (trans.). Minneapolis, MN: University of Minnesota Press.

Originally published as *Les noms de l'histoire: Essai de poétique du savoir* (Paris: Seuil, 1992).
Rancière, J. 1995. *On the Shores of Politics*, L. Heron (trans.). London: Verso. Originally published as *Aux bords du politique* (Paris: La fabrique, 1998).
Rancière, J. 1996a. *Lire le Capital*. Paris: PUF.
Rancière, J. 1996b. *Mallarmé: Politique de la sirène*. Paris: Hachette.
Rancière, J. 1997. "L'inoubliable". In *Arrêt sur histoire*, J.-L. Comolli and J. Rancière, 47–60. Paris: Centre Pompidou.
Rancière, J. 1998a. *Disagreement: Politics and Philosophy*, J. Rose (trans.). Minneapolis, MN: University of Minnesota Press. Originally published as *La Mésentente: Politique et philosophie* (Paris: Galilée, 1995).
Rancière, J. 1998b. *La parole muette: Essai sur les contradictions de la littérature*. Paris: Seuil.
Rancière, J. 2000. "Dissenting Words: A Conversation with Jacques Rancière", D. Panagia (trans.). *Diacritics* 30(2): 113–26.
Rancière, J. 2001. "Ten Theses on Politics", D. Panagia (trans.). *Theory and Event* 6(4), http://muse.jhu.edu/login?uri=/journals/theory_and_event/v005/5.3ranciere.html (accessed April 2010).
Rancière, J. 2002. "The Aesthetic Revolution and Its Outcomes: Emplotments of Autonomy and Heteronomy". *New Left Review* 14: 133–51.
Rancière, J. 2003a. "Comments and Responses". *Theory and Event* 6(4), http://muse.jhu.edu/login?uri=/journals/theory_and_event/v006/6.4ranciere.html.
Rancière, J. 2003b. *Les scènes du peuple*. Paris: Horlieu [Rancière's articles in *Révoltes logiques*].
Rancière, J. 2004a. *The Flesh of Words: The Politics of Writing*, C. Mandell (trans.). Stanford, CA: Stanford University Press. Originally published as *La Chair des mots: Politiques de l'écriture* (Paris: Galilée, 1990, 1998).
Rancière, J. 2004b. *The Politics of Aesthetics*, G. Rockhill (trans.). London: Continuum. Originally published as *Le Partage du sensible: Esthétique et politique* (Paris: La fabrique, 2000).
Rancière, J. 2004c. "The Politics of Literature". *SubStance* 33(1): 10–24.
Rancière, J. 2004d. "The Sublime from Lyotard to Schiller: Two Readings of Kant and Their Political Significance". *Radical Philosophy* 126: 8–15.
Rancière, J. 2004e. "Is there a Deleuzian Aesthetics?" *Qui parle?* 14(2): 1–14.
Rancière, J. 2004f. "Who is the Subject of the Rights of Man?" *South Atlantic Quarterly* 103(2/3): 297–310.
Rancière, J. 2005. "From Politics to Aesthetics". *Paragraph* 28(1): 13–25.
Rancière, J. 2006a. *Film Fables*, E. Battista (trans.). Oxford: Berg. Originally published as *La Fable cinématographique* (Paris: Seuil, 2001).
Rancière, J. 2006b. *Hatred of Democracy*, S. Corcoran (trans.). London: Verso. Originally published as *La Haine de la démocratie* (Paris: La fabrique, 2005).
Rancière, J. 2006c. "Thinking Between Disciplines: An Aesthetics of Knowledge". *Parrhesia* 1: 1–12.
Rancière, J. 2007a. "Art of the Possible: Fulvia Carnevale and John Kelsey in Conversation with Jacques Rancière". *Artforum* 45(7): 256–69.
Rancière, J. 2007b. "The Emancipated Spectator". *Artforum* 45(7): 271–81.
Rancière, J. 2007c. *The Future of the Image*, G. Elliott (trans.). London: Verso. Originally published as *Le Destin des images* (Paris: La fabrique, 2003).
Rancière, J. 2007d. "On Medium Specificity and Discipline Crossovers in Modern Art", interview by A. McNamara & T. Ross. *Australian and New Zealand Journal of Art* 8(1): 99–107.

Rancière, J. 2007e. *Politique de la littérature*. Paris: Galilée.
Rancière, J. 2007f. "Theatre of Images". In *Alfredo Jaar: La Politique des Images*, 71–80. Zurich: JRP/Ringier.
Rancière, J. 2008a. "Aesthetics against Incarnation: An Interview by Anne Marie Oliver". *Critical Inquiry* 35: 172–90.
Rancière, J. 2008b. "Jacques Rancière and Interdisciplinarity". Interview with M.-A. Baronian & M. Rosello, G. Elliott (trans.), *Art and Research* 2(1), www.artandresearch.org.uk/v2n1/pdfs/jrinterview.pdf (accessed May 2010).
Rancière, J. 2008c. "Why Emma Bovary had to be Killed". *Critical Inquiry* 34: 233–48.
Rancière, J. 2009a. *The Aesthetic Unconscious*, D. Keates & J. Swenson (trans.). Cambridge: Polity. Originally published as *L'inconscient esthétique* (Paris: Galilée, 2001).
Rancière, J. 2009b. *Aesthetics and its Discontents*, S. Corcoran (trans.). Cambridge: Polity. Originally published as *Malaise dans l'esthétique* (Paris: Galilée, 2004).
Rancière, J. 2009c. "Contemporary Art and the Politics of Aesthetics". In *Communities of Sense: Rethinking Aesthetics and Politics*, B. Hinderliter *et al.* (eds), 31–50. Durham, NC: Duke University Press.
Rancière, J. 2009d. *The Emancipated Spectator*. London: Verso. Originally published as *Le spectateur émancipé* (Paris: La fabrique, 2008).
Rancière, J. 2009e. *Et tant pis pour les gens fatigués: Entretiens*. Paris: Editions Amsterdam.
Rancière, J. 2009f. *Moments politiques: Interventions 1977–2009*. Paris: La fabrique.
Rancière, J. 2010. *Dissensus: On Politics and Aesthetics*, S. Corcoran (trans.). London: Continuum.

Other works

Agamben, G. 1998. *Homo Sacer: Sovereign Power and Bare Life*. Stanford, CA: Stanford University Press.
Althusser, L. 1973. "Letter of March 15 1969". In M. A. Macciocchi, *Letters from inside the Communist Party to Louis Althusser*, 301–20. London: NLB.
Arendt, H. 1958. *The Human Condition*. Chicago, IL: University of Chicago Press.
Aristotle. 1981. *Politics*. T. A. Sinclair (ed. & trans.), T. J. Saunders (rev.). London: Penguin.
Aristotle. 1996. *Poetics*, M. Heath (trans.). Harmondsworth: Penguin.
Auerbach, E. 1953. *Mimesis: The Representation of Reality in Western Literature*, W. Trask (trans.). Princeton, NJ: Princeton University Press.
Badiou, A. 1994. "Casser en deux l'histoire du monde". Paris: Les Conférences du Perroquet.
Badiou, A. 2005a. *Metapolitics*, J. Barker (trans.). London: Verso.
Badiou, A. 2005b. "Rancière and the Community of Equals". In *Metapolitics*, J. Barker (trans.), 107–13. London: Verso.
Badiou, A. 2005c. "Rancière and Apolitics". In *Metapolitics*, J. Barker (trans.), 114–23. London: Verso.
Badiou, A. 2009. "The Lessons of Jacques Rancière: Knowledge and Power after the Storm". In *Jacques Rancière: History, Politics, Aesthetics*, G. Rockhill & P. Watts (eds), 30–54. Durham, NC: Duke University Press.

Balibar, E. 2009. "What is Political Philosophy? Contextual Notes". In *Jacques Rancière: History, Politics, Aesthetics*, G. Rockhill & P. Watts (eds), 95–104. Durham, NC: Duke University Press.
Barthes, R. 1982. *Camera Lucida: Reflections on Photography*, R. Howard (trans.). New York: Hill & Wang.
Barthes, R. 2007. *The Neutral: Lecture Course at the Collège de France (1977–1978)*, R. Krauss & D. Hollier (trans). New York: Columbia University Press.
Baudrillard, J. 1983. *In the Shadow of Silent Majorities*. New York: Semiotext(e).
Baudrillard, J. 1994. *The Illusion of the End*. Cambridge: Polity Press.
Bazin, A. 1967. "The Evolution of the Language of Cinema". In *What Is Cinema?* vol. 1, H. Gray (trans.), 23–40. Berkeley, CA: University of California Press.
Bell, D. 2004. "Writing, Movement/Space, Democracy: On Jacques Rancière's Literary History". *SubStance* 33(1): 126–40.
Benton, T. 1974. "Discussion: Rancière on Ideology". *Radical Philosophy* 9: 28–9.
Benveniste, E. 1966. "Les relations de temps dans le verbe français". In *Problèmes de linguistique générale*, 237–50. Paris: Gallimard.
Berrebi, S. 2008. "Jacques Rancière: Aesthetics is Politics". *Art and Research* 2(1), www.artandresearch.org.uk/v2n1/berrebirev.html (accessed June 2010).
Bingham, C. & G. Biesta (Introduction by Rancière) 2010. *Jacques Rancière: Education, Truth, Emancipation*. London: Continuum.
Bosteels, B. 2009a. "Rancière's Leftism, Or, Politics and Its Discontents". In *Jacques Rancière: History, Politics, Aesthetics*, G. Rockhill & P. Watts (eds), 158–75. Durham, NC: Duke University Press.
Bosteels, B. 2009b. "Afterword: Being, Thinking, Acting, or, On the Uses and Disadvantages of Ontology for Politics". In *A Leftist Ontology: Beyond Relativism and Identity Politics*, C. Strathausen (ed.), 235–51. Minneapolis, MN: University of Minnesota Press.
Bosteels, B. 2010. "Metapolitics". In *Encyclopedia of Political Theory*, M. Bevir (ed.), 878–80. New York: Routledge.
Bourdieu, P. 1979. *The Inheritors: French Students and Their Relations to Culture*. Chicago, IL: University of Chicago Press. Originally published in 1964.
Bourdieu, P. 1987. *Distinction: A Social Critique of the Judgment of Taste*. Cambridge, MA: Harvard University Press.
Bourdieu, P. & J.-C. Passeron 1990. *Reproduction in Education, Society and Culture*. London: Sage.
Bourriaud, N. 2002. *Relational Aesthetics*, S. Pleasance & F. Woods (trans.). Paris: Les Presses du Réel.
Bourriaud, N. 2009a. *The Radicant*. New York/Berlin: Sternberg Press.
Bourriaud, N. 2009b. "Precarious Constructions. Answer to Jacques Rancière on Art and Politics", www.skor.nl/article-4416-nl.html?lang=en (accessed April 2010).
Bowman, P. 2009. "Aberrant Pedagogies: JR, QT and Bruce Lee", *Borderlands* 8(2), www.borderlands.net.au/vol8no2_2009/bowman_abberant.htm (accessed April 2010).
Braudel, F. 1995. *The Mediterranean and the World in the Age of Philip II*, S. Reynolds (trans.). Berkeley, CA: University of California Press. Originally published in 1949.
Chambers, S. 2003. *Untimely Politics*. Edinburgh: Edinburgh University Press.
Chambers, S. 2004. "Ghostly Rights". *Cultural Critique* 54:148–77.
Chambers, S. 2005. "The Politics of Literarity". *Theory and Event* 8(3), http://muse.

jhu.edu/login?uri=/journals/tae/v008/8.3chambers.html (accessed April 2010).
Chambers, S. 2009. "A Queer Politics of the Democratic Miscount". *Borderlands* 8(2), www.borderlands.net.au/vol8no2_2009/chambers_miscount.htm (accessed April 2010).
Chambers, S. & M. O'Rourke 2009. "Jacques Rancière and the Shores of Queer Theory". *Borderlands* 8(2), www.borderlands.net.au/vol8no2_2009/chambersorourke_intro.htm (accessed April 2010).
Christofferson, M. S. 2004. *French Intellectuals Against the Left: The Anti-Totalitarian Movement of the 1970s*. New York: Berghahn Books.
Citton, Y. 2007. *Lire, interpréter, actualiser: Pourquoi les études littéraires?* Paris: Éditions Amsterdam.
Citton, Y. 2009. "Political Agency and the Ambivalence of the Sensible". In *Jacques Rancière: History, Politics, Aesthetics*, G. Rockhill & P. Watts (eds), 120–39. Durham, NC: Duke University Press.
Conley, T. 2004. "A Fable of Film: Rancière's Anthony Mann". *SubStance* 33(1): 91–107.
Conley, T. 2009. "Cinema and its Discontents". In *Jacques Rancière: History, Politics, Aesthetics*, G. Rockhill & P. Watts (eds), 216–28. Durham, NC: Duke University Press.
Cook, R. 2009. "Aesthetic Revolution, the Staging of ('Homosexual') Equality and Contemporary Art". *Borderlands* 8(2), www.borderlands.net.au/vol8no2_2009/cook_aesthetic.pdf (accessed April 2010).
Cornu, L. & P. Vermeren 2006. *La philosophie déplacée: Autour de Jacques Rancière*. Paris: Horlieu.
Craib, I. 1975. "Rancière and Althusser". *Radical Philosophy* 10: 28–9.
Critchley, S. 2001. *Continental Philosophy: A Very Short Introduction*. Oxford: Oxford University Press.
Dasgupta, S. 2009a. "Conjunctive Times, Disjointed Time: Philosophy between Enigma and Disagreement". *Parallax* 15(3): 3–19.
Dasgupta, S. 2009b. "Jacques Rancière". In *Film, Theory and Philosophy: The Key Thinkers*, F. Colman (ed.), ch. 31. Durham: Acumen.
Davis, O. 2009. "Rancière and Queer Theory: On Irritable Attachment". *Borderlands* 8(2), www.borderlands.net.au/vol8no2_2009/davis_irritable.htm (accessed April 2010).
Dean, J. 2009. "Politics without Politics". *Parallax* 15(3): 20–36.
Debord, G. 1994. *The Society of the Spectacle*. New York: Zone Books.
Deleuze, G. 1986. *Cinema 1: The Movement-Image*, H. Tomlinson & B. Habberjam (trans.). Minneapolis, MN: University of Minnesota Press.
Deleuze, G. 1989. *Cinema 2: The Time-Image*, H. Tomlinson & R. Galeta (trans.). Minneapolis, MN: University of Minnesota Press.
Deleuze, G. & F. Guattari 1986. *Kafka: Towards a Minor Literature*, D. Polan (trans.). Minneapolis, MN: University of Minnesota Press.
Deleuze, G. & F. Guattari 1987. *A Thousand Plateaus: Capitalism and Schizophrenia*, B. Massumi (trans.). Minneapolis, MN: University of Minnesota Press.
Déotte, J.-L. & R. Lapidus 2004. "The Differences Between Rancière's 'Mésentente' (Political Disagreement) and Lyotard's 'Différend'". *SubStance* 33(1): 77–90.
Deranty, J.-P. 2003a. "Jacques Rancière's Contribution to the Ethics of Recognition". *Political Theory* 31(1): 136–56.
Deranty, J.-P. 2003b. "Rancière and Contemporary Political Ontology". *Theory and Event* 6(4), http://muse.jhu.edu/login?uri=/journals/theory_and_event/voo6/6.4deranty.html (accessed June 2010).

Deranty, J.-P. 2007. "Democratic Aesthetics: On Jacques Rancière's Latest Work". *Critical Horizons* 8(2): 230–55.
Deranty, J.-P. et al. (eds) 2007. *Recognition, Work, Politics: New Directions in French Critical Theory*. Leiden: Brill.
Dikeç, M. 2007. *Badlands of the Republic: Space, Politics and Urban Policy*. Oxford: Blackwell.
Dillon, M. 2003. "(De)void of Politics: A Response to Jacques Rancière's Ten Theses on Politics". *Theory and Event* 6(4), http://muse.jhu.edu/login?uri=/journals/theory_and_event/voo6/6.4dillon.html (accessed June 2010).
.Dillon, M. 2005. "A Passion for the (Im)possible: Jacques Rancière, Equality, Pedagogy and the Messianic". *European Journal of Political Theory* 4: 429–52.
During, E. 2001. "What Pure Aesthetics Can't do". *Art Press* 267: 56–8.
Elliott, G. 2006. *Althusser: The Detour of Theory*. Leiden: Brill.
Engelibert, J.-P. 1998. "Sur Jacques Rancière". *Literary Research/Recherche Littéraire* 30: 23–32.
Farge, A. 1997. "L'Histoire comme avènement". *Critique* 601–2: 461–6.
Fénelon, F. 1994. *Telemachus*, P. Riley (ed. & trans.). Cambridge: Cambridge University Press.
Ferris, D. 2009. "Politics after Aesthetics: Disagreeing with Rancière". *Parallax* 15(3): 37–49.
Foucault, M. 1979. "Omnes et Singulatim: Towards a Criticism of *Political Reason*". Tanner Lectures on Human Values, Stanford University, 10 and 16 October.
Furet, F. 1981. *Interpreting the French Revolution*. Cambridge: Cambridge University Press.
Game, J. & A. Wald Lasowski (eds) 2009. *Jacques Rancière: Politique de l'esthétique*. Lyon: Centre d'Etudes Poétiques.
Garneau, M. & J. Cisneros 2004. "Film's Aesthetic Turn: A Contribution from Jacques Rancière". *SubStance* 33(1), 108–25.
Gibson, A. 2001. "'And the Wind Wheezing Through that Organ Once in a While': Voice, Narrative, Film". *New Literary History* 32(3): 639–57.
Gibson, A. 2005. "The Unfinished Song: Intermittency and Melancholy in Rancière". *Paragraph* 28(1): 61–76.
Godard, J.-L. 1988–98, *Histoire(s) du cinéma* (film). Gaumont.
Gossez, R. 1968. *Les Ouvriers de Paris*. Paris: Mouton.
Gramsci, A. 1996. "Notes for an Introduction and an Approach to the Study of Philosophy and Culture". In *The Antonio Gramsci Reader*, D. Forgacs (ed.), 323–43. New York: New York University Press.
Guénoun, S. 2000. "An Interview with Jacques Rancière: Cinematographic Image, Democracy, and the 'Splendor of the Insignificant'". *Sites: The Journal of Twentieth Century Contemporary French Studies* 4(2): 249–58.
Guénoun, S. 2004. "Jacques Rancière's Freudian Cause". *SubStance* 33(1): 25–53.
Guénoun, S. 2009. "Jacques Rancière's Ethical Turn and the Thinking of Discontents". In *Jacques Rancière: History, Politics, Aesthetics*, G. Rockhill & P. Watts (eds), 176–92. Durham, NC: Duke University Press.
Guénoun, S., J. H. Kavanagh & R. Lapidus 2000. "Jacques Rancière: Literature, Politics, Aesthetics: Approaches to Democratic Disagreement". *SubStance* 92: 3–24.
Guerlac, S. & P. Cheah 2009. *Derrida and the Time of the Political*. Durham, NC: Duke University Press.
Guha, R. 1994. "The Prose of Counter-Insurgency". In *Culture/Power/History: A Reader in Contemporary Social Theory*, N. Dirks, G. Eley & S. B. Ortner (eds), 336–71. Princeton, NJ: Princeton University Press.

BIBLIOGRAPHY

Hallward, P. (ed.). 2004. *Think Again: Alain Badiou and the Future of Philosophy*. London: Continuum.

Hallward, P. 2005a. "Jacques Rancière and the Subversion of Mastery". *Paragraph* 28(1): 26–45.

Hallward, P. 2005b. "The Politics of Prescription". *South Atlantic Quarterly* 104(4): 769–89.

Hallward, P. 2006. "Staging Equality. On Rancière's Theocracy". *New Left Review* 37, www.newleftreview.org/?view=2601 (accessed June 2010).

Hallward, P. 2009. "Rancière's Theocracy and the Limits of Anarchic Equality". In *Jacques Rancière: History, Politics, Aesthetics*, G. Rockhill & P. Watts (eds), 140–57. Durham, NC: Duke University Press.

Harvey, D. 2003. *Paris, Capital of Modernity*. New York: Routledge.

Hegel, G. W. F. 1998. *Aesthetics: Lectures on Fine Art*, T. M. Knox (trans.). Oxford: Clarendon Press.

Hewlett, N. 2007. *Badiou, Balibar, Rancière: Re-thinking Emancipation*. London: Continuum.

Hirst, P. 1979. "Rancière, Ideology and Capital". In his *On Law and Ideology*, 79–95. Basingstoke: Macmillan.

Hobbes, T. 1983. *De Cive*. Oxford: Clarendon Press.

Hobbes, T. 1997. *Leviathan*. New York: Norton.

Ieven, B. 2009. "Heteroreductives – Rancière's Disagreement with Ontology". *Parallax* 15(3): 50–62.

Ingram, J. 2006. "The Subject of the Politics of Recognition: Hannah Arendt and Jacques Rancière". In *Socialité et reconnaissance: Grammaires de l'humain*, G. Bertram *et al.* (eds), 229–45. Paris: L'Harmattan.

Kollias, H. 2009. "How Queer is the *Demos*? Politics, Sex, and Equality". *Borderlands* 8(2), www.borderlands.net.au/vol8no2_2009/kollias_demos.htm (accessed April 2010).

Labelle, G. 2001. "Two Refoundation Projects of Democracy in Contemporary French Philosophy: Cornelius Castoriadis and Jacques Rancière". *Philosophy and Social Criticism* 27(4): 75–103.

Larrain, J. 1979. *The Concept of Ideology*. London: Century Hutchinson.

Lecourt, D. 2001. *The Mediocracy: French Philosophy since the mid-1970s*, G. Elliott (trans). London and New York: Verso.

Linhart, R. 1981. *The Assembly Line*, M. Grosland (trans.). Amherst, MA: University of Massachusetts Press.

Lyotard, J.-F. 1984. *The Postmodern Condition: A Report on Knowledge*. Minneapolis, MN: University of Minnesota Press.

Lyotard, J.-F. 1989. *The Differend: Phrases in Dispute*. Minneapolis, MN: University of Minnesota Press.

Lyotard, J.-F. 1991. "After the Sublime, The State of Aesthetics". In *The Inhuman: Reflections on Time*, G. Bennington & R. Bowlby (trans.), 135–43. Cambridge: Polity.

Lyotard, J.-F. 1993. *Political Writings*. Minneapolis, MN: University of Minnesota Press.

MacCormack, P. 2009. "Inhuman Evanescence". *Borderlands* 8(2), www.borderlands.net.au/vol8no2_2009/maccormack_inhuman.htm (accessed April 2010).

McClure, K. 2003. "Disconnections, Connections and Questions: Reflections on Jacques Rancière's Ten Theses on Politics". *Theory and Event* 6(4), http://muse.jhu.edu/login?uri=/journals/theory_and_event/v006/6.4mcclure.html (accessed June 2010).

May, T. 2008. The *Political Thought of Jacques Rancière: Creating Equality*. Philadelphia, PA: University of Pennsylvania Press.
May, T. 2009. "There are no Queers: Jacques Rancière and post-identity Politics". *Borderlands* 8(2), www.borderlands.net.au/vol8no2_2009/may_noqueers.htm (accessed April 2010).
May, T. 2009. "Rancière in South Carolina". In *Jacques Rancière: History, Politics, Aesthetics*, G. Rockhill & P. Watts (eds), 105–19. Durham, NC: Duke University Press.
Mecchia, G. 2009. "The Classics and Critical Theory in Postmodern France: The Case of Jacques Rancière". In *Jacques Rancière: History, Politics, Aesthetics*, G. Rockhill & P. Watts (eds), 67–82. Durham, NC: Duke University Press.
Méchoulan, E. 2004. "Introduction: On the Edges of Jacques Rancière". *SubStance* 33(1): 3–9.
Méchoulan, E. 2009. "Sophisticated Continuities and Historical Discontinuities; Or, Why Not Protagoras?". In *Jacques Rancière: History, Politics, Aesthetics*, G. Rockhill & P. Watts (eds), 55–66. Durham, NC: Duke University Press.
Mehlman, J. 1976. "Teaching Reading: The Case of Marx in France". *Diacritics: A Review of Contemporary Criticism* 6(4): 10–18.
Mufti, A. 2003. "Reading Jacques Rancière's Ten Theses on Politics: After September 11th". *Theory and Event* 6(4), http://muse.jhu.edu/login?uri=/journals/theory_and_event/voo6/6.4mufti.html (accessed June 2010).
Nancy, J.-L. 2009. "Rancière and Metaphysics". In *Jacques Rancière: History, Politics, Aesthetics*, G. Rockhill & P. Watts (eds), 83–92. Durham, NC: Duke University Press.
Nordmann, C. 2007. *Bourdieu/Rancière: La politique entre sociologie et philosophie*. Paris: Editions Amsterdam.
Panagia, D. 2001. "*Ceci n'est pas un argument*: An Introduction to the Ten Theses". *Theory and Event* 5(3), http://muse.jhu.edu/login?uri=/journals/theory_and_event/voo5/5.3panagia.html (accessed June 2010).
Panagia, D. 2006. *The Poetics of Political Thinking*. Durham, NC: Duke University Press.
Panofsky, E . 1995. "Style and Medium in the Motion Pictures". In *Three Essays on Style*, I. Lavin (ed.), 93–122. Cambridge, MA: MIT Press.
Parker, A. 2009. "Impossible Speech Acts: Rancière's Erich Auerbach". In *Jacques Rancière: History, Politics, Aesthetics*, G. Rockhill & P. Watts (eds), 249–59. Durham, NC: Duke University Press.
Pelletier, C. 2009a. "Emancipation, Equality and Education: Rancière's Critique of Bourdieu and the Question of Performativity". *Discourse: Studies in the Cultural Politics of Education* 30(2): 137–50.
Pelletier, C. 2009b. "Rancière and the Poetics of the Social Sciences". *International Journal of Research and Method in Education* 32(3): 267–84.
Perrot, M. 1987. *Workers on Strike*, C. Turner (trans.). New Haven, CT: Yale University Press.
Phillips, C. 2009. "Difference, Disagreement and the Thinking of Queerness". *Borderlands* 8(2), www.borderlands.net.au/vol8no2_2009/phillips_difference.htm (accessed April 2010).
Plato 1927. *The Republic*, B. Jowett (ed. & trans.). Oxford: Clarendon Press.
Plato. 2005. *Phaedrus*, C. Rowe (trans.). London: Penguin.
Power, N. 2009a. " Which Equality? Badiou and Rancière in Light of Feuerbach". *Parallax* 15(3): 63–80.
Power, N. 2009b. "Non-Reproductive Futurism. Rancière's Rational Equality

against Edelman's Body Apolitic". *Borderlands* 8(2), www.borderlands.net.au/vol8no2_2009/power_futurism.pdf (accessed April 2010).

Prothero, I. 1997. *Radical Artisans in England and France 1830–1870*. Cambridge: Cambridge University Press.

Rajaram, P. K. & C. Grundy-Warr 2007. *Borderscapes: Hidden Geographies and Politics at Territory's Edge*. Minneapolis, MN: University of Minnesota Press.

Reid, D. 1989. "Introduction". In J. Rancière, *The Nights of Labour: The Workers' Dream in Nineteenth Century France*, J. Drury (trans.), xv–xxxvi. Philadelphia, PA: Temple University Press.

Rifkin, A. 2005. "Il y a des mots qu'on ne souhaiterait plus lire". *Paragraph* 28(1): 96–109.

Rifkin, A. 2009a. "JR Cinéphile, or the Philosopher who loved Things". *Parallax* 15(3): 81–7.

Rifkin, A. 2009b. "Oh I do Like to be Beside the Seaside (Now Voyager)... On Misunderstanding Rancière and Queer Theory". *Borderlands* 8(2), www.borderlands.net.au/vol8no2_2009/rifkin_afterword.htm (accessed April 2010).

Rifkin, A. & R. Thomas 1998. *Voices of the People: The Social Life of 'La Sociale' at the End of the Second Empire*, J. Moore (trans.). London: Routledge & Kegan Paul.

Rimbaud, A. 1957. "Democracy". In *Illuminations and Other Prose Poems*, L. Varèse (trans.), 128. New York: New Directions.

Robson, M. (ed.). 2005. "Hearing Voices". Introduction to special issue of *Paragraph* 28(1) (March).

Robson, M. 2005. "Jacques Rancière's Aesthetic Communities". *Paragraph* 28(1): 77–95.

Robson, M. 2009. "'A Literary Animal': Rancière, Derrida, and the Literature of Democracy". *Parallax* 15(3): 88–101.

Rockhill, G. 2004. "The Silent Revolution". *SubStance* 33(1): 54–76.

Rockhill, G. 2009. "The Politics of Aesthetics: Political History and the Hermeneutics of Art". In *Jacques Rancière: History, Politics, Aesthetics*, G. Rockhill & P. Watts (eds), 195–215. Durham, NC: Duke University Press.

Rockhill, G. & P. Watts (eds) 2009. *Jacques Rancière: History, Politics, Aesthetics*. Durham, NC: Duke University Press.

Rogozinski, J. *et al.* (eds) 1983. *Le Retrait du politique: travaux du Centre de recherches philosophiques sur le politique*. Paris: Galilée.

Ross, K. 1991. "Rancière and the Practice of Equality". *Social Text* 29: 57–71.

Ross, K. 2002. *May '68 and its Afterlives*. Chicago, IL: University of Chicago Press.

Ross, K. 2009. "Historizing Untimeliness". In *Jacques Rancière: History, Politics, Aesthetics*, G. Rockhill & P. Watts (eds), 15–29. Durham, NC: Duke University Press.

Rousseau, J.-J. 1987. *The Basic Political Writings*. Indianapolis, IN: Hackett.

Ruby, C. 2009. *L'Interruption: Jacques Rancière et la politique*. Paris: La fabrique.

Schaap, A. 2009. "The Absurd Proposition of Aboriginal Sovereignty". In *Law and Agonistic Politics*, A. Schaap (ed.), 209–23. Aldershot: Ashgate.

Schwartz, F. J. 1996. *The Werkbund: Design Theory and Mass Culture before the First World War*. New Haven, CT: Yale University Press.

Sewell, W. 1980. *Work and Revolution in France. The Language of Labour from the Old Regime to 1848*. Cambridge: Cambridge University Press.

Shapiro, W. 2008. "Radicalising Democratic Theory: Social Space in Connolly, Deleuze and Rancière". In *The New Pluralism. William Connolly and the Contemporary Global Condition*, D. Campbell & M. Schoolman (eds), 197–220. Durham, NC: Duke University Press.

Stamp, R. 2009. "The Torsion of Politics and Friendship in Derrida, Foucault and Rancière". *Borderlands* 8(2), www.borderlands.net.au/vol8no2_2009/stamp_torsion.pdf (accessed April 2010).
Stendhal. 1970. *Racine et Shakespeare*. Paris: Garnier.
Strauss, L. 1959. *What is Political Philosophy? And Other Studies*. Chicago, IL: University of Chicago Press.
Swenson, J. 2009. "Style Indirect Libre". In *Jacques Rancière: History, Politics, Aesthetics*, G. Rockhill & P. Watts (eds), 258–72. Durham, NC: Duke University Press.
Tambakaki, P. 2009. "When Does Politics Happen?" *Parallax* 15(3): 102–13.
Thompson, E. P. 1966. *The Making of the English Working Class*. London: Vintage.
Tocqueville, A. de 1995. *The Old Regime and the French Revolution*, S. Gilbert (trans.). Peterborough: Anchor Books.
Van Munster, R. 2009. "Rancière". In *Critical Theorists and International Relations*, J. Edkins & N. Vaughan-Williams (eds), 266–77. London: Routledge.
Valentine, J. 2001. "The Hegemony of Hegemony". *History of the Human Sciences* 14(1): 88–104.
Valentine, J. 2005. "Rancière and Contemporary Political Problems". *Paragraph* 28(1): 46–60.
Vallury, R. 2009. "Politicising Art in Rancière and Deleuze: The Case of Postcolonial Literature". In *Jacques Rancière: History, Politics, Aesthetics*, G. Rockhill & P. Watts (eds), 229–48. Durham, NC: Duke University Press.
Watts, P. 2002. "Le Cinéma entre *mimesis* et zone d'ombre". *Critique* 58: 830–37.
White, H. 1994. "Foreword: Rancière's Revisionism". In J. Rancière, *The Names of History: On the Poetics of Knowledge*, H. Melehy (trans.), vii–xx. Minneapolis, MN: University of Minnesota Press.
Whyschogrod, E. 1998. *An Ethics of Remembering: History, Heterology and the Nameless Others*, 1–40. Chicago, IL: University of Chicago Press.
Williford, D. 2009. "Queer Aesthetics". *Borderlands* 8(2), www.borderlands.net.au/vol8no2_2009/williford_queer.htm (accessed April 2010).
Wolfe, K. 2006. "From Aesthetics to Politics: Rancière, Kant and Deleuze". *Contemporary Aesthetics* 4, www.contempaesthetics.org/newvolume/pages/article.php?articleID=382 (accessed April 2010).
Žižek, S. 1999. "Political Subjectivization and Its Vicissitudes". In his *The Ticklish Subject*, 171–244. London: Verso.

Index

Achilles 123
action
  collective 70, 79
  creative 130, 184–5
  in film 175
  of masses 106–12
  noble 120, 140–41
  political 51, 53, 68, 72, 74, 76–7, 82, 87, 96–9, 103
  representation of 122–6, 138, 156
  of spectators 101
  versus pathos in aesthetic regime 129, 159, 179
Adorno, Theodor. W. 101, 142
aesthetic, *see also* regimes of the arts
  autonomy 152, 161–5, 172
  dimension of politics 95–6, 99–103, 134–5
  experience 36–7, 161, 168
  regime 113, 121–9, 137, 155–7, 161–5, 170–72
  unconscious 129
Agamben, Giorgio 52–3
Algerian War 2, 50
Althusser, Louis 2–4, 33, 35, 39–40, 42, 50, 95, 97–8, 101, 112, 148
Arendt, Hannah 57, 65
Aristotle 10, 45–8, 57, 73–4, 77, 86–9, 108, 121–2, 124, 146
Auerbach, Erich 118, 120, 138

Arts and Craft Movement 162

Bacon, Francis 159
Badiou, Alain 1, 4, 11, 81, 8–6, 91–2, 183–5
Ballanche, Pierre-Simon 102, 137
Balzac, Honoré de 114, 126, 134, 156
Barthes, Roland 109, 154, 157–8
Bataille, Georges 160
Baudelaire, Charles 125
Baudrillard, Jean 50, 182
Bazin, André 170, 177
Behrens, Peter 162–3
Benoist, Alain de 92
Blanchot, Maurice 134, 145
Bourdieu, Pierre 33, 35, 43, 80, 84–5, 101, 109–10
Bourriaud, Nicolas 167
Bouvard and Pécuchet 144
Bovary, Emma 126, 140, 142, 146, 171
Braudel, Fernand 105–7

Cabet, Etienne 21
Chardin, Jean-Siméon 160
Chateaubriand, François-René de 111
Commune (Paris) 18, 86
communism 2, 106
Communist Party 3, 8, 39, 40, 106
Courbet, Gustave 157

Deleuze, Gilles 1, 4, 135, 148–9, 159–60, 164, 170, 176–81
"Democracy" (Rimbaud) 5, 18
democracy see also politics
 anarchic 108, 113
 ancient 45, 47, 66
 hatred of 13, 53–4, 64, 153
 liberal/bourgeois 46, 90, 173
 modern 134
 radical 9, 11, 54, 147
 representative 47, 54, 66
 scandal of 30, 47, 64–5, 80
 synonymous with politics 53, 66–8, 70, 81
demos 46, 49, 65, 70–75, 78–9, 81, 83, 88–9
Denis, Maurice 159
Deroin, Jeanne 21
Derrida, Jacques 1, 10, 108, 129, 153
Despard, Edward 112
Diderot, Denis 36
disagreement 10, 51, 73–6, 82, 100, 185
dissensus 53, 95–100
domination see oligarchy, police
 and ideology 3, 109
 in political orders 59, 64, 67, 78, 80–82
 social 3–5, 11, 110

education see also knowledge and learning
 Bourdieu's sociology of 109–10
 Jacotot's theory of 6–7, 27–37, 77, 114
 and the republic 48, 84–5
emancipation see also democracy, politics
 and "distribution of the sensible" 98–103
 intellectual 6, 23, 25–37, 98
 political 21, 41, 82
 universal 90
Enfantin, Barthélémy Prosper 21
Epstein, Jean 170–72, 175
equality see also democracy, wrong, police
 axiom/presupposed 11–12, 32, 72, 77, 109, 144, 150, 152, 183
 of intelligences 28–33, 37, 77, 98, 109

 in literature and aesthetics 11–12, 24, 133–4, 137–8
 and political action 77–8, 122
 in political theory 69–71, 91
 radical 3, 6–7, 9, 13, 43, 184
"everything speaks" 12, 126, 157
expressivity 129, 134–5, 146, 149, 170–78

fable 119, 169–82
Farge, Arlette 110
Faure, Elie 181
Ferry, Jules 85
Ferry, Luc 58
Flaubert, Gustave 42, 114, 126, 134, 140–47, 156, 171–2, 175
Foucault, Michel 1, 4, 9–10, 53, 61, 78, 105, 155, 185
Fourier, Joseph 20
freedom
 as equality 85, 183–5
 political 38
Frost, John 112
Furet, François 106–7

Gauny, Louis-Gabriel 6, 21, 111
Godard, Jean-Luc 166, 170, 177, 179–81
Goethe, Johann Wolfgang von 111, 115
Goncourt, Edmond and Jules 160
Gramsci, Antonio 40–42
Greenberg, Clement 154, 159
Guha, Ranajit 113

Haacke, Hans 165
Habermas, Jürgen 9–10, 101
Heartfield, John 165
Hegel, G. W. F. 39, 117, 127–8, 139, 153, 157–8, 168, 169
Henson, Gravener 112
hierarchy see domination, oligarchy, police
history
 of art 151, 153, 155, 160–61
 of film 175, 177
 Godard's Histoire(s) 179–82
 heretical 110–12
 "history from below" 5–6, 10, 104, 111

INDEX

Michelet's 107–8, 135, 142, 146–7, 179
"names of" 112, 188
of philosophy 38, 43, 54
subjects of 41, 44–6, 108, 146, 179
versus poetry (Aristotle) 146
writing/historiography 12, 96, 104–14, 135, 146–9, 179–81
Hitchcock, Alfred 178–81
Hobbes, Thomas 38, 48–9, 53, 80, 88
Hölderlin, Friedrich 127
Homer 127
Hugo, Victor 142, 157
human
  equality 3, 6, 38, 43, 49
  inhuman (critique of) 52–3, 164
  intelligence 7–8, 26, 30
  language 74, 102, 117, 126–8
humanism
  Rancière's thinking 184–5
  tendency of contemporary art 167

ignorance
  expert versus ignorant 30, 37, 65, 125
  schoolmaster 27–8, 98
image
  in aesthetic regime 155–6
  definition 118
  fate of 119
  sentence-image 163–4
  versus text 124, 128
inequality
  and the "distribution of the sensible" 11, 98
  and knowledge 28–32, 98, 101–2
  and politics 73, 96, 184
  as structure of social orders 7–8, 59, 64
Intellectuals 3–5, 18, 33, 38, 42, 45, 53–4, 110

Jaar, Alfredo 159
Jacotot, Joseph 6–9, 25–37, 77, 98, 114, 143
Joyce, James 172

Kant, Immanuel 138, 151, 153, 161, 164, 168
knowledge
  and authority 28–30, 37, 98
  distribution of 84
  as ideology 43–4
  poetics of 95, 104–10, 145–6, 150

labour
  division of 3–4, 29, 111, 128, 136
  history of 1, 5, 12, 19, 49, 119
  intellectual 3–4, 41
  manual 3–4, 46, 109, 111
  movement 1, 5–6, 12, 20–23, 31, 119
  "nights of" 18–22
"Land of the People" 18, 23–4
Lang, Fritz 170, 173, 175–6, 182
learning 7, 26–8, 31, 36
liberal
  democracy 45–6
  state 10
  theory 70–72
liberalism see also neo-liberalism, social-liberalism
  interest-group- 61
literarity 13, 133–50
Levinas, Emmanuel 10
Lubitsch, Ernst 180
Lyotard, Jean-François 1, 4, 10, 50–51, 53, 129, 164, 185

Malevich, Kazimir 172
Mallarmé, Stéphane 12, 18, 134, 145, 162–3, 166
Manet, Edouard 157
Mao Tse-Toung 8
Marx, Karl 2–4, 9–10, 19, 40, 42–3, 57, 80, 90, 117
Marxism 3, 9, 17, 19–20, 38–45, 90–91
materiality
  chaotic 158
  of image 124–5, 154–5
  of language 7, 161, 163
materialism
  historical 3, 33
  Rancière's 183, 187
May '68 1–5, 17, 19, 40, 50
Melville, Herman 134, 148
Menzel, Adolph von 157
Michelet, Jules 104, 107, 108, 135, 142, 146, 147, 179
mimesis 108, 118, 120, 126, 155–6, 173–6

205

Mitterrand, President François 8
modernity
   aesthetic 13, 18, 124, 134, 151–8, 165
   cinematographic 170–77
   political 23, 46, 87
   montage 14, 155, 163–8, 170, 172, 177–82
   "mute speech" 13, 134–5, 143, 145–6, 148

neo-liberalism 9, 106

oligarchy 57–8, 61, 64–8
Oedipus 123–4, 129, 138

Paine, Thomas 112
parataxis *see* materiality
partage du sensible (distribution of the sensible) 11, 63, 95–103, 117, 136, 145, 147, 152, 187
people (the) *see also demos* 9, 12, 20, 34, 37, 42, 50–54, 65–6, 70–73, 75, 81, 83–5, 89, 92, 108, 122, 142, 179
philosophy *see* political and politics
Plato 10, 43–7, 57–60, 64–5, 68, 80–86, 108, 121, 143
police *see also* oligarchy, politics
   definition of 62
   and distribution of the sensible 97–9
   order 70–76
   in Plato's *Republic* 59–60
   violence 2, 72
political, the 10, 71, 87
political movement 73, 78
political philosophy/theory 9, 10–13, 38, 43–9, 52–4, 57–9, 69–70, 80–86, 136, 184–6
political subject (subjectification) 10, 31–4, 44–6, 50–52, 75–8, 84–5, 100–102
Politics (Aristotle) 73–4, 87
politics *see also* democracy
   and aesthetics 100–101, 116–20, 133–6, 179
   archipolitics 10, 46, 80–81, 83–6
   and art 152, 159–68, 175
   biopolitics 53–4
   and equality of intelligences 29–32
   and literature 136–9, 141–3, 150
   metapolitics 10, 80–81, 89–92
   parapolitics 10, 46, 80–81, 86–90
   and philosophy 80, 82, 86, 92
   and poetics 12, 37
   versus police 10, 60–67, 70–71
Pop Art 157
post-revolution 11, 13, 139–40
post-romanticism 13–14
power *see also* politics
   of art 158
   distribution of 87
   Foucault 20, 78
   of images 110, 163–4, 175–81
   of intelligence 28, 30–31, 36–7, 54, 157
   and knowledge 30, 34, 110, 112
   sovereign 48–9, 53, 88–9
   and speech 4, 59, 84, 123–6
   state 2, 5, 8, 66, 106

Rawls, John 9, 57
regimes of the arts 13, 116–31, 137–40, 144–8
Renaut, Alain 58
revolts
   Canuts 20
   logical 4–5, 17–18, 21
   workers 17–18, 20
revolution *see also* post-revolution
   of 1830 21
   of 1848 20
   aesthetic/poetic 12, 37, 133
   Cuban 2
   cultural 3
   democratic 20, 96
   French 86, 106–8, 112, 114
   political 13, 90, 124
   Russian 41
rights
   citizen 52
   civil 67, 72
   civil rights movement 72
   human 22, 53, 79, 82
Rimbaud, Arthur 5, 18
romantic art/aesthetics 134, 139, 149, 155, 182
romantic literature/poetry 12, 107, 126–8
romanticism *see also* expressivity, literarity, post-romanticism

British 125
German 153
Hegel's critique of 127, 128, 139
and realism 155–6
Rosler, Martha 165
Ross, Kristin 19, 33, 34, 106
Rosselini, Roberto 110
Rousseau, Jean-Jacques 49, 97

Saint-Simonianism 20–21, 186
Sartre, Jean-Paul 38, 43–5, 142, 145
Schiller, Friedrich 127
Schönberg, Arnold 172
Soboul, Albert 106
social-liberalism 9
socialism 19, 70
"Socialisme ou Barbarie" 50
socialists 8, 18, 33, 70
socialist realism 37
Socrates 29, 59, 83, 86
Soviet socialism 44
Spenser, Thomas 112
Spivak, Gayatri Chakravorty 113
Stael, Anne L. G. de 113
Stendhal 108
struggle
  class 3, 5, 17, 19, 39–44, 49, 89–91
  democratic 67–8
  against domination 22, 152
  political 79, 97
subject, subjectification *see* political
symbol/symbolic *see also* aesthetic
  regime

of collective life 161–3
montage 165–8
principle of aesthetic regime 125, 129
violence and social hierarchy 4, 43, 61, 85, 102

Tacitus 113–14
Thompson, E. P. 5, 111–13
Tolstoy, Leo 126

Ulysses 123

Véret, Désirée 21
Vietnam War 2, 165
Vinçard, Pierre 21
Voilquin, Suzanne 20
Voltaire 108

Werkbund 162
Winterbotham, William 112
Wollstonecraft, Mary 112
Woolf, Virginia 134, 139, 172, 175
Wordsworth, William 23, 112
workers
  "dream" 17, 21
  and the philosopher 43–5, 59
  "voice" 8, 11, 18, 20
Wrong 10, 52, 75–8, 81, 100

Zola, Emile 126, 145

For Product Safety Concerns and Information please contact our EU representative GPSR@taylorandfrancis.com
Taylor & Francis Verlag GmbH, Kaufingerstraße 24, 80331 München, Germany

www.ingramcontent.com/pod-product-compliance
Lightning Source LLC
Chambersburg PA
CBHW071354290426
44108CB00014B/1549